HOOTENANNY

HOOTENANNY

The Craze and Controversy of TV's Folk Music Series

By

Michael J. Hayde

BearManor Media
2023

*HOOTENANNY: The Craze and Controversy
of TV's Folk Music Series*

© 2023 Michael J. Hayde
All rights reserved.
The United States Copyright Office, 2006

Published in the United States of America by:

Bear Manor Media
P.O. Box 71426
Albany, GA 31708

bearmanormedia.com

Typesetting and layout by Michael Hayde

ISBN 979-8-88771-176-8

DEDICATION

To John J. Hayde, Jr., who is 50% responsible for the author and 100% responsible for the author's interest in this show. Love you, Dad.

Jackie Miller, Barry McGuire and Gayle Caldwell, then with The New Christy Minstrels, rehearse for *Hootenanny* at Fordham University, November 13, 1963. Miller and Caldwell would form a pop duo (Jackie & Gayle) the following spring. McGuire would hit #1 with "Eve of Destruction" in 1965. *From the author's collection.*

TABLE OF CONTENTS

A *Hootenanny* is under way at UCLA, as Jack Linkletter introduces The Brothers Four. *From the author's collection.*

INTRODUCTION

Join us! You're just in time for the HOOTENANNY!

It's been called "The Folk Era," "The Folk Revival" and sometimes "The Golden Age of Folk Music." Or maybe, like folk-blues artist Dave Van Ronk, who was present for it all, you prefer "The Great Folk Scare." However you term it, folk is the music that gave birth to the 1960s, the decade that promised to remake America into a New Frontier and a Great Society but delivered the assassination of a sitting President, heightened racial tension, increasing poverty, escalating drug addiction and a troublesome foreign war, all of which would be commented upon by the genre's writers and performers. Without folk, popular music as we've known it for the last 60 years couldn't have existed.

The music, of course, had been around for centuries: tragic ballads from Western Europe; joyful drinking songs heard in English taverns (Francis Scott Key cribbed the melody for one of these, "To Anacreon in Heaven," when he wrote "The Star-Spangled Banner" in 1814); African songs of life and labor plucked on a stringed instrument known as the akonting, the predecessor of the banjo. Every nation, territory or region had its own brand of local music; for most, it was the only entertainment available. When mass immigration to America occurred in the 19th century, its practitioners brought their songs… and, like messages passed from person-to-person over time, they changed. Work songs, drinking songs, children's songs, songs of loves won and lost, songs of hope and despair, songs of faith and redemption: all created, polished and performed by people who'd lived—or at least *believed*—the stories they told.

As recording became an industry during the first half of the 1900s, 'Folk Music' was a blanket term that encompassed hillbilly, rhythm and blues, and pretty much everything in between. Performers of what we now call 'Blues' and 'Country' were originally marketed as folk singers. Most recording was done in the northeast, and so these musicians—a few could be considered itinerant—brought their tunes to the big cities, catching the fancy of several budding singers in the process. These city dwellers, for whom labor meant working in steel mills, automobile factories and the like, put their own spin on lyrics, such as turning spirituals into anthems for unionization. Once those songs took root, they also laid claim to the term "folk music," leaving hillbilly (or "country-western music") and rhythm and blues (or "race music") to describe the originals. Unintended or not, the folk genre became as segregated as anything else in the nation.

With the sudden, unexpected popularity of The Kingston Trio (so sudden and unexpected that their Grammy for "Tom Dooley" was awarded in the 'Best Country & Western Performance' category), folk music became a commercial force. Similar groups sprouted and charted hits: The Highwaymen ("Michael, Row the Boat Ashore"), The Brothers Four ("Greenfields"), The Rooftop Singers ("Walk Right In") and especially Peter, Paul & Mary (too many to name). More importantly, new singer-songwriters came along, providing material, much of it topical, for these groups, other singers and themselves, none more prominently than Bob Dylan. By the end of 1963, folk music was literally everywhere.

Less than six months later, the British Invasion had revitalized rock 'n' roll and forced folk out of the mass marketplace, but even The Beatles acknowledged Dylan's influence as they made their journey from "yeah, yeah, yeah!" to "All You Need is Love." In America, members of such groups as The Byrds, The Mamas & the Papas and The Lovin' Spoonful began their careers in folk music... and as such had appeared on a short-lived, yet highly influential musical variety show on the ABC-TV network called *Hootenanny*.

This program, simultaneously beloved and reviled, once thought completely lost, stands as an illustration of everything that was important and everything that was meaningless and trivial about the Folk Era. It has a legacy of showcasing only the most vapid, commercial aspects of the music, while ignoring its traditions and especially its messages. The truth, however, is not so cut-and-dried, and the purpose of this book is to document evidence, culled mostly from surviving video and/or audio, that will hopefully give future musicologists and historians a foundation upon which to make their own judgements.

I've written about this show before: at *TVParty.com*, Wikipedia, and my blog *Better Living Through Television*. The TV Party piece served as a simple overview with a few audio clips; the Wikipedia entry (which I formatted and contributed about 90% of the content) is a nuts-and-bolts overview; the blog entry speaks mainly to the controversy surrounding the show owing to a decision not to include Pete Seeger or his former group The Weavers for political reasons.

Hootenanny was hardly television's first controversial series; that dubious label probably resides with *Amos 'n' Andy* (1951-53). But its particular controversy shed light on the social and political imbalance between network and advertising executives on one side, and the folk audience on the other. In its modest (*too* modest, according to critics) way, *Hootenanny* tried to redress this imbalance by granting time to anti-war and other political songs; to showcase a few little-known folksingers and singer-songwriters; to bring together artists that, due to management or record label restrictions, couldn't otherwise join forces; to welcome white and black American, Canadian, Polynesian, European, African, Australian and Latino talent, sometimes on a single stage. All of this punctuated by the visible enthusiasm of American university and college students, a.k.a. tomorrow's leaders.

And it did that while simultaneously banning the guy who'd essentially birthed the hootenanny more than twenty years before.

No matter what you've read elsewhere, *Hootenanny* was committed to videotape, not film, and the tapes were erased and re-used per network policy. However, many ad agencies received kinescopes (16mm films from a camera pointed at a TV screen) of the shows on which their commercials aired, and those who sponsored this series were not exempt. Eighteen of the 43 total programs (originally 13 half-hours for season one and 30 hours for season two) exist whole or in part in this format, and most of these survivors were used to assemble the *Best of Hootenanny* DVD set from Shout Factory. All of the kinescopes reside in archives or private collections; most are available for licensing selected footage to a reputable production house. Those held by The Library of Congress, The Paley Center for Media and UCLA may be viewed by researchers on site, by appointment.

There were also home viewers who audio taped the broadcasts for their own repeated enjoyment. My father was one of these, and it's from his collection, plus that of a gentleman with whom I have traded material, that the soundtracks I've referenced originated. (Any readers who have their own audio tapes of *Hootenanny*, whether on reel-to-reel or other formats, and would like to have digitized copies of them and/or trade for copies of mine, please email me, especially if they can help fill in the remaining gaps: MikeH0714@yahoo.com.)

Program guides are incorporated within chapters three and five. When the structure of a show is known via existing video, audio, or a reliable published source, the songs and artists are sequenced accordingly. For those that aren't known to exist or are otherwise undocumented, lineups are taken from newspaper and TV magazine listings, and all songs known to have been performed by each act are grouped together. In cases when audio and/or video are incomplete, published TV listings were used to supplement. In cases where the *listings* are incomplete… *please* check your audio tape libraries, ladies and gentlemen! Then contact me at the above email address.

In this book, you'll learn exactly what *Hootenanny* was and what it wasn't, who liked it and who didn't, what certain artists who performed on it thought of the experience, and why it couldn't hold on when the times, they were a-changin'.

PROLOGUE:
Progressivism, Pete Seeger and the 'hootenanny'

Upon the conclusion of World War II, two opposing political forces took root in America: Progressivism and Anticommunism. Adherents of Progressivism saw the evil of the war, namely fascism that decreed some human beings were not equal to others and therefore should be repressed, and even eliminated, for the good of the master race. With visions of citizens ripped from their homes and businesses, forced like cattle into railroad boxcars, herded into concentration camps, starved, beaten and finally led into ovens or shot outright, progressives looked at their own country and saw essentially the same thing: black Americans treated as third-class citizens in the north and targets for beatings and lynching in the south.

Progressivism also supported the organizing of labor unions, believing that "big bosses" were reaping entirely too much profit off the sweat and toil of their barely-scraping-by employees. They held that free markets were a sham that harmed the working class by widening the economic gap between them and their employers. This distrust of capitalism was borne out of abuses that culminated in the Great Depression. Similarly, they felt it was the responsibility of government to care for its poorest citizens, through welfare and other programs, which neatly dovetailed with its focus on civil rights.

All of these stances were also held by the Communist Party of the United States of America (CPUSA), which had reached peak membership during the Depression years. By 1947, citizens were well aware of atomic warfare and feared what might transpire should such weapons be controlled by nations with a penchant for aggressive expansion, such as the Soviet Union. With the Truman Doctrine designed to prop up free countries facing Soviet invasion and the establishment of the House Un-American Activities Committee (HUAC) and its hearings into Communist infiltration, the CPUSA was in decline.

A new political player, the United States Progressive Party, came into being in time for the 1948 presidential election. Its founders were mainly from the left-most wing of the Democratic Party, who were appalled at President Truman's hardline stance against the Soviets, fearing it would lead to future armed conflict, as well as the idea that anyone's personal politics could be censured as "un-American." Former Vice-President under Franklin Roosevelt, Henry A. Wallace, entered the race as the Progressive candidate; at the party's July convention in Philadelphia, Glen H. Taylor, Democratic senator from Idaho, was selected as his running mate. Both were staunch anti-segregationists and firmly believed that, as Taylor put it, "We can get along with Russia if we elect [a] man of peace... [Wallace] is the only great man we can expect the Russians to have any confidence in." With that kind of platform, disenfranchised CPUSA members hopped aboard.

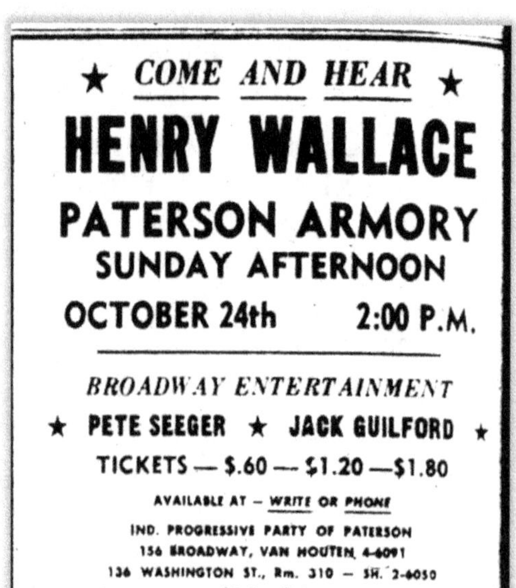

A New Jersey rally for Henry A. Wallace includes music by Pete Seeger and comedy by Jack Gilford. This "Broadway Entertainment" for the Progressive Party candidate would contribute to both men being blacklisted from radio and television in 1950.

Performing at the convention, as well as on the campaign trails for both men, was young folk balladeer Pete Seeger.

* * * * *

"I had no idea of becoming a musician when I left school" at 19 years old, Seeger told a reporter in January 1955. "I carried a banjo, more as an introduction than as a musical instrument. Then I found that people wanted to hear my songs."

Born in 1919, the son of pioneering musicologist and instructor Charles Seeger, he was introduced to the banjo at age 16 when he heard black musicians at Ashville North Carolina's Folk Song and Dance Festival in 1935. Later that same summer, he attended the Pennsylvania Folk Festival in Lewisburg, in which he was first exposed to the "the great field of folk music that was as yet unexplored," according to Sunbury, Pennsylvania's *Daily Item*.

Leaving Harvard in 1938 after completing only a single year, Seeger hitchhiked across the country and "sang everywhere—churches and barrooms and street corners—anywhere [people] asked me to sing," collecting songs along the way. In 1939, a family friend, Alan Lomax, invited him to help catalog the music of the Archive of American Folk Song for the Library of Congress, which had been recorded throughout the 1930s by Alan and his father, John Lomax. This exposed Seeger to still more songs, including one that would prove pivotal in his professional life: Huddie "Leadbelly" Ledbetter's "Irene." In 1940, he met folksinger Woody Guthrie and traveled across the country again, this time as a companion. Raised in Oklahoma, Guthrie was a CPUSA member who witnessed first-hand what the Depression and devastating dust storms had done to the country's heartland and took to songwriting and performing to spread the news; his messages resonated with the populist Seeger.

Back in New York, Seeger made Greenwich Village his home base, and together with Guthrie, journalist Millard Lampell and Lee Hays, the son of a Little Rock, Arkansas Methodist church elder, formed The Almanac Singers. This group, all avowed leftists with or without other part-time members, made a handful of records and concert performances, mostly in support of labor unions.

World War II interrupted this endeavor, and Seeger was drafted into the Army. "Military intelligence got interested in my politics," he later told journalist Amy Goodman. "My outfit went on to glory and death, and I stayed there in Keesler Field, Mississippi, picking up cigarette butts for six months." After that he was transferred to Saipan and helped organize entertainment for hospitalized soldiers.

Returning to New York after war's end, he resumed performing, usually under the auspices of People's Songs, Inc. Folksinger and fellow activist Oscar Brand recalled that Seeger, "wanted to put out a magazine in which we'd put out the new songs that we were writing, rather than… antique songs that everyone seemed to be depending on." With that and $135 in capital, People's Songs, Inc. was founded. Seeger's title was "National Director in Charge;" board members included Guthrie, Hays, Brand, Alan Lomax, singer Paul Robeson and editor Irwin Silber, who soon became its executive director.

Publishing and distributing a monthly newsletter of songs was the priority: "We believe that songs should be concerned with more than just 'June-moon-croon,'" read an early issue. "There is a need for songs about things in the world about us, and songs expressing the deepest aspirations of all people for freedom and equality." In the quest to fulfill this need, *People's Songs* didn't always take artistry into account. "I wasn't crazy about all the songs and I asked to be taken off the board," Brand told author Robbie Woliver. "By this time, they had also become a booking group, called People's Artists." In the Spring of 1946, this sub-organization initiated a series of folk music concerts dedicated to keeping *People's Songs* solvent. Intended, too, at these performances was audience participation; with this in mind, Seeger gave them a special title.

"Something new in the world of music are 'hootenannies,' or more simply, 'hoots,' which are evenings devoted to folk music, presented by People's Songs," wrote Isabel Turnbull for the *Windsor Ontario Star* in September 1946. "This new development in music is a by-product of World War II…. Nervous tension was relieved by singing, and in the case of Americans, songs from widely separated parts of the United States were made familiar to new audiences. Soldiers from backwoods cabins in the mountains of Virginia or Kentucky, from the western plains, from northern lumber woods or southern tobacco and cotton country pooled the ballads they knew at home. They found it an interesting and stimulating exchange, and though the war is over, many of them want to keep on hearing new songs.”

Until the advent of community folk singing, the word 'hootenanny' had various definitions and nearly as many spellings. A completely unscientific sampling of vintage newspapers turns up the following timeline:

Entering the 20th century: The prevalent use of "hootenanny" is as a synonym to "dingus," "thingumajig" or "whatchamacallit." As late as 1961, this was also the primary definition found in *Webster's Third International Dictionary.*

Late 1910s: The word, occasionally spelled as "hootin' nanny," becomes slang for the automobile; synonymous with "tin lizzie."

May 1923: A Belleville, Kansas newspaper, *The Republic County Democrat,* advises us, "There is a big black bird in Africa called the Hootenanny which according to Natural Histories lives on what it can steal from the young of other birds." Around this same time, the word is used as a synonym for the crawling creatures that would frequently plague farmers' crops.

January 1924: Dayton Ohio's Marion McKay and His Greystone Artists release a tune called "Hootenanny," described by Gennett Records as "The New Dance Sensation That's Sweeping the Country. A Peppy Melody." This appears to be the earliest association of the word with music.

Late 1920s into the 1930s: 'Hootenanny' makes its debut in politics, describing trucks equipped with loudspeakers so candidates wouldn't have to shout while delivering campaign speeches.

May 1936: Clark Hickman, Mayor of Cortez, Colorado, writes his local newspaper, the *Sentinel*, asking for a definition: "Hootenanny is a funny word and I used to think that it meant the little doo-dad hanging down in front of a Scotchman's kilt. But after trying in vain to find it in the dictionary and having it heard used for many things, I have concluded it is one of the words that might mean anything. Once when ill in a hospital, my nurse would say, 'Do you want to use the hootenanny?' and then again she would say, 'Get your little hootenanny over,' so I'm still in doubt about the word. Can anyone enlighten me?" It appears no one could.

May 1937: One year after Mayor Hickman's lighthearted letter, the *Kansas City Star* reassigned the word to primitive automobiles, specifically, "that vehicle technically described as consisting of a motor chassis, four wheels and no brakes," built and operated by unlicensed teenagers. "The decision of the police to take more active measures against the hootenanny and its drivers would seem entirely justified.... The presence of a brakeless car on the streets today cannot be treated as a harmless prank."

July 1938: Texas Jim Lewis and His Lone Star Cowboys headline at the Beverly Hills Country Club in Cincinnati, Ohio with a contraption Lewis labeled a hootenanny. "This is a band on wheels," said the city's *Enquirer*, which also called it the "top feature of the new show. Its bells, whistles, and gadgets turn up a lot of hot syncopation."

August 1939: 'Hooten-anny' shows up in Alabama to describe a musical gathering... but not, according to the *Luverne Journal* newspaper, in an uplifting way: "Last week a negro woman of Luverne lost her life by being stabbed by another negro woman at the 'honky-tonk' operated by the colored for the colored people almost a stone's throw from the main street of Luverne. This is the second negro killing that has taken place at this 'honky-tonk' since its opening. Much complaint is being heard from citizens over the town of this place being a nuisance and especially at night when the negroes congregate there and begin playing the 'hooten-anny' full blast. The thing can be heard in all parts of the town on a still night… and unless it is stopped or at least this loud music playing at night when people are trying to sleep, the place may be visited most any night by some of the citizens who are annoyed by the loud playing of the so-called 'hooten-anny.'" No veiled threat there.

July 1940: The word finally turns up synonymous with a musical jamboree, used by *The New Dealer*, a progressive paper housed in Seattle, Washington, to advertise a fund raiser they called their "Midsummer Hootenanny," which promised an evening of music, dancing, refreshments, and door prizes. Per a January 1941 blurb in the *Tacoma Times*, Paul Ashford, Seattle's noted music reviewer and folklorist, performed at these events. Ashford collected folksongs along the Puget Sound, wrote a few of his own, and had been visited by Woody Guthrie and his young associate Pete Seeger during their travels the previous year. The question is, did they give Ashford the word… or did he give it to *them*?

Whatever the case, by 1943, Guthrie, Seeger and company were using it for their own fund raisers, after which it spread to straight-up folk concerts. In her article, Turnbull enthused, "The success of 'hootenannies' was immediate, and surprised even the organizers… 300 were turned away [from the first one]. There was no formal program, but each singer went to the platform and sang what he pleased, with the audience clamoring for more. Two successive concerts crowded Town Hall—one a Union Hoot, the other a Freedom Hoot. Bills of fare now offered are varied and timely, with current events translated into words and music. Original songs have dealt with the housing shortage, O.P.A., the fight for freedom in other countries, the fight against prejudice in America, the shortcomings of Congressmen, woes of union members, and so on."

* * * * *

When the 1948 Presidential election results were tallied, the Wallace/Taylor ticket had garnered 2.4% of the popular vote, won zero electoral college votes, and bankrupted People's Songs, Inc., which had poured a lot of capital into Wallace's campaign.   Accusations flew that the Progressive party had solicited and received funds from Soviet Russia, and suddenly anyone who'd been involved found themselves tainted in the extreme right-wing press.   Seeger kept right on singing, though, "anywhere and everywhere I have been asked… to bring the folk music to the people."   He also kept writing, and around that time he and Lee Hays composed one of the best-remembered songs of the Folk Era: "The Hammer Song," a.k.a. "If I Had a Hammer."   Irwin Silber and some of the original People's Songs backers, including Seeger behind the scenes, used it as a springboard for a new folk magazine: *Sing Out!* The name was taken from the third verse of "The Hammer Song," which graced the cover of issue #1, released in May 1950.

Some months prior, Seeger and Hays met two Brooklyn-native singers and activists: Fred Hellerman and Ruth "Ronnie" Gilbert.   The foursome made an interesting blend: baritone and guitarist Hellerman and contralto Gilbert meshed seamlessly with Hays' bass voice and Seeger's tenor harmonies and accomplished banjo playing.   Dubbing themselves the "No-Name Quartet," they eventually became The Weavers and signed with Decca records under the guidance of bandleader and arranger Gordon Jenkins.

The label permitted them to record on their own, but Jenkins also wanted to work with them.   Their first record, "Tzena, Tzena, Tzena," based on an Israeli folk dance, was released in two different versions: as a Jenkins-orchestrated, up-tempo number with English lyrics (also provided by Jenkins), and on their own with a folk arrangement "less commercial but more moving," according to *Variety*.   The B-side of the folk record was "Around the World," a medley of international songs, but it was the flip of Jenkins' version that caught lightning: Huddie Ledbetter's "Goodnight, Irene."   *Variety* termed this one "a pleasant Ozark-flavored item."   Little did they know it had been composed by a black Louisiana-born musician who was discovered while serving time in his home state for attempted homicide.

Released in June 1950, "Goodnight, Irene" took off like a rocket; the first folk tune to reach number one on the popular music charts.   A string of hits followed over the next year-and-a-half, including Woody Guthrie's "So Long, It's Been Good to Know Yuh," originally written about the Dust Bowl in 1935. With the substitution of more lighthearted lyrics, it reached number four in 1951 and drew attention to Guthrie's backlog.

The Weavers at the start of their checkered career. Clockwise from top left: Pete Seeger, Lee Hays, Fred Hellerman, Ronnie Gilbert. *From the author's collection.*

Also released in June 1950 was *Red Channels*, an alphabetical list of suspected Communists in radio and TV and the organizations to which they belonged or at least sympathized with, published by *Counterattack*, the self-styled "newsletter of facts to combat Communism." As they put it, "The purpose of this compilation is threefold. One, to show how the Communists have been able to carry out their plan of infiltration of the radio and television industry. Two, to indicate the extent to which many prominent actors and artists have been inveigled to lend their names, according to these public records, to organizations espousing Communist causes. This, regardless of whether they actually believe in, sympathize with, or even recognize the cause advanced. Three, to discourage actors and artists from naively lending their names to Communist organizations or causes in the future."

Seeger is the only Weaver named in *Red Channels*, but the organizations to which he and the others belonged, including People's Songs, Inc., the Wallace for President Campaign, etc., meant they'd all eventually be tarred and barred… which is exactly what happened. Dispirited by the sudden loss of radio play, the termination of their Decca contract, cancelled concerts and hecklers at the few gigs they were given, The Weavers disbanded in 1952.

Seeger resumed his career as best he could, performing solo at various folk festivals, labor union meetings and political rallies for the next three years. "Seeger… had the entire audience singing along with him as he plucked out 'work songs' and other old favorites" at St. Louis' National Folk Festival of 1953, per the *Globe Democrat*. He recorded for Folkways, a label begun by yet another activist, Moses Asch, a Polish immigrant whose family came to the U.S. in 1912 when he was 7 years old. An early interest in recording Yiddish music led to the formation of Asch Records in 1940. When that firm went bankrupt eight years later, he quickly followed up with Folkways, widening the scope to include American blues and folk. Guthrie, Leadbelly and Seeger were among the earliest artists on the label.

In 1955, HUAC turned its attention to Broadway and New York's nightclub scene. Seeger knew what was coming: "It's a terrible thing to be accused of being a Communist," he told *The Daily Item* that January.

"My only defense can be to let people come and hear what I sing. But these accusations follow me everywhere." He was called to testify on August 18, and when asked whether or not he was a Communist, replied, "I am not going to answer any questions as to my associations, philosophical or religious beliefs, or my political beliefs, or how I voted in any election, or any of these private affairs. I think these are very improper questions for any American to be asked, especially under such compulsion as this." Instead, he offered to play his banjo and sing, which the committee rebuffed. "I have sung to many audiences," he said in conclusion. "I have sung in hobo jungles and I've sung for the Rockefellers. I've never refused to sing for anybody. That's the only answer I can give. I'm proud I've sung for Americans of every political persuasion."

Seeger was one of 23 witnesses; only one, actor George Hall, disclosed his past involvement with Communism. Most of the others invoked the First, Fifth, Sixth, Tenth and/or Fourteenth amendments of the U.S. Constitution. Seeger made his simple statement and six years later was charged, tried and convicted in U.S. District Court for contempt of Congress. Sentenced to a year in prison, he promptly appealed and the conviction was overturned in May 1962.

Shortly after the committee hearing, perhaps desiring to kick HUAC in the teeth for attacking his client, Seeger's manager, empresario Harold Leventhal, arranged for The Weavers to reunite. He did it by telling Hays, Gilbert, Hellerman and Seeger individually that the other three had already agreed. Carnegie Hall was booked for December 24. That night, New York City received an early Christmas present, one recorded for posterity by Vanguard Records, an independent label that ordinarily specialized in classical releases. Beginning with the success of *The Weavers at Carnegie Hall*, Vanguard would become a force in the folk world.

The original Weavers remained intact until 1957 when Seeger departed for good, wishing to return to life as a traveling troubadour. He personally recommended his successor, Erik Darling, most recently a member of a folk trio called The Tarriers. This lineup continued until 1962, when Darling pulled out. Frank Hamilton, then Bernie Krause stepped in until the group called it quits once and for all in December 1963.

* * * * *

In 1956, rock 'n' roll was king of the pop charts, and Elvis Presley was king of rock 'n' roll, but a new form of music was also getting significant airplay. It was called calypso, hailed originally from Trinidad and popularized (and, critics would say, bastardized) by Harry Belafonte. His RCA-Victor recording of "Banana Boat (Day-O)" became a signature tune, begat subsequent releases in a similar vein, and even generated a Stan Freberg parody record, but The Tarriers' version, released on the small Glory label, charted slightly higher, peaking at #4, with Belafonte's holding at #5. The group even lip-synched to it in a quickie movie for Columbia Pictures, *Calypso Heat Wave* (1957).

The following year, another trio literally burst on the scene, with a name directly inspired by the calypso tunes they'd been honing along with other folk and foreign language material. Dave Guard, Nick Reynolds and Bob Shane, friends and former classmates all in their mid-to-late twenties, formed a partnership with talent agent Frank Werber; donned identical striped shirts; turned a one-week engagement at San Francisco's Purple Onion nightclub into six months; released an album and single on Capitol Records that each shot to number one and went gold; established a concert circuit made up of college auditoriums, a strategy other acts would quickly utilize.

The Kingston Trio had arrived. So had the Folk Era.

CHAPTER 1

"What The Hell Is a 'Hootenanny?'"

"What I try to do is identify and work with the most talented people I can get." So said producer Daniel Melnick in 1990, describing his filmmaking philosophy to *The Los Angeles Times*. It was no less true in 1962, when he was the 30-year-old Vice President of Programming for the ABC-TV network.

Melnick's was a meteoric rise by most standards, having gone from college, to a hitch in the Army, to CBS-TV as a line producer, to an ABC vice-presidency within a dozen years. At what was then a network perpetually in distant third place to CBS and NBC, Melnick oversaw the production and/or scheduling of shows that closed the gap: *77 Sunset Strip*, *The Donna Reed Show*, *The Untouchables*, *The Flintstones*, *Ben Casey*. A folk music fan, in mid-Fall of 1962 he and the Ashley-Steiner Talent Agency envisioned a different kind of variety show with what *TV Guide* later called "an offbeat approach, something other than a string of folk singers parading across a TV-studio stage." To achieve that, Melnick dove into his pool of "most talented people" and emerged with the one who specialized in producing a compelling pilot: Gil Cates.

Another meteoric riser, Gilbert Cates was only 28 when presented with the concept, and it was his suggestions that stuck. First, he knew folk concerts had taken place on college campuses and that this would be the ideal venue for such a show. Network executives agreed, realizing, as one later explained, "By doing the show in a college gym or field house, we could play off the audience, generating excitement among viewers by showing the excitement of the college kids." To emphasize the student presence, Cates insisted the show should be staged as theater-in-the-round, with students seated on the floor. His vision was "a sea of humanity, the faces that could be caught on our cameras only if the kids sat on the floor."

For guidance in booking appropriate talent, Melnick turned to yet another rising star: Fred Weintraub, owner of the Greenwich Village nightclub, The Bitter End. Although only 34, Weintraub was the eldest of this triumvirate and his venue was one of the most respected among performers. He took over the lease of what had been a modest coffee-house in mid-1961, and within a year, according to *Variety*, "built The Bitter End into one of New York's most unorthodox and thriving niteries sans booze." Folksingers and stand-up comedians were the club's bread-and-butter and such future icons as Peter, Paul & Mary and Woody Allen became professionals on its stage. Tuesday nights were set aside for open-mic hootenannies, undoubtedly the inspiration for the title Cates selected.

Weintraub later described his role as talent consultant: "I don't book people on the show. But I know all the acts and particularly all the new acts on the way up. I make suggestions as to whom to go after, what songs they should do and how the acts should be staged. Some of my suggestions are followed."

Arrangements were made with Cates' alma mater, Syracuse University, for the show to be videotaped on Sunday, November 18, 1962. Thirteen-hundred free tickets were distributed to university officials, who in turn parceled them out in various ways. According to the student newspaper *The Daily Orange*, 900 were made available on a "first come, first serve" basis at the student government office. Another approximately 400 were given to campus organizations that "have rendered service to the university for many years, receiving very little recognition for their efforts." Finally, 30 tickets would be awarded to the winner of the Homecoming Weekend house decorating contest. Similar distribution methods would become the norm for the subsequent series.

Jean Shepherd, the radio personality and humorist who'd been a popular college attraction since the mid-fifties, was selected to host. Cates determined that Shepherd, who'd produced folk and jazz concerts at Carnegie Hall and Central Park, would not be a traditional emcee but rather a "guide and commentator… [conducting] his commentary while seated in the audience," as stated in an early press release. A veteran lyricist, Broadway librettist, radio and television scribe, David Greggory, was tasked with writing the casual yet informative performer intros that Shepherd would deliver. Cates and Weintraub chose an eclectic talent lineup for the pilot, expected to air as a special the following January, that included a young male balladeer, Mike Settle; a young female balladeer, Jo Mapes; and a gospel group, Clara Ward and Her Gospel Singers. Headlining would be one of the most omnipresent—especially on television—of the commercial folk trios: The Limeliters.

Ticket distribution for the *Hootenanny* pilot is announced in Syracuse University's *Daily Orange*, November 12, 1962. *Image courtesy of The Daily Orange*

The group that would literally appear every other week during *Hootenanny's* first season had what its on-stage spokesman, Dr. Louis Gottlieb, would likely term "a curious history." In the mid-1950s, Gottlieb was a member of The Gateway Singers, a folk quartet closely patterned after The Weavers with a progressive twist: *their* contralto, Elmerlee Thomas, was black. The other two members were, like Gottlieb, white males: Travis Edmonson and Jerry Walter. Barred from some venues as well as network TV simply for being biracial, various Gateway Singers came and went; Gottlieb was the first to depart in 1958.

HOOTENANNY TICKETS READY TODAY

"Hootennany" tickets may be picked up beginning at 5 p.m. today at the Student Government office, 907 University Ave. Tickets will be given out on a first come, first served basis.

Each student must present his ID card to receive a ticket, and no student will be given more than one ticket, or may present more than one ID card.

After earning his Ph.D. in Musicology, by mid-1959 Dr. Gottlieb was writing arrangements for the Kingston Trio. Evenings, he'd perform stand-up comedy at various clubs, primarily the Ash Grove in Los Angeles. Thinking only in terms of recording demos for the Trio, he found two soloists who occasionally joined forces on coffee house stages, and had recently purchased one for themselves: baritone Alex Hassilev and tenor Glenn Yarbrough. Once they started singing together, Gottlieb was impressed with their blend and decided to work up an act. They broke it in at Hassilev's and Yarbrough's venue, The Limelite, located in Aspen, Colorado, from which the group took its name.

Yarbrough had recorded a couple of albums for the folk-centric Elektra Records, and the fledging label took on his bandmates for a 1960 release that frankly went nowhere. But after spending most of the year at the Ash Grove and the hungry i in San Francisco, they were signed by RCA. The much bigger and better-distributed label put out *Tonight: In Person* in early 1961; recorded at the Ash Grove, the disc remained on *Billboard's* album chart for 74 weeks, topping out at #5.

Other successful albums followed, as did television guest shots and concert tours; at their peak, the group was playing 310 live shows per a year. But they made their biggest splash with TV commercial jingles, most notably L&M cigarettes ("Start Fresh, Stay Fresh") and Coca-Cola ("Things Go Better with Coke," which they were the first to perform).

And then, less than a month after completing the *Hootenanny* pilot, it all literally came crashing down.

On Tuesday, December 11, the group had performed a concert in Denver, and were to appear the following evening at the University of Utah. On Wednesday, a heavy fog settled over Salt Lake City and their scheduled commercial flight was cancelled. Their road manager, Burt Zelnigher, chartered a twin-engine plane in order to make the gig. Due to poor visibility, pilot Harlan Mitton was unable to land at Salt Lake City and turned toward a smaller airport in Provo. He had the runway in sight while descending, but ran into a bank of fog and went off course by about a mile. Once Mitton got below the fog and saw a farmer's field instead of a runway, "I applied full power and started to pull up, and that's when we hit," he told the press the next day. The plane "pancaked into the field… scattering plane parts for hundreds of feet," reported the *Salt Lake Telegram*. "The crash knocked both engines loose, ripped off the wheels and heavily damaged the craft, although the cabin stayed fairly intact…. The tail hit the ground first and the plane lurched into the plowed field, skidding through the loose earth."

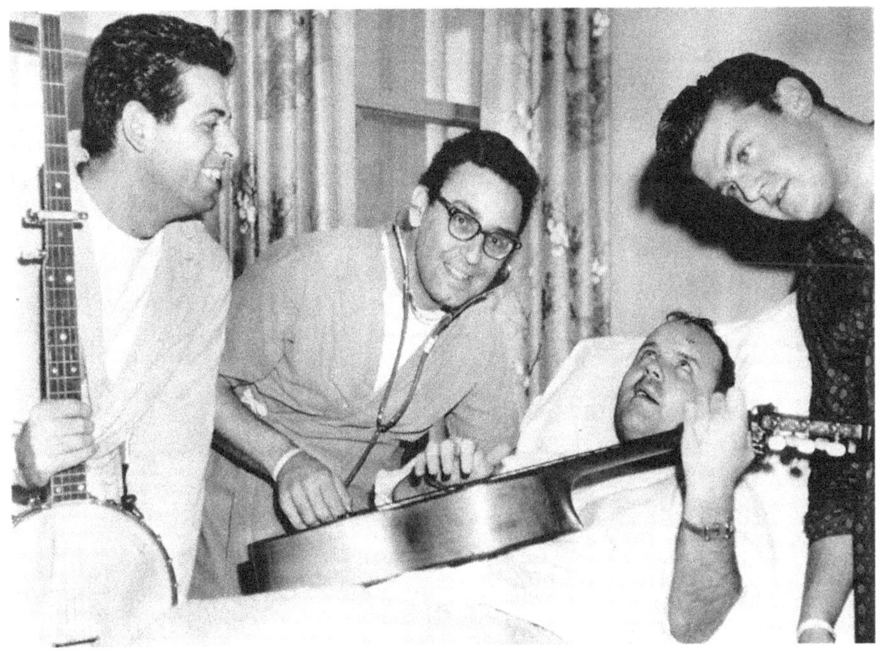

Alex Hassilev, Lou Gottlieb and road manager Burt Zelnigher flank Glenn Yarbrough the day after surviving an airplane crash. Even when hospitalized, The Limeliters can't keep from singing, nor from promoting themselves. *From the author's collection*

Mitton and Zelnigher wound up with minor face cuts; Hassilev and Yarbrough with forehead lacerations and various bruises. Gottlieb got the worst of it, with two broken ribs for which he was given morphine. "What a recovery!" he cracked the next day. "They stuck a little needle in my chest and now I'm well." Jokes aside, the incident convinced all three Limeliters to "reassess [our] priorities," as Yarbrough put it. The distinctive tenor would be the first to leave in the coming year.

* * * * *

ABC loved the pilot. With Melnick's enthusiastic input, they scrapped the idea of airing a special and immediately planned a 13-week summer series, which meant twelve more shows were required. They also needed a producer, since Cates had moved on to a new project. In mid-December, Melnick approached Richard Lewine, a Broadway composer and former CBS-TV vice president known for producing highly acclaimed musical specials such as *The Mary Martin-Noel Coward Show* (1956) and *Rodgers and Hammerstein's Cinderella* (1957), as well as four seasons of the *Young People's Concert* series alongside its host, Leonard Bernstein. Reportedly, the conversation between Melnick and the 52-year-old Lewine went something like this:

MELNICK: "How would you like to produce a hootenanny?"

LEWINE: "What the hell is a 'hootenanny?'"

To answer, Melnick needed only to screen the pilot and although folk music was "a whole new world to me," Lewine instantly saw the appeal of a musical program originating from college campuses. "The whole thing thrives in an atmosphere like that," he told the *New York Times'* John P. Shanley shortly after the premiere. "We could get an ordinary studio audience to applaud—or to stand on their heads—but we couldn't influence a college audience if it didn't want to be influenced. At the same time, a college audience gets the best out of the people who are performing, because they know they're being understood." He especially liked the idea of seating the students on the floor so the cameras could roam across their singing faces. "A proscenium kills a folksing," he asserted. "You can understand they'd sing a lot more than someone seated formally in the eighth row of an orchestra. When the audience is seated in chairs, it's far more inhibited. It's not inclined to join in. But when they're sitting on the floor, they respond."

Richard Lewine: renowned Broadway composer, respected theatrical historian, and beleaguered producer of *Hootenanny*.

The only change Lewine wanted to make was the show's host. Disregarding Jean Shepherd's proven rapport with college audiences, he wanted someone nearer in age to the students, yet still a professional. That led him to Jack Linkletter.

As personable and ambitious as his father, Art, the younger Linkletter found himself emulating his dad's yen for showbiz success and business acumen almost instinctively. At age 4, homemade tapes of his impromptu conversations with Pop were airing on the latter's San Francisco radio show, *Who's Dancing Tonight?* "Mail came in from all over northern California, saying, 'What a wonderful thing it is to hear a little boy talking to his daddy,'" Art Linkletter recalled late in life, "and it struck me that there were no interviews with children as children…. Jack opened my eyes for the first time to the joy of just hearing kids say the darndest things." With that, a toddler unknowingly became the key influence for one of his father's most memorable successes.

While attending University of California, Jack would occasionally substitute for Art on the latter's *House Party*, and then hosted a summer game show, *Haggis Baggis* (which had been produced by Gil Cates). After graduating he took on hosting chores for two interview shows: *On the Go* (1958-59) and *Here's Hollywood* (1960-62). Both consisted in the main of remote interviews. "Mobility is a concept I believe in," he said in 1963. "I feel it is more meaningful for viewers. The person being interviewed is most himself in his own environment. It makes things more interesting for viewers and listeners. I think people have come to expect more depth." He admitted to signing for *Hootenanny* because "my three previous series were daytime and I've been looking for a nighttime show. [Plus] I'm still going to college myself… working for my Master's degree in Business Education at UCLA. But most important of all, from my point of view, is the mobility of the show." (Lewine liked this as well. "We've got a different look every week," he told radio-TV columnist Alan Gill. "The room's different. The kids are yelling in a different way. You won't find yourself saying, 'Gee, this looks like last Saturday's show.'")

As for the occasional accusation that his father had more to do with his career aspirations than he did, Jack had a ready answer: "I never felt that I lived in Dad's shadow because I never had a pedestal image of him. I've grown up in the business world as much as I have in show business…. When I was a kid, if I was interested enough to ask questions, he'd let me sit in on the meetings he and his partners would have at our house." The Business Ed degree would wind up taking him much farther than his TV jobs, which he foresaw even then: "The yardsticks are different. Business is both tangible and creative; I love it. In show business, on the other hand, your own efforts are not necessarily the molders of your future.

"I consider myself most fortunate to be able to combine the two."

Art and Jack Linkletter, around the time of *Hootenanny*. The son would eventually manage his father's extensive business holdings. *From the author's collection*

Behind the scenes, Weintraub was retained as Talent Consultant and Greggory as head writer. Lewine formed a producing company, Dankar Productions, and engaged Garth Dietrick to direct. A television veteran since 1951, breaking in at NBC's flagship station, WNBT in New York, Dietrick was currently associated with ABC's network news programming, most recently its *Politics '62* series. He brought along a 45-pound portable camera regularly used for on-the-spot reports, informally known as the "creepy peepie," which could easily be swept across a row of student faces as they sang along.

Dankar then arranged with six East Coast universities to host. Melnick's right-hand man, network executive producer John Green, would accompany Lewine, Weintraub and Dietrick to each institution. To expedite production and keep costs to a minimum, two separate shows would be taped back-to-back at every school, with at least one act— usually the headliner—appearing in both.

While all this pre-production hubbub was going on, ABC execs were scrutinizing the first quarterly ratings report for 1962-63, and suddenly *Hootenanny* became a mid-season replacement for a series in its death throes: *Mr. Smith Goes to Washington.* The Oscar-winning 1939 feature starring Jimmy Stewart was now an insipid sitcom starring Fess Parker, and audiences were not amused. *Mr. Smith* aired at 8:30 PM Saturday evening, a far-too-lucrative timeslot to waste on a loser.

Cynthia Lowry was first with the news in her Associated Press column *TV News and Views* on February 13: "The April title of an ABC show may well be 'Mr. Smith Goes to Oblivion,' when the series… will be dropped. It will be replaced by a country-music, folk-song half hour called 'Hootenanny,' with Jack Linkletter, son of Art, as head man." *TV Guide's* <u>TV Teletype: New York</u> department made a similar announcement in the February 16 issue, confirming *Mr. Smith's* final airing would be March 30. Proctor & Gamble, Remington and Miles Laboratories signed on as participating sponsors.

February 20 saw the production of Lewine's initial two programs, for which the weekly show biz bible, *Variety,* gave a quick overview: "'Hootenanny' taping at George Washington [University] drew a 'bursting at the seams' audience of GWU undergraduates, and ABC-TV looks for a similar outpouring of students next Monday and Tuesday (March 4 and 5) when executive producer Richard Lewine and ABC-TV program exec John Green take their crew to the Brown campus in Providence for a taping at Sayles Hall. Judy Collins and Theodore Bikel are among the guest stars slated for the Brown U. taping, the former coming in from Denver for the program. Host Jack Linkletter will fly in from Hollywood. High interest is being evinced in this folk singing program, first regular network tv series based on folk music."

High interest indeed: *Newsweek* sent a reporter to Providence to cover the event and gave it a three-column spread in its March 18 issue under the title "The Folknik Show." "After years of toe-in-the-water specials, TV is at long last preparing to play folk music in prime time… [The] show's makers have had the sense to let folk music enter the mass medium on its own terms, which are strictly informal and spontaneous." Of course, *Newsweek* couldn't resist pointing out the contradiction between 'spontaneous' music and rigidly timed commercial TV, and the resulting headaches afflicting the production people; all quoted anonymously: "'The basis of folk music is informality,' said the Journeymen's John Phillips. A harassed 'Hootenanny' executive put it differently. 'It's a smear of music,' he said. 'You ask them how many bars they have in their introduction and they look at you as though you just came down from Mars. Some of these groups are so undisciplined musically that they never do the same number in the same amount of time twice.'"

Nevertheless, the artists were optimistic… guardedly. "Before, they tried to dramatize folk music in a studio," Judy Collins knowingly replied, having experienced it first-hand in a January appearance on CBS's *Dinner With the President*, a live special featuring President Kennedy commemorating the 50th anniversary of the Anti-Defamation League of the B'nai B'rith. "This is the home territory, the colleges," Collins continued. "It was the obvious thing." Theo Bikel agreed, seeing the same advantages and pitfalls of performing for university students as did Lewine: "They're very enthusiastic. They're also critical. If they don't like, they don't like. Other audiences, they're not critical—but they're not enthusiastic, either." Bikel also understood that every TV series needs a large audience to remain on the air. "Even the people doing the show are afraid in their heart of hearts that there may not be enough [viewers], so they try to do it fast and snappy to attract everybody."

Theodore Bikel, Judy Collins and Jack Linkletter chat between songs at Brown University. *From the author's collection*

Bikel's manager was Harold Leventhal, still managing Pete Seeger and The Weavers, as well as The Tarriers and Joan Baez. When Leventhal periodically inquired about having Seeger on the show, the silence on Dankar's end was deafening. When *they* inquired about Joan Baez, she pointedly asked if Seeger would also be invited.

What happened next threatened to sink *Hootenanny* even before it reached the air.

CHAPTER 2

"Why Pick on This Show?"

Jazz critic and *Village Voice* columnist Nat Hentoff could be infuriating; even his friends thought so. Although he leaned leftward politically, in his eyes, free speech was free speech, whether you agreed with what was being said or not. No one should be silenced, he maintained, including himself, unafraid over the years to argue against some of his side's sacred cows, such as legalized abortion. In the spring of 1963, though, free speech was still hard to come by for those who openly supported progressive causes like labor unions and civil rights. And when Hentoff got wind of what was happening between *Hootenanny* and Pete Seeger, he went digging for the facts, which were spelled out and spiced with generous helpings of disgust in his *Voice* column of March 14:

"I've checked out the story at ABC and with several other sources, and it's true. Worth adding is the fact that this is not the first time Joan Baez has turned down television offers because Pete isn't 'pure' enough politically to be on the same show with her....

"The Kafkaesque judge at ABC, by the way, has also ordained that The Weavers do not belong in 'Hootenanny....' It is also true that a couple of performers who once were blacklisted are now 'safe' enough to be hired... and I have heard it said in the past few days that 'at least we've broken the blacklist to this extent, and that's a sign of progress.' Another, non-musical participant in 'Hootenanny' added, 'Well, at least we'll be getting folk music to a lot more people than ever before through this series, and that's a sign of progress. It's tough on Pete, but after all, he's been turned down by all three networks. Why pick on this show?'

"It seems to me that it's not necessary to dwell long on this grubby, upwardly mobile morality. Joan Baez is absolutely correct in her position. I do wonder, however, whether some of the other performers who have agreed to be on 'Hootenanny'—and they include a number of resplendent liberals—know about the Seeger blacklisting. And I wonder how, if they do know about it, they rationalize their abandonment of Pete…. It would be far better for folk music, for the performers involved, and for the public moral health if there were no 'Hootenanny' series rather than a series from which one man has been egregiously excluded.

"I suspect that the absence of [Seeger's] presence will gnaw at some of the folk singers who are cooperating in the expunging of his voice from network television. It'll be extremely interesting to see if any one of them, however, joins Joan Baez in saying 'No' to scared power. But then again, there is all that bread and all that exposure. On the other hand, what are you exposing when you go out there and leave Mr. Seeger behind?"

A few newspapers also picked up the story. *Variety* noted the brouhaha on March 20 with a bit more detail: "ABC-TV, seconding previous actions by NBC-TV and CBS-TV has turned down folksinger Pete Seeger and The Weavers for the weekly folk music series scheduled for April…. Joan Baez, who received national attention recently via a [*TIME* magazine] cover story, has refused to do the show….

"Other top folk acts plan to meet within the next few days in New York to decide whether they should follow Miss Baez's lead (first step, however, will probably be a group appeal to the network and 'Hootenanny's' producers to allow Seeger and the Weavers to appear).

"Personal manager Harold Leventhal… who in the last year has tangled with all three networks on The Weaver ensemble appearances, says, 'There's never any official statement on the blacklisting. You have to read between the lines when you don't know what they mean anyway. And it comes down to the same old passing of the buck from network top management to ad agency to client.'"

Sing Out! and another Seeger-backed folk music newsletter, *Broadside* (which specialized in newly-composed topical songs), chimed in loudly. Each reprinted Hentoff's *Voice* column in full and would later follow up with their own editorials. As for the man himself, he used his *Sing Out!* column to lament what he predicted would be an artistic disappointment: "All strictly professional performers will be used. Real folk musicians such as Doc Watson, Horton Barker, or Bessie Jones and the Sea Island Singers will not stand a chance of being considered."

After describing the show's college audience layout, Seeger admitted, "It could be a nice format. The folk song revival on its home grounds. With good performers allowed to ad-lib, with meaningful songs and youthful participation, it could be a breath of fresh air on TV. But with the producers of the show knowing little about folk music besides what they learn from the pages of *Billboard* and *Variety* (listing 'top sellers'), and with their usual concern that every song be 'socko!' it will be a miracle if much meaningful music gets to reach the TV screens."

As if to claim true ownership of the word, Folkways Records and *Sing Out!* release the *Sing Out! Hootenanny* LP a month ahead of the TV series' debut. *Billboard*: "The set consists of early performances, going back as many as 20 years.... Many collectors will regard this as a gem." *From the author's collection*

The day after Lewine returned from the University of Michigan, where his third pair of *Hoots* were taped on March 20 (one of which featured The New Lost City Ramblers, a group that included Seeger's half-brother, Mike), he spoke with a reporter from the Long Island-based *Newsday*. "[Seeger and The Weavers] were not banned and I was under no pressure of any blacklist. I don't really know if there is a list." The uncredited reporter continued that Lewine "explained he chose groups such as the Limeliters, the Chad Mitchell Trio and the Smothers Brothers because they are 'far better' than the Weavers.... He said he was not going to use the Weavers or Seeger just because they had pioneered in the business."

Newsday also sought out Leventhal, who couldn't believe his ears. "What [Lewine]'s saying is a fraud and the highest form of hypocrisy conceivable. How can he say that Pete, who originated the term 'hootenanny' in concerts 15 years ago, and the Weavers, with six million records sold, are not as good as other groups?" He also accused the network of handing Lewine the "dirty job" of enforcing their blacklist.

The *Newsday* article appeared on Friday, March 22. The following week, Judy Collins "helped found a committee protesting ABC's position," as told in her autobiography *Trust Your Heart*. "The protesters included Erik Darling, Leon Bibb, Tommy Makem and Izzy Young [owner of the Folklore Center in Greenwich Village]. We met at the Village Gate, gathering place for so many social and political causes, and drafted a letter to the press, the attorney general and the FCC, asking them to outlaw hiring decisions made on political grounds." Chairing the meeting was Bill Faier, singer, banjoist and recent host of a folk music program on New York's WBAI-FM. Four of the six principals had already done the show: Collins and Darling at Brown, Bibb at GWU and Makem at both.

Variety reported all of this in their March 27 issue, and also reached out to Lewine, who insisted there was "no political talk in my office or any word from the ABC management over who is or is not to appear. Our only consideration has been to seek the most entertaining talent suitable for this particular show." They also contacted Leventhal, who reiterated that Lewine's excuses were "sheer hypocrisy. There is a blacklist, and that's that."

By now, Lewine was also aware that Joan Baez had publicly announced her boycott and informed *Variety* she "had insisted on doing a minimum of 15 minutes.... Since she would not settle for less, she was not used." Another "person connected with the show," possibly Weintraub, confirmed Baez had made time demands, but also admitted "she would not do the show without Seeger and The Weavers being included on the roster."

Variety also got in touch with Seeger, who was vacationing in Miami. "I have no desire to be a cause celebré," he told them, "but, in a way, somebody has to be the person around whom the cause revolves. I'd love to do the show on the assumption I do good music." In closing, he assured *Variety's* readers, "I'm not at all bitter. I'm a lucky musician who's making a living singing the songs I love."

Interviewed by Ralph Gleason of the *San Francisco Chronicle*, Lewine labeled Seeger "too slow and thoughtful" and The Weavers not "peppy and funny" enough for *Hootenanny*, adding, "We wanted groups who could carry a national audience, a much larger audience than the Greenwich Village coffee houses. We want to take folk music out to the public without jamming groups down their throat. After all, we want to get away from the esoterics."

The upshot: the committee sent their "telegrams of concern," in *Variety's* words, to ABC, Lewine and the FCC. The network, as they'd been doing since the Baez announcement, punted to Lewine. He spoke with Faier on the telephone but refused to put his words in writing and maintained his public stance that Seeger was rejected on "artistic merit," not politics. ("We aren't taking that bait," Faier commented dryly.) The FCC also received a telegram from the ACLU specifically protesting the Seeger-Weavers issue, and were compelled to issue a statement. Said *Variety*, "FCC declared, in effect, that neither blacklisting nor the application of a political test as a precondition of employment was involved. Rather, 'because of the nature of the cold war and the Communist Party' the practice of inquiring into possible CP membership of performers is 'not inconsistent with the public interest.'"

Faier told *Variety*, "We are confident we have practically full strength of the entire folk singing industry behind us on this issue. At the moment, we are formalizing this strength in terms of signatures on a strongly-worded statement indicating our feelings."

Theodore Bikel weighed in: "The criteria for performance should be only how a man performs," he told *Detroit Free Press* columnist Bettelou

Peterson. "How can it be said that one man singing 'John Henry' and using the same lyrics as another man can sway people to a particular creed?" He also shared details of a second controversy: "Before I did my shows, I learned The Tarriers, a racially mixed group, had been dropped from the show. It was not stated, but the reason undoubtedly was sponsor pressure because of possible Southern reaction. I objected strongly. I don't know if it was my protest or not, but they will be on."

Folk and blues singer Barbara Dane was approached to guest on a *Hootenanny* to be taped at Penn State University, and declined. So did The Greenbriar Boys, an east-coast Bluegrass troupe, when they were invited to appear on the show at Rutgers. Along with up-and-coming singer-songwriter Tom Paxton, each declared they would not accept *Hootenanny* invitations unless Seeger was included. Both Dane and the Greenbriars issued statements through Faier's committee:

Dane: "Please feel free to include my name with those of our craft who realize that without Pete Seeger there would be no 'Hootenanny,' or at least it would not be about to make all that money for somebody in this decade."

Greenbriar Boys: "Pete Seeger should be on this show. He should not only be on it, he should also be a unifying factor throughout the whole series. He has been the backbone of the younger generation which this series highlights. He is obviously being blacklisted and we don't wish to support this practice, therefore we have refused to participate in the show."

Clearly a boycott was on; only time would tell if Faier's claim to having the "full strength of the entire folk singing industry" was genuine or hyperbole, and whether it would break the blacklist or the show. In the meantime, the series made its debut on schedule.

CHAPTER 3

SEASON ONE: "The Hit of the Spring"

Several newspapers subscribed to a wire service called *TV Key*, which provided capsule reviews for each day's line up, usually the networks' prime time offerings. For April 6, they called the *Hootenanny* premiere the evening's BEST BET: "**Hootenanny**, a new program, attempts to capitalize on the rage for folk music. Producer Richard Lewine is taping his shows at college campuses, with his artists giving concerts for the undergraduates. The camera will watch this concert, with host Jack Linkletter—they're calling him a 'describer'—standing on the sidelines and talking about what is being performed, rather than introducing the acts. In this first one, we're at the University of Michigan. As the show begins, the concert is already under way with The Limeliters working. Bud and Travis, Bob Gibson and Bonnie Dobson are the other acts you'll watch. Anyone who enjoys folk music will welcome this, television's first regularly scheduled folk music show."

1-01: University of Michigan, Ann Arbor #1

Recording Date: March 20, 1963.

Airdate: April 6, 1963. *Repeat*: July 6, 1963

The Limeliters: "I Had a Mule," "Wake Up, Dunia," "The Riddle Song."

Bud and Travis: "Raspberries, Strawberries," "Delia's Gone."

Bob Gibson: "Good News," "Yes I See" (with *The Limeliters*).

Bonnie Dobson: "She's Like a Swallow," "Fare Thee Well" (with *Bob Gibson*).

FINALE: "Mary Don't You Weep" (*Everyone*).

Jack Linkletter, looking very collegiate, and The Limeliters, looking anything but, in a publicity still for *Hootenanny's* premiere. *From the author's collection*

The first *Hootenanny* to air was the sixth taped. Already recorded were the two shows each at George Washington University and Brown University, plus the pilot... although the latter would at some point be re-edited with inserts of Jack Linkletter replacing Jean Shepherd. Throughout the show's history, ABC would be anxious to get the most recent segments on the air, preferring that audiences be exposed to the *Hootenanny* format after its bugs had been worked out.

That might not have worked to their advantage. Based on some of the reviews, the Michigan students were not visibly enthusiastic.

Possibly it was the weather, with temperatures hovering around 30 degrees, and wind and flurries in the forecast.

Bob Gibson: handsome, witty, unpredictable, and immensely talented.

Bob Gibson was playing at the Bitter End while Melnick, Weintraub and the Ashley-Steiner people were brainstorming the series. According to Gibson's autobiography, *I Come For To Sing*, it was his idea to close with a group sing featuring all the performers. By that time, he'd been performing for the better part of a decade and authored several folk classics like "Well, Well, Well" and "There's a Meetin' Here Tonight." At the first Newport Folk Festival, he brought 18-year-old Joan Baez to the stage and launched her stellar career. He was a respected folk ambassador whose only problem was an over-dependence on stimulants that he'd mix with marijuana to take the edge off, a combination that at times led to unpredictable behavior.

Gibson makes his first of eight appearances, the most of any solo performer. His recurring presence affirms Lewine and company were unafraid that one banjo-playing folksinger leading the students in frothy sing-alongs like "Good News" wouldn't hold audience interest. But Gibson was never the headliner, although certainly talented enough to handle the role; furthermore, he was younger and infinitely more photogenic than Seeger, which counted for much with Madison Avenue. What Lewine *should* have told *Variety* was, "We're seeking the most entertaining talent suitable for selling Oxydol and Alka Seltzer."

Conversely, Bonnie Dobson, best remembered for writing the haunting post-nuclear apocalypse ballad "Morning Dew," was absolutely a Seeger disciple, and after completing this one show, she never returned. "The first time I heard Seeger sing was a revelation," she told *Shindig!* magazine in 2014. "He had a gift for making anybody relax and be happy and sing. It sounds corny but he really strove for understanding between people. Everybody who emerged during that '60s folk period, we were all Seeger's babies. He was real and wonderful."

Most of the newspaper and trade critics weren't overly impressed. "If ABC expects to make its college 'Hootenanny' series a TV success, somebody may have to start rehearsing the student audiences," wrote *The New York Post's* Bob Williams. "The searching cameras turned up nothing in the undergraduate gathering suggesting unrestrained enthusiasm or total absorption. The viewer was left wondering whether shyness or disinterest… may have been responsible. [The show] must capture the student audience if it is to capture living-room interest."

Variety's reviewer 'Gros' concurred: "For the past several years, the folkniks have been hitting the campus circuit for a big [box office] score via the loyal support of the cleancut(*sic*) college crowd. It therefore follows that tv should pick up on the folk trend…. Unfortunately, though, ABC-TV's venture into the folk arena, with a series tagged 'Hootenanny,' is built along the lines of routine vaudeo fare. The preem show lacked the spark and spirit that is found in 'live' college and concert dates and even though the show was taped at the U. of Michigan at Ann Arbor, the undergrads seemed inhibited and too aware that they and the show were on camera. The introductory patter prepared for the series emcee, Jack Linkletter, was of elementary school nature and did nothing to enliven the proceedings. The guestars(*sic*), too, seemed to lack their usual zest and delivered as though it were just another shot on an ordinary variety bill…. The series will move to a different college each week with a different lineup of performers so there's bound to be a pickup in buoyancy along the line. Even so, the folk bit is still a special taste and it's doubtful if the series will broaden the palatability."

Ben Gross of the *New York Daily News* took Seeger's point of view that the show lacked authentic folk talent: "I don't know about you… but as far as I'm concerned I've had my fill of folk singing. It has become too civilized since leaving the farms and backwoods to become 'sophisticated' night club entertainment." The same stance was taken by Howard Abrams of the university's student paper, *Michigan Daily*: "As folk music, it stunk…. Perhaps the TV producers are right [that] the average American does have an idiot mentality and taste to match."

UPI's Rick DuBrow brought more than a touch of sarcasm to an otherwise favorable review: "A folk-singing show hosted by Jack Linkletter is something akin to a symposium on Henry Miller presided over by Donna Reed…. Happily, Linkletter kept almost entirely out of things, which was almost enough; and the result was that 'Hootenanny' had a number of pleasant things to recommend it. To start with, it replaces the 'Mr. Smith Goes to Washington' series. Furthermore, it is good to see a show that is virtually 'live,' and pays some attention to an intelligent group of college students. I don't know how pure the folk singing was. But it was nice again to hear the Limeliters singing something other than a commercial; and Gibson picks a pretty mean, rollicking banjo. I continue to maintain, however, that the lyrics of most folk songs are as purely idiotic as opera plots."

More impressed by both the show and Linkletter was the *Atlanta Constitution's* Paul Jones: "It doesn't seem possible that something called 'Hootenanny' could be entertaining—but it is. ABC-TV's new series devoted to folk music made its debut Saturday night and turned out to be one of the most agreeable surprises of the season…. The presentations are informal with Jack Linkletter… spotted in various parts of the auditorium, on stage, seated in the audience [or] on steps…. His introductory remarks are brief and to the point. I hope that this program… will serve to acquaint teen-agers with a type of music that is far better than the rock 'n' roll mumbo-jumbo now heard on nine out of 10 radio stations in the land. Let's hope that the sudden popularity of folk music continues and that TV's 'Hootenanny' grows and prospers."

Harry Harris of *The Philadelphia Inquirer* also liked it, at least compared to *Sing Along with Mitch*: "Now, thanks to ABC's half-hour 'Hootenanny,' TV audiences can sing along with those favorites of campus and coffee house, the guitar-strumming folkniks. There are no lyrics on the screen, no satanic arm-waver to guide the beat, but the words are simple, the rhythms clear and the melodies irresistible. In fact, 'simple' and 'irresistible' just about sum up the show."

Alone among his Big Apple colleagues, only Jack Gould of *The New York Times* waxed enthusiastic, complete with his own dig at Mitch Miller's *Sing Along*: "The naturalness of the setting, which on the first show was an auditorium at the University of Michigan, adds immensely to the show's interest…. When the student body joined in, the ensemble effect had a delightful charm and warmth. The Michigan undergraduates certainly put it all over Mitch Miller's creaky chorale." Overall, thought Gould, "the American Broadcasting Company appears to have made both a thoroughly pleasant and enterprising departure from the staid programming norm. Mark it down as the hit of the spring."

However, Gould's enthusiasm was tempered by "one disquieting note. Apparently, Pete Seeger's private political concerns continue to keep him off all network shows of folk singing. Since he is at liberty to appear on stages and can be heard at home on recordings, why should TV prolong its blacklist? Mr. Seeger's credential for TV is his art, which is in order."

As for Nat Hentoff, he thought the premiere "was a drag. Musically and in terms of camera work.… Above all, the show was dull. And Seeger, whatever his occasional stylistic deficiencies by my way of listening, is never that. The point, of course, is that there is no likelihood whatsoever that Seeger was absent for musical reasons. An aesthetician Mr. Lewine is not. A scared man he is."

At present, only an audio snippet posted to YouTube by a fan circulates from this show.

1-02: Brown University, Providence RI #1

Recording Date: March 5, 1963.

Airdate: April 13, 1963. *Repeat*: July 13, 1963

Theodore Bikel: "Daddy Roll 'Em" (with *The Journeymen*)

The Journeymen: "I May Be Right"

Ian & Sylvia: "Mary Ann"

The Rooftop Singers: "Good Time"

Theodore Bikel: "Two Brothers," "A Mighty Day" (with *The Journeymen*).

Ian & Sylvia: "Rocks and Gravel"

The Journeymen: "500 Miles"

The Rooftop Singers: "Walk Right In"

Theodore Bikel: "Dodi Lee"

FINALE: "Railroad Bill" (*Everyone*).

No known video or audio survives from the broadcast as of this writing. *TV Key* affirmed, "Actor-folksinger Theo Bikel's talent helps make this second 'hoot' a lively show. His rendition of the poignant folk ballad 'Two Brothers' is a highlight. Bikel receives able musical support from the Journeymen, Ian and Sylvia, and the Rooftop Singers, who offer their popular hit, 'Walk Right In.' The appreciative audience is made up of students from Brown University in Providence, R.I." Actually, as is known from the surviving audio of show #8, the male students were from Brown and the females from Pembroke College.

"Folk singing is an avocation. I am still primarily an actor," Bikel told Leslie Blatt of the *Brown Daily Herald*. "I have been an actor for some twenty years and a professional folk singer for about seven." An actor he indeed was, but his "avocation" served him in good stead.

Bikel was born in Vienna in 1924; when the Nazis took over in 1937, he and his family fled to Palestine. He joined the Habima Theater in Tel Aviv, moved on to the Royal Academy of Dramatic Arts in London and, under the direction of Laurence Olivier, played in the October 1949 British production of *A Streetcar Named Desire*; first as an understudy, then eventually taking the role of Mitch. Two years later, director John Huston cast him as the Nazi gunboat captain in *The African Queen* (1951). More film appearances swiftly followed, including an Oscar-nominated role in *The Defiant Ones* (1958). Between acting assignments, Bikel could be found singing in Greenwich Village and other places, and was an early signee to the Elektra label. His reputation grew so quickly that when he was cast as Captain Von Trapp in the original Broadway production of *The Sound of Music* in 1959, Rodgers and Hammerstein created "Edelweiss" for him. "Oscar Hammerstein was by then very ill," he liked to remind interviewers, "and it was the last song he ever worked on. The last word he wrote was the final one in the song: 'Forever.'"

When asked, ex-Tarrier and Weaver Erik Darling made clear why he'd formed The Rooftop Singers: "To make a hit record of 'Walk Right In.'" The song, which went to the top of *Billboard's* Hot 100, was written by Gus Cannon in 1913 and recorded by him and his Memphis Jug Stompers in the late 1920s. Cannon lived in Memphis all his life and in later years would sit on the porch playing the banjo upon which he'd written his song. Aspiring local musicians would sometimes come by, listen, and occasionally join in; one of these was a door-to-door appliance salesman named Johnny Cash.

Darling allegedly heard "Walk Right In" on a tape housed at the Library of Congress. William Svanoe, a left-handed 12-string guitar virtuoso, and Lynne Taylor, a jazz vocalist who'd sung with Benny Goodman's orchestra, joined forces with Darling and recorded it for Vanguard. The week it reached number one, the nearly-destitute Cannon had hocked his banjo. Eventually the publishing company discovered the song was not an adaptation but an original composition. That led to a visit by the label-credited Darling and Svanoe, who got his banjo out of hock and offered him $500 plus one-fourth of royalties. Cannon's hopes of getting rich didn't materialize. "[The publishing company] didn't hardly send him over $300 to $400 year," his niece, Mrs. Rosetta Taylor, told the *Memphis Commercial-Appeal* in 1979. "He was mostly living on his Social Security." Cannon died that year on October 15, age 104.

Billboard's Barry Kittleson waited until he'd seen this show before writing a scathing review: "ABC-TV's Saturday Night 'Hootenanny' is in more hot water than was created by the stir over its alleged blacklisting of Pete Seeger and the Weavers. It is in desperate need of a suitable format to bring the show to life…. (The) second show in the series… as in the case with its premiere, missed coming off. The lineup of talent was first rate… [but] only made it double apparent that anyone can be made to look dull. The producers of the show try very hard to create an authentic college concert atmosphere. Instead, they've whipped up a monster that is reminiscent of the amateur days of early television."

Kittleson's biggest gripes were the very things Melnick and Lewine believed set *Hootenanny* apart: its intimacy and immediacy. "Linkletter lurks in the background only to come on like a reporter at a wrestling match, hand-mike, tweedy jacket and all, whispering over the first few bars of each selection in 'You Are There' fashion. The audience is thoroughly uncomfortable and intimidated by the awareness that they may at any moment be panned by [the] camera. The performers give the impression that they have been manipulated into a straight jacket and can't wait to get out. The whole business is uneasy and self-conscious."

Consequently, he maintained the solution was the very thing Lewine *didn't* want to do: "The producers might well benefit by going back to the use of the proscenium set-up which puts everybody where they belong. They might create the enthusiasm of an authentic college concert if they do."

The Journeymen—Dick Weissman, John Phillips and Scott McKenzie—make the first of their two *Hootenanny* appearances. Weissman would later become a respected author and instructor of music history, Phillips would co-organize The Mamas and the Papas, and McKenzie would score a hit with the Phillips-penned "San Francisco (Be Sure to Wear Flowers in Your Hair)." *From the author's collection*

The critic's perception of "uncomfortable" students "intimidated" by the presence of TV cameras was contradicted by another young reporter for Brown's own *Daily Herald*. "Tuesday night, after two days of hauling lights and cameras, of constant script reading and rewriting, and of positioning the groups and their guitars, the doors finally opened to let in the long-patient line of students that had stretched back through the Faunce House Arch," Charles Hartman proclaimed in the next day's issue. "They arrived eager for good seats on the floor, with their blankets, pillows and a few secretly-appropriated lounge cushions. Frantic ushers packed students into corners they didn't know existed…. Finally, the long-awaited call was heard and Theodore Bikel and the Journeymen stepped up onto the platform, surrounded by an abstraction of blinding lights and expectant faces. The show was on…. Rapt faces and applause greeted each individual act. The students yelled for more and more…."

Brown was among the five universities that hosted tapings prior to the show's debut. Associate Producer Don Silverman was an alumnus who influenced the school's selection. What was perceived as audience intimidation was more likely awe that they were getting all this entertainment for free. Once *Hootenanny* started airing, students at other colleges would circulate petitions and otherwise lobby for a visit, and if successful, they knew what to expect… and what was expected of *them*.

During the coming week, Hentoff would pen a follow-up to his *Village Voice* column: "Singers Tom Paxton and Barbara Dane and the Greenbriar Boys (a bluegrass unit) have turned down appearances on ABC's 'Hootenanny' series for the same reason that Joan Baez refused to appear…. [Their] decision was particularly selfless. They do not as yet have reputations outside of a relatively small nucleus of listeners, and being on the program could have benefitted them considerably. It is easy enough for an outsider to challenge ABC and 'Hootenanny' in *The Voice*, but the action of these folk performers is of a different order of courage and deserves respect as well, I hope, as emulation."

Broadside published its editorial, by Gordon Friesen, recapping the controversy and asserting, "ABC, and the other networks, should be reminded once more that the airwaves still belong to the American public; the TV industry is only chartered to use these airwaves as long as its output serves 'the interests of the public.' We all have the right to see and hear Pete Seeger on TV, regardless of how Mr. ABC or any other TV outfit feels about it…. It is hoped that the drive against TV network blacklisting started by Nat Hentoff's article will lead to common sense and reason prevailing and this evil kicked into the ashcan."

Despite all the negativity, the ratings were better on the second week than for the premiere, according to *Variety*: "The show garnered a 32% share, compared to a 33.6 for CBS-TV's 'The Defenders' and a 27.1 for NBC-TV's 'Joey Bishop Show.' Opening week for the folksing showed a 26 share in the Nielsen 30-market survey. Boost in ratings during the second week was wholly at the expense of 'The Defenders.'"

1-03: Pennsylvania State University, University Park #1

Recording Date: April 3, 1963.

Airdate: April 20, 1963. *Repeat*: July 20, 1963

The Limeliters: "The Bear Chase" (*Jack Linkletter intro*)

The Limeliters: "Western Wind"

The Carter Family: "Sun's Gonna Shine"

The Limeliters: "When I First Came to This Land"

The Phoenix Singers: "The Music Train"

The Limeliters: "Yerakina."

Will Holt: "Lemon Tree"

The Phoenix Singers: "Mighty Joe Macarack"

The Carter Family: "Foggy Mountain Top" (with *The Limeliters*).

FINALE: "Goodnight, Irene" (*Everyone*).

"Not a dull moment in tonight's folk song fest," *TV Key* assured its readers, and the surviving audio confirms it. It's a sprightly show with an interesting line-up: the all-white female Carter Family ("Mother" Maybelle and daughters Helen, June and Anita) from southwestern Virginia and the all-black male Phoenix Singers (Roy Thompson, Ned Wright and Arthur Williams), ex-Broadway musical vocalists who met as members of The Belafonte Folk Singers chorale. If this was Lewine's or ABC's idea of prepping southern affiliates for interracial performances, it was an impressive one, although no one at *Sing Out!* or *Broadside* would ever admit it. Each group did two songs. For balance, there is singer-songwriter Will Holt performing his own composition, "Lemon Tree," which had already become a folk standard thanks to Peter, Paul & Mary.

The Limeliters, rehearsing at Penn State, remain smartly dressed. *From the author's collection*

Headlining, of course, were the Limeliters. "I have been informed that there is a relatively small group of the specially initiated among the student body whose esoteric sensibilities are offended at the thought that the the Limeliters, who topped the bill here, being classed as true folk singers." This from *Pittsburgh Post-Gazette* TV columnist Win Fanning, whose paper sent him to cover the taping. Fanning, who thought the Limeliters and Kingston Trio "represent the best thing that has happened to popular vocal music in more than a decade," couldn't resist adding that his informant classed this group of probable *Sing Out!* devotees as "definitely in the out group on campus."

The jovial columnist reported that dress rehearsals were taped as well as 'final' evening performances for both shows, presumably to give Lewine and company another choice for every song. Tickets were issued for both rehearsal and performance, so there'd be an audience for each. He also informed readers that songs were selected the night before, and in listing out the guest lineup for each performance, revealed this show was the second of the two segments taped at the end of what was described as a very long day.

Which might explain Jack Linkletter's two flubs. First, in introducing The Carter Family as having originated in the 1920s, he twice refers to the remaining founding member as "Marybelle" instead of Maybelle. One tune by the Limeliters later, he introduces The Phoenix Singers and erroneously changes Ned Wright's first name to "Nick." Fanning observed Linkletter rehearsing with a mass of curious students gathered around him. "Ego-wise, I don't like the kids reading the cards with me," he told another columnist a couple of weeks later, "but I need 'em, especially for singers' names and song titles."

In his review of the broadcast, Fred Remington of the *Pittsburgh Press* termed the series "a delightful half-hour" that "brings good folk-singing groups together on various college campuses. The college audiences are responsive without being hysterical like 'The Price is Right' or 'Queen For a Day' audiences. Last night, 'Hootenanny' was at Penn State and the singing groups included the witty, beautifully-blended Limelighters(*sic*). A group previously unknown to me, The Phoenix Singers, also performed with gusto and dash and a dazzling interplay of voices. It was as swift a half-hour as television has given us in a long while."

During the week between this show and the next, *Variety* announced that *Hootenanny* was being considered as an hour-long series for the Fall season, planning for which was well under way, "if the ratings continue to hold up." They'd also announce that Ramblin' Jack Elliot, a long-time admirer of Seeger and his mentor, Woody Guthrie, had joined the boycott. "If I did the program, I couldn't stand up and sing again, or sit down to dinner again, with Pete Seeger, the greatest folk singer of them all and the originator of the whole idea of hootenanny," he wrote to Bill Faier, who added, "We want the show to succeed, but it never will as long as they eliminate the best people in the field before they even start."

Behind the scenes, though, Seeger was advocating against a boycott, apparently having seen enough good in what had aired so far. He told Theo Bikel it was more important that the series be given the chance to present folk music to a mass audience than to appear on it himself. As Bikel told *Variety*, "If we were to boycott the show, they might have to say 'All right, forget the whole thing,'" and suggested a more effective protest would be to "flood the sponsor with letters telling them they're going to stop buying his product."

1-04: Rutgers University, New Brunswick, NJ #1

Recording Date: April 15, 1963.

Airdate: April 27, 1963. *Repeat*: July 27, 1963.

Video: UCLA Film & Television Archive: 16mm archival copy, T3359; VHS non-circulating Research & Study Center copy, VA635_T.

The Chad Mitchell Trio: "Leave Me if You Want To" (*Jack Linkletter intro*)

The Chad Mitchell Trio: "Ain't No More Cane on This Brazos"

Judy Henske: "Wade in the Water"

The Smothers Brothers: "Marching to Pretoria"

The Chad Mitchell Trio: "DuBarry Done Gone Again"

The Simon Sisters: "Wynken, Blynken and Nod"

The Smothers Brothers: "Daniel Boone," "Sail Away Lady" (with Judy Henske)

The Chad Mitchell Trio: "Moscow Nights"

FINALE: "Joshua Fit the Battle of Jericho" (*Everyone*)

The earliest *Hootenanny* to survive in full, it's also the first for The Chad Mitchell Trio, who made nine separate appearances, the most of any group. Chad Mitchell, Mike Kobluk and Mike Pugh formed the Trio in 1959 at Gonzaga University in Spokane, Washington. Mitchell and Kobluk had been members of the university's glee club, and together with Pugh, they "were singing pretty regularly at various social functions, for kicks and beer money," Kobluk wrote for the Trio's website, chadmitchelltrio.com.

A priest friend of Mitchell's family, Fr. Reinard Beaver, had heard the three and thought they had real potential. In the summer of 1960, he needed to attend Army Chaplain School in New York, and convinced the others they could "sing their way across the country, spend 6 or 7 weeks in New York… and drive back in time for the fall semester." Fr. Beaver's enthusiasm was catching and all agreed. By taking catch-as-catch-can singing jobs along the way, they made it to the Big Apple and ended up with a record deal, a musical director named Milt Okun, appearances on Arthur Godfrey's radio show, and a gig at the Blue Angel nightclub. They worked for several months, until Pugh decided to return to school for Spring 1961. The others held auditions and in December 1960, Joe Frazier from Lebanon, Pennsylvania, was selected.

Like any college-educated son of a steelworker, Frazier's politics were, in his words, "progressive, working class" and although that sensibility had already formed within Mitchell and Kobluk, his presence brought it to the forefront on stage. The group mixed satirical and serious message songs into their repertoire, which earned them a level of respect not shown to the Kingston Trio, the latter's record sales notwithstanding. They strove to get that material on the air and, in subsequent *Hootenanny* appearances, would succeed. For now, they had to settle for a chain gang song and a Tom Paxton composition that were slated for the first album on their new label, Mercury Records, plus a Russian-language song, "Moscow Nights," the lyrics for which, Linkletter assures us, were "a simple poem that promotes moonlight, midnight, snow and, of course, romance."

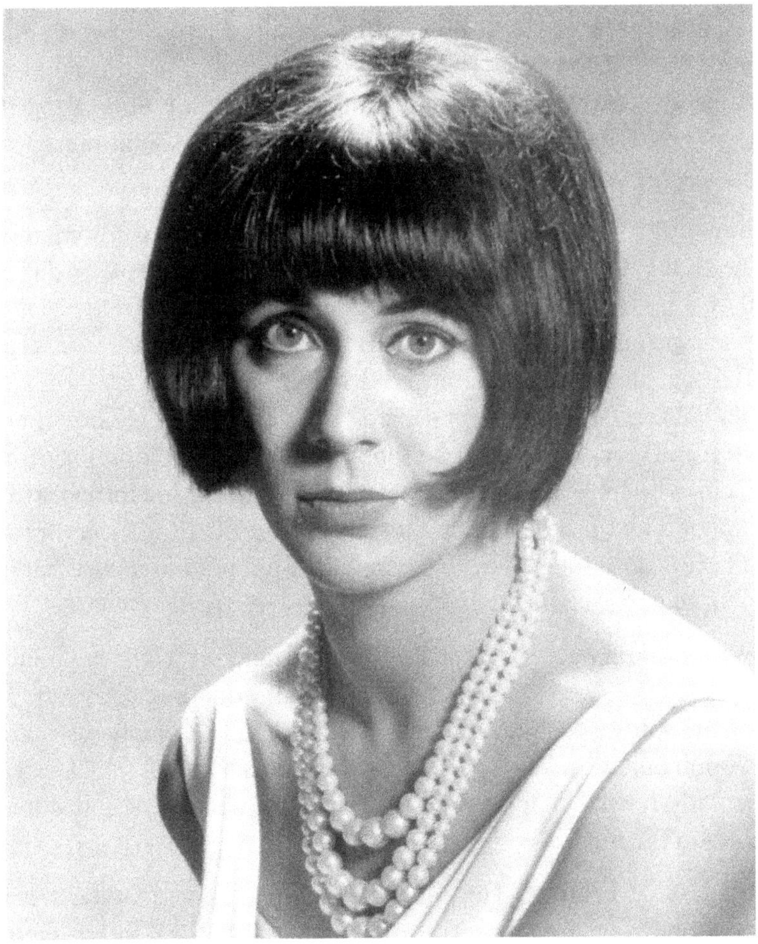

The extraordinary Judy Henske, at the outset of her career. *From the author's collection*

Judy Henske makes her first of three appearances. Born in Chippewa Falls, Wisconsin in 1936, Judith Anne Henske sang in church and school choirs while growing up. By her senior year at McDonnell High School, her talent was obvious. On May 23, 1954, a reporter for the *Chippewa Herald-Telegram* attended a school recital where Henske performed selections by Schubert, Mendelssohn and Dvorak, and was deeply impressed: "This beautiful young singer made a striking appearance on the stage and gave every evidence of intensive training during all of the intricate phases of the various composers. A bright future in the musical world is assured Judy Henske should she follow it through as a career." After getting kicked out of two Midwest colleges, she opted for California in 1959, where she debuted in an establishment called the Zen Coffee House and Motorcycle Repair Shop for $30 per week. "The coffeehouse was behind the cycle shop. It attracted a kind of Hell's Angels crowd," she recalled.

In early 1961, Dave Guard, fed up with the growing commercialism of The Kingston Trio, recruited Henske for his new group, The Whiskeyhill Singers, which also featured a former classmate of Guard's, Cyrus Faryar on guitar, and David "Buck" Wheat on bass. She recalled in 2013 that the Kingston Trio "did all these songs that didn't cause trouble, were nicely sung… but then Dave wanted to get down and be funky. And Dave could never be funky, so he went looking for people in the group to be funky. And he chose me." The quartet recorded an album for Capitol and a brace of songs for the MGM film *How The West Was Won* (1962), only four of which were used, but not much else happened and Henske departed in July 1962.

With a bluesy style meshed with folk material, Henske "comes on long and strong," says Linkletter in his introduction. That she does, wailing the spiritual "Wade in the Water" here with enough gusto to blow Janis Joplin out of the room. It's a kick to watch some of the Douglas co-eds behind Henske snapping fingers, shaking shoulders and otherwise grooving to the music.

By way of contrast, The Simon Sisters, Lucy and Carly, were still wide-eyed newcomers to the folk scene, and here they are, in their first network TV appearance, chirping Lucy's arrangement of Eugene Fields'

"Wynken, Blynken and Nod." The duo didn't as yet have a record deal; *that* oversight would be rectified by the Kapp label almost immediately after this show aired.

A publicity photo of The Smothers Brothers from around the time of their *Hootenanny* appearance captures their on-stage personae. *From the author's collection*

The Smothers Brothers seemingly went straight from San Jose State University to San Francisco's Purple Onion nightclub in 1959. The comedic duo had already scored nationwide success on the Jack Paar edition of *The Tonight Show* and recorded three successful albums for

Mercury when they appeared here. Lewine was enough of a fan to sign them for both Rutgers shows, the first non-headliner act to get that distinction. Given the hardline political stance they took with their own starring series four years later, one wonders what they thought when they looked at what was going on outside that evening.

Ten days earlier, Pete Seeger had performed before an enthusiastic, appreciative crowd of 2,500 in the campus gymnasium. Now, four students—seniors Jim Egen, Dave Grossman and Robert Rosen, plus junior Anthony Boyle—announced in the Letters column of the *Rutgers Daily Targum*, "we believe that a protest against Seeger's blacklisting is in order.... Rutgers students turned out en masse at his recent appearance on this campus [while] the *Hootenanny* people would have us believe that he is unwanted by the public. We invite all Rutgers students to join with us in a picket of the *Hootenanny* program on Monday evening, at 7:00 pm, in front of The Ledge. We also exhort all students who plan to be part of the show's audience to stay away from a program which is directed by those who would destroy our democratic heritage."

"Nearly 400 singing, sign-carrying students at Rutgers University staged a demonstration tonight against what they termed the blacklisting of certain folksingers by the television networks," reported the Associated Press wire service. "The pickets, strumming guitars, plucking banjos and enjoying their own songfest, gathered in front of The Ledge, a social center at Rutgers, the state university. Inside, some 600 students were attending the American Broadcasting Company's 'Hootenanny'.... Bob Rosen, an organizer of the demonstration, said it was to protest particularly the 'blacklisting' of the folksinger Pete Seeger." Carrying signs that read "Rutgers won't tolerate intolerance" and "The ABC of freedom demands ABC end blacklist," the picketers marched and sang for about 60 minutes before disbanding, although a few gathered beside the truck that housed the taping control room to continue singing. The AP contacted ABC for comment and they punted to Lewine yet again.

On a positive note, the show earned another rave from a newspaper critic. "Last Saturday night, at the teasing of my oldest daughter, I consented to watch for a few minutes," wrote the *San Mateo Times'* Bob Foster for his "TV Screenings" column the following Monday. "As it turns out, 'Hootenanny' is one of the most delightfully refreshing shows to come along in some time. Starring Jack Linkletter, a young man who exceeds his father in personality and ability, the show features the currently popular 'folk singing' type [of] groups…. The decision to do a show featuring this kind of musical group was indeed a smart step on ABC's part."

1-05: George Washington University, Washington DC #1

Recording Date: February 15, 1963.

Airdate: May 4, 1963. *Repeat*: August 3, 1963.

The Limeliters: "Lonesome Traveler," "Hard, Ain't it Hard," "I'm Goin' Back," "Whistling Gypsy."

The Clancy Brothers & Tommy Makem: "Port Lairge," "Bold O'Donohue."

Bob Gibson: "Where I'm Bound," "This Train" (with *The Limeliters*).

Lynn Gold: "Come All Ye Fair and Tender Ladies."

FINALE: "This Little Light of Mine" (*Everyone*).

This was Dankar's first college visit; whether it's show one or two from that taping is unknown. Precious little video and audio exists for the moment, but from the sound of what *does* exist, the audience was suitably enthusiastic and may have been over-mic'd. The hand-clapping is loud and there's a reverb to the singing voices that isn't present in other shows. (Then again, it could be just the reproduction quality of a hand-held Wollensak microphone against a GE Television speaker.) There's also a surprising lack of variety in the song choices: except for Lynn Gold's ballad, all of the selections are up-tempo.

The Clancy Brothers and Tommy Makem perform "Port Lairge" at GWU. That's Makem on the tin whistle, and brothers Pat, Tom and guitarist Liam Clancy. *From the author's collection*

Surviving video comes from a one-minute promo for the show that has been available online for years. A pair of doors open and the camera moves toward The Limeliters as they're performing "Lonesome Traveler." The commercial's remaining 40 seconds are from the original pilot. The existing audio comes from the author's collection: "Bold O'Donohue," "I'm Goin' Back" (a song that, on record, dates back to the 1920s and Uncle Dave Macon, one of the earliest stars of the *Grand Ole*

Opry) and a few seconds of the closing, during which no verses are sung, just the chorus four times.

It's said that the Clancy Brothers and Tommy Makem resurrected traditional Irish songs that had been ignored for years in their homeland. If so, they did it very *un*traditionally, infusing them with the theatrical sensibilities of four working actors who'd left the Auld Sod for North America beginning in the late 1940s and were performing classic drama in Greenwich Village playhouses since that time, singing while between shows mostly for the fun of it, as did their friend Theo Bikel. In 1956, eldest brother Patrick Clancy helped found Tradition Records and the foursome recorded an album of rebellion songs, *The Rising of the Moon*, in the Bronx apartment of a fellow musician.[1] Incredibly, the thing sold. They recorded an album of drinking songs, and that, too, scored a reasonable success. Finally, they took on singing as a full-time endeavor, appeared on *The Ed Sullivan Show* for St. Patrick's Day 1961, were signed to the mighty Columbia label, and their future was assured.

Soprano Lynn Gold, after having moved to Los Angeles from her native Brooklyn while still a teenager, had reserved her love of singing for friends and family until she was heard at a party in 1958 by Ed Pearl, the owner of L.A.'s Ash Grove nightclub. Pearl booked her and she remained for eight months, appearing on an LP for World Pacific records, *A Night at Ash Grove* with Barbara Dane, Bud Dashiell, Travis Edmonson and others. From there, she appeared at Chicago's Gate of Horn. As the folk boom heated up toward the end of 1962, she recorded an album for the Warner Bros. label and in January 1963 appeared on *Dinner with the President*, singing "Shenendoah" with Judy Collins and Will Holt. After her lone *Hootenanny* appearance, she toured with a "Traveling Hootenanny" package show hosted by Lou Gottlieb. A reviewer for the *Emporia Kansas Gazette* enthused, "Lynn Gold… possesses perfect pitch and control, and extraordinary range that maintains its strength and purity in both low and upper registers. [She has] a singing style which is a joy to folk-music lovers." It was also a style strongly reminiscent of the now-internationally famous Joan Baez.

---

[1] Some months later, they re-recorded the tunes in a proper studio and re-released the record.

When the tour ended, Gold worked the coffeehouse circuit, returned to the Ash Grove (along with Gottlieb) in 1965, and continued in this vein until mid-'66 when she faded out of the limelight.

Lynn Gold, one of many sopranos whose vocal style, intentional or not, evoked Joan Baez. *From the author's collection*

Bob Gibson's return is highlighted by "Where I'm Bound," his take on the spiritual "Come And Go With Me To That Land." Based on the recording he released the following year, Rick DuBrow should've found it suitably "rollicking."

"As I write this, TV's 'Hootenanny' is in its fifth week on the ABC network," wrote *Sing Out!* editor Irwin Silber for his magazine's summer issue. "In the heat of the civil liberties issue, the show itself has become almost of secondary interest. TV, which seems destined to be a follower rather than an innovator, has done little more than attempt to trade on the current popularity of folksinging. In the process, the 'Hootenanny' series has become merely a hodge-podge of unrelated songs and performers, with an occasional number or sequence really capturing the spirit and sound of the music…. The net result has been a vaguely unsatisfying half-hour every Saturday night, containing little more than a kiss-and-a-promise of the vast riches of our folk heritage. 'Hootenanny' desperately needs the inimitable art and presence of Pete Seeger."

1-06: University of Virginia, Charlottesville #1

Recording Date: April 30, 1963.

Airdate: May 11, 1963. *Repeat*: August 10, 1963

Video: 16mm kinescope minus commercials. Licensing: Historic Films Archive, LLC, #V-1011. Viewing: The Library of Congress, catalog # MAVIS 2899698. Excerpted on ***The Best of Hootenanny***.

The Chad Mitchell Trio: "Hello Susan Brown" (*Jack Linkletter intro*)

The Travelers 3: "Light From the Lighthouse"

Miriam Makeba: "Umqokozo"

Molly Scott: "Texas River Song (Down By the Brazos)"

The Chad Mitchell Trio: "Whup Jamboree"

The Travelers 3: "Cotton Fields"

Miriam Makeba: "Love Tastes Like Strawberries"

The Chad Mitchell Trio: "The John Birch Society," "Mbube" (with *Miriam Makeba*)

FINALE: "I'm On My Way" (*Everyone*)

Perhaps Silber should have waited another week before penning his editorial, as *this* show took some risks. South Africa's Miriam Makeba, soon to become a prominent anti-Apartheid voice, steps into the spotlight provocatively dressed (her shoulders are bare, save for a silky shawl that keeps slipping down) and sings one song in her native tongue and, a little later, another in English. Then The Chad Mitchell Trio join her for "Mbube," the Zulu warrior tale of a lion hunt that became The Weavers sing-along "Wimoweh" and The Tokens' 1961 chart topper, "The Lion Sleeps Tonight." The performance here is stunning: Makeba's dynamic vocal and the Trio's solid backing surpasses anyone else's version, while seeing all four arm-in-arm at the close, southern affiliates be damned, is arguably the highest moment of the series.

As Mitchell hints at when introducing the song, his group had a history with Makeba. "Our first nightclub appearance in New York was at The Blue Angel, and for about two of the six or eight weeks we spent there, Miriam Makeba was also on the bill," Mike Kobluk recalled for the author. "She was a 'protégé' of Harry Belafonte, so Harry came in often to see her, and in so doing, saw us. Harry suggested we sing two or three numbers with Miriam after each of us completed our individual sets. It went over well with New York audiences, especially considering that the march from Selma to Montgomery, and the racial riots that preceded, were still years away… and yes, three white guys performing with a black lady from South Africa was unique to live performance… and of course to national television in 1963." Belafonte would take the Trio under his wing, inviting them to perform at Carnegie Hall, along with Makeba, Odetta and the Belafonte Men's Chorus, for an RCA two-disc album, *Belafonte Returns to Carnegie Hall*. After that, "we signed a recording contract with Harry, and those albums were released on Kapp Records," says Kobluk. "So the Trio owed a lot to our association with Miriam and the association that developed with Belafonte as a result."

As if "Mbube" wasn't daring enough, the Trio also take a swipe at the mentality that was keeping Seeger off the program by doing one of their most popular satiric numbers, "The John Birch Society." Although it's missing a verse (technically, two half-verses have been cut) and the tempo races a bit, the witty spoofing of the rabidly anticommunist organization remains sharp and gets laughs.

The Travelers 3 were an unusual lineup: two native Hawaiians and an ex-television art director from Oregon. The three met in Eugene in 1958, where banjoist Charlie Oyama was a counselor for the city's school system and guitarist Pete Apo was a University of Oregon undergraduate. Along with bassist Dick Shirley, they spent a half-year performing at local functions and the reception convinced them to turn professional. This is the first of three appearances and their lively performance style is impressive.

Although only 25, Molly Scott had been singing professionally since before her graduation from Massachusetts' Smith College in 1959, first as one-third of 3 Folk Sing, with Walt Winter and Brooks Jones, then as a soloist, actress and children's TV hostess. With Dick Shirley on bass plus her own guitar accompaniment, she entices students to join in on her sole number, "Texas River Song" (also known as "Down By the Brazos"), which had originated in the southwest in the 1800s. "It was not in my repertoire," she recalled for the author in 2023. "It's a sweet song, and I probably sang it here and there. [The producers] wanted something that had a nice audience reciprocity, which it certainly did." The complete song mentions all fourteen of the state's rivers, hence the title, but for time reasons only verses one and three are sung.

After performing and acting in various touring companies, and earning her master's and doctoral degrees in Counseling Psychology at the University of Massachusetts, Dr. Molly Scott specializes in both Equine Assisted Psychotherapy and Resonance Therapy. In recent years, she has also been acclaimed for her poetry, winning the Robert Frost Foundation award in 2015, and publishing a collection of her work, *Up to the Windy Gate: Poems of Grief and Grace.* Her website is *mollyscott.com.*

As superb as the others were, though, *TV Key* affirmed, "Miriam Makeba's unmistakable artistry makes this show a must."

The cast rehearses the finale. From left to right: The Chad Mitchell Trio, Miriam Makeba, Molly Scott and The Travelers 3. *From the author's collection*

By this point, a few *Sing Out!* readers felt compelled to defend the series. In a lengthy response to Irwin Silber's editorial, David Williams wrote in part, "The millions that are watching 'Hootenanny' and buying the record albums are interested in entertainment… and not in the folk traditions…. The producers… know that 99% of the program's viewers have never heard of folk music before. Therefore, they will not find the program a 'hodge-podge of unrelated songs and performers' and 'vaguely unsatisfying….' They have never heard of Pete Seeger and certainly do not 'desperately need him.' Indeed, the program was very daring by TV standards when they allowed the Chad Mitchell Trio to perform their satire of the John Birch Society…. And, too, 'Hootenanny' is the only place some of us, located hundreds of miles from any kind of folk center, can see some of the folksingers we hear on records."

Josh White, accompanied by Bob Mathews, gives a rousing performance at U-MI. *From the author's collection*

1-07: University of Michigan, Ann Arbor #2

Recording Date: March 20, 1963.

Airdate: May 18, 1963. *Repeat*: August 17, 1963.

The Limeliters: "Joy Across the Land," "Hold On," "Where Shall I Be," "Molly Malone"

Josh White: "Cindy," "Nobody Knows You When You're Down and Out"

Elan Stuart: "Melora," "Angus McFergus McTavish Dundee" (with *the Limeliters*).

The New Lost City Ramblers: "New River Train"

FINALE: "Going Down That Road" (*Everyone*)

"Some behind-the-scenes drama makes 'Hootenanny' particularly interesting," wrote *TV Key's* reviewer. "Featured soloist in this folk concert from the University of Michigan is Josh White. He reported in great pain from a pinched shoulder nerve and was hospitalized between rehearsals. He did the show after the doctors doped him up but you'd never know it; he is his usual rousing self." More's the pity there's no known audio or video for this, White's first of three appearances.

TV Key continued: "The Limeliters have four songs, with Glenn Yarbrough's tenor solo on 'Molly Malone' outstanding. Elan Stuart, a Scottish girl discovered by the Limeliters, and some representatives of Blue Grass(*sic*) music, The New Lost City Ramblers, complete the bill."

John Cohen, Tracy Schwarz and Mike Seeger comprised the Ramblers, who were always termed a "Bluegrass" trio in the TV listings. In fact, they patterned themselves like an old-time string band straight out of the 1927 *Opry*, with Cohen flailing away on banjo like Uncle Dave Macon reincarnated, Schwarz on guitar and Seeger on fiddle, although they'd each trade instruments at times. They were perennials at the Newport Folk Festival, and of course recorded for Folkways. *Hootenanny* sure could've used them or a similar-sounding group in the coming year… but no such luck. According to the *Michigan Daily*, Lewine and company refused to let them choose which songs to play. "The producers felt that their material sounded too much like 'hillbilly' music, which wasn't the right sound for a folk music show." Consequently, they were the "one-and-done" of this episode; even Elan Stuart would return the following season.

The New Lost City Ramblers at their home territory, the Newport Folk Festival. From left to right: Mike Seeger, John Cohen and Tracy Schwarz. *From the author's collection*

1-08: Brown University, Providence RI #2

Recording Date: March 5, 1963.

Airdate: May 25, 1963. *Repeat*: September 7, 1963.

Theodore Bikel and The Clancy Brothers & Tommy Makem: "King's Highway" (*Jack Linkletter intro*)

The Clancy Bros. & Tommy Makem: "Holy Ground"

Judy Collins: "Maid of Constant Sorrow"

Theodore Bikel: Woody Guthrie Medley ("Car-Car, Ladies Auxiliary")

Allen and Grier: "Work Song" (a.k.a. "Counterman")

The Clancy Bros. & Tommy Makem: "Haul Away Joe" (with *Theodore Bikel*).

Judy Collins: "Greenland Whale Fisheries" (with *Theodore Bikel*)

The Clancy Bros. & Tommy Makem: "Johnson's Motor Car," "Barnyards of Delgaty" (with *Theodore Bikel*).

Theodore Bikel: "Yekhali Tsigane"

FINALE: "So Long, It's Been Good to Know Ya/Saturday Night" (*Everyone*)

Theodore Bikel and Judy Collins perform "Greenland Whale Fisheries" at Brown. In July, they'd reprise it at the Newport Folk Festival. *From the author's collection*

The second go-round at Brown University is, as Bikel told *Newsweek*, a "fast and snappy" mélange of music, most of it ethnic in character if not execution. The returning Clancy Brothers and Tommy Makem give out with five robust tunes, accompanied on three of them by headliner Theo Bikel, who also contributes an all-too-brief Woody Guthrie medley, a fine duet with Judy Collins and a lively Russian Gypsy number, accompanied by Sasha Polinoff on balalaika. The up-and-coming Collins makes her *Hootenanny* bow with "Maid of Constant Sorrow," title track of her debut album. There's even a bit of satire: Allen and Grier's "Counterman" (introduced by Linkletter under a working title, "Work Song").

In a subsequent issue of *Sing Out!* Pete Seeger overlooked the contributions of his friends and chose instead to excoriate Allen and Grier's one-off: "I don't know the duo personally and I've got nothing against them except this song.... And I've nothing against satire, but with all the things in the world that can be satirized, they decided they were going to do a take-off on a Negro work song. In effect, what their song said was that Leadbelly was just a silly old man and anybody who would give the song 'Take This Hammer' more than a snicker was just plain naïve."

Allen and Grier were John "Jake" Grier Holmes and Kathryn "Kay" Allen Reynolds, a young husband-and-wife. Having met and married while Reynolds was a senior at Vermont's Bennington College, both subsequently trained in opera, but they enjoyed folk music and after moving to Long Island would participate in the informal sing-alongs held at Washington Square Park. In 1962, they worked up a satirical act and took it to The Bitter End, using each other's middle names as billing. Writer Paul Colby, in his book about the iconic nightclub, described "Counterman" as "a chain-gang song relocated in a Chock Full O' Nuts restaurant," which is on target. Consisting of little more than the jargon of diner personnel and featuring such couplets as:

Employees must wash hands / before mixing salad

the number is basically harmless, although the pair's affected dialect would never fly today. The duo would record an album, *It's Better To Be Rich Than Ethnic*, and tried to make a living at performing, but were certainly no threat to The Smothers Brothers or Allan Sherman. Fred Weintraub managed them for a time, until Jake was drafted and entered the Army in July for a brief hitch. After that, he formed "Jim, Jake and Joan" with actor Jim Connell and comedienne Joan Rivers, but eventually scored success with advertising jingles, writing "Be All That You Can Be" for the U.S. Army and "Wouldn't You Like to Be a Pepper?" for Dr. Pepper soda. Billed as Grier Reynolds, Kay would return to *Hootenanny* during season two, as would all the other acts.

Audio from most of this episode survives in the author's collection.

1-09: Pennsylvania State University, University Park #2

Recording Date: April 3, 1963.

Airdate: June 1, 1963. *Repeat*: September 14, 1963.

Video: 16mm kinescope minus commercials. Licensing: Historic Films Archive, LLC, #V-1011. Viewing: The Library of Congress, catalog # MAVIS 2899699. Excerpted on **The Best of Hootenanny**.

The Limeliters: "Midnight Special" (*Jack Linkletter intro*)

The Limeliters: "Wondrous Love/Old Time Religion,"

Ian & Sylvia: "C.C. Rider"

Martha Schlamme: "Johnny, I Hardly Knew Ye"

The Limeliters: "Done Laid Around"

Richard & Jim: "Charming Betsy" (with *The Limeliters*)

Ian & Sylvia: "Ole Blue"

Richard & Jim: "East Virginia"

The Limeliters: "I'm Goin' to Leave Old Texas Now"

FINALE: "Michael, Row the Boat Ashore" (*Everyone*).

The kinescope for this installment opens with Jack Linkletter on the terrace outside the Hetzel Union Ballroom (or HUB). One thousand tickets were distributed for the performance, but the student paper, *The Daily Collegian*, announced "if the weather is good on Wednesday, the terrace adjacent to the ballroom will be lighted and students without tickets will be seated there." The weather cooperated.

Sylvia Fricker and Ian Tyson, two gifted composers as well as performers. *From the author's collection*

This was the show for which Barbara Dane was sought; thankfully Martha Schlamme proves a more than capable replacement. Will Holt (present for his spot in the previously aired Penn State show) likely had a hand in getting her involved; the two were partners in interpreting the work of composer Kurt Weill and would, in two months, be opening a Weill program in New York City that stayed into the following year.

Schlamme's dramatic interpretation of the Irish ballad "Johnny" is beautifully crafted and includes a verse not often heard: "They're rollin' out the guns again / But they never will take our sons again!" Like most other female soloists this season, she didn't return for future shows.

Canada's Ian & Sylvia, in their second of four appearances, excel in a couple of tunes from their debut Vanguard LP: the driving "C.C. Rider" and the wistful "Ole Blue." The pair had been singing together for four years, were linked romantically as well as musically, and would wed the following year. Both were songwriters and each would pen a classic: Ian's "Four Strong Winds" and Sylvia's "You Were On My Mind." Since the couple never wrote together, they were separately inducted into the Canadian Songwriter's Hall of Fame in 2019.

Richard (Lockmiller) & Jim (Connor) mesh the driving speed of Bluegrass with old-time flailing banjo and it works. They certainly give Lou Gottlieb, graciously providing bass accompaniment, a workout on "East Virginia." The pair teamed up in their hometown of Gadsden, Alabama in 1961, appeared on local television, made their way to New York, Canada, England, Scotland and France, and finally to network television. This is their first of two *Hootenanny* appearances.

A student named Bernie Kamoroff was another disgruntled *Sing Out!* reader who took time to write: "A 'Hootenanny' was filmed(*sic*) here at Penn State. It was advertised as a hoot featuring the Limeliters. The Limeliters drew the crowds, but it wasn't the Limeliters that the crowds talked about when they left. It was the powerful Phoenix Singers, Martha Schlamme, the 'ethnic' Carter Family, two guys called 'Richard and Jim' (whose instrumental styles awed the audience), Ian and Sylvia from Canada, and Will Holt. Can you imagine people swarming to the TV to see the Carter Family? Or Martha Schlamme? This is truly a credit to ABC."

Kamoroff clearly saw what Hentoff, Silber and others couldn't or wouldn't see: *Hootenanny* was presenting interesting, relatively obscure folk talent along with popular names. Seeger, in his pre-airing critique of the show, wrote, "The great thing about the old Hootenannies was their ability to put together on one stage the old-timer and the new-timer, the citybilly and the hillbilly. The professional and the amateur. But the TV networks have not learned this lesson." Maybe not entirely—everyone at Penn State for both shows had recorded at least one album—but ABC was drawing nearer to Seeger's idea of folk music than anyone else's TV show.

It's ironic an outsider had to point that out.

1-10: Rutgers University, New Brunswick, NJ #2

Recording Date: April 15, 1963.

Airdate: June 8, 1963. *Repeat*: August 24, 1963.

Oscar Brand with The Tarriers: "Raise A Ruckus" (*Jack Linkletter intro*)

The Tarriers: "Ride Up."

Shirley Abicair: "I Know Where I'm Goin'."

The Smothers Brothers: "John Henry," "I Never Will Marry."

The Tarriers: "Swing Down Chariot."

Oscar Brand: "Copper Kettle."

The Smothers Brothers: "My Old Man."

The Tarriers: "Jordan's River."

FINALE: "Li'l Liza Jane" (*Everyone*).

New York TV columnist Alan Gill was present for the taping of both Rutgers shows and his resulting piece was simply pulled from notes he took throughout. About this show's rehearsal, Gill wrote, "[The] Smothers Brothers frisked through [their] number on [the] platform; then Tom Smothers, one with the stammers, said, 'Let's b-b-bring out the integrated group now,' and the Tarriers came on."

The Tarriers during their brief span as a quartet. From left: Eric Weissburg, Clarence Cooper, Marshall Brickman and charter member Bob Carey.

The Tarriers formed in 1956 and, as stated earlier, had a hit the following year with their own version of the calypso "Banana Boat Song." At that time, the group consisted of Erik Darling, Alan Arkin and Bob Carey. Arkin left early on, deciding an actor's life beat that of a folksinger's, especially one in a group that couldn't get work south of the Mason-Dixon line *or* on national TV, because they were biracial. Replacing him was versatile instrumentalist Eric Weissburg. Not long after, Darling left to join The Weavers; his replacement was the vibrant baritone of Clarence Cooper. That made Weissburg the only white in the troupe. A few years later, Bob Carey started planning a solo career, and Weissburg suggested adding a former U. of Wisconsin classmate and fellow musician, Marshall Brickman. For a brief period, The Tarriers were an equally-mixed quartet and that's the lineup for this show. They and Oscar Brand begin the festivities with "Raise a Ruckus," which they'd recorded for Decca.

Brand had been named in *Red Channels* all those years ago, but as he told Robbie Woliver for the latter's *HOOT! A 25 Year History of the Greenwich Village Music Scene*, "I had also been blacklisted by the left wing. It seemed that my dropping out of *People's Songs*, and the feelings that I had expressed on occasion about the very rigorous dictatorship of the Communists, had me blacklisted by *People's Songs*." Editor Irwin Silber all but confirmed it to Woliver: "The leading force of the Left at this time was the Communist Party, so the natural position to take was usually the same position the Communist Party took." Since Brand was no longer espousing that position (if he ever did), he was "cleared" for network TV. Nevertheless, this was his only appearance on the show; possibly due to his personal convictions over blacklisting, possibly because that autumn he became host of *Let's Sing Out*, Canadian television's version of *Hootenanny*, sponsored, like its U.S. counterpart, by Proctor & Gamble.

Known as "the Australian zither-girl" in England, where she made her first success in the mid-1950s, Melbourne-born Shirley Abicair studied at the Sydney Conservatorium of Music. "I used to take my zither along to parties and sing for friends," she wrote in 1957. This led to cabaret engagements in Sydney and London, followed by several appearances on U.K. and Australian television, including a 6-episode series in 1960, *Shirley Abicair in Australia*, a travelogue filmed during a concert tour in her native land. Here, she accompanies herself on the Scottish ballad, "I Know Where I'm Goin'."

All three of The Smothers Brothers' numbers come from their most recent album, *Think Ethnic*. The third, "My Old Man," was written by Brand. The students clearly love these guys; their reaction to the payoff of the otherwise straight-sung "I Never Will Marry" threatens to blow the roof off The Ledge.

Oscar Brand and Shirley Abicair rehearsing for the finale. *From the author's collection*

From Gill's notes: "Brand… turned to a cluster of nearby undergrads and said, 'You all be here at 7 o'clock, now. Wear clothes.' Lewine frantically paced [the] ballroom floor muttering that 'Little Liza Jane' wasn't running long enough." His solution was to have the refrain intoned twice between each verse.

Audio from all but the opening of this episode survives in the author's collection.

1-11: George Washington University, Washington DC #2

Recording Date: February 15, 1963.

Airdate: June 15, 1963.

The Limeliters: "Jehosephat," "John Henry," "Hey Li Lee."

Flatt & Scruggs: "Worried Man Blues," "This Land is Your Land" (with *The Limeliters*).

Carolyn Hester: "Summertime"

Leon Bibb: "Red Rosy Bush," "Mule Skinner Blues."

FINALE: "Mama Don't 'low" (*Everyone*).

"Not the best of the series," said *TV Key*, "but still a lively half-hour songfest with a standout number, 'Hey Li Lee,' delivered by the Limeliters with an assist from various members from the student audience…. Leon Bibb, Flatt and Scruggs and Carolyn Hester round out the talent roster."

"Hey Li Lee" had been a Limeliters perennial from their start, one that Gottlieb brought from his Gateway Singers days. It's a song in which audience members are encouraged to make up their own verses. The trio released two recordings of it for RCA: one at the Ash Grove on their first LP for the label, the other in a London, England concert issued two years after their split. Only the informality of *Hootenanny* audience seating could make it possible for televising.

With all due respect to Joan Baez, Carolyn Hester was the original queen of folk music. Born in Waco, Texas, her family moved to Washington DC when she was two years old but returned to the home state by the time she entered high school. Now living in Dallas, she took voice lessons that brought out her crystal pure soprano, learned to play a Sears Roebuck guitar and headed for the Village after finishing high school. She hit the coffeehouse circuit, recorded for Pat Clancy's Tradition, toured and paid her dues. Columbia Records signed her in 1961 and she recruited Bob Dylan to play harmonica on her first effort for the label, which led to *his* signing.

Two things mitigated against Hester. First, by the time she got her major label deal, Baez and Judy Collins had arrived and were making waves. It didn't take long for the press, including Irwin Silber in *Sing Out!*, to decry "the battle of the Folk Queens." As she recalled for Robbie Woliver, "Harold Leventhal [told me], 'Well, you know, the kids only have so much money. They can only buy a few of the women's records every year.' That kind of made me sad.… There was always room for all of us, and I thought the competition thing was dangerous for the movement."

Second, she had impulsively wed Richard Fariña, an advertising copywriter and eventual novelist; their union was a stormy one, primarily because she was the more successful spouse. Striving to make the marriage work, she bought him a dulcimer so they could perform together and, disrupting her momentum in New York, followed him to Europe, where he hoped to finish his novel and find his own successes. While there, he fell in love with Baez's 16-year-old sister, Mimi, who was attending school in France. When the marriage ended in 1963, Hester flew home, arranged for a quickie Mexican divorce, and set about resurrecting her career.

Neither video nor audio are known to exist for this broadcast, the only one of Lewine's from this season that was not repeated. It's especially tough to have lost Leon Bibb's *Hootenanny* debut since his subsequent appearances, all of which survive in one form or another, are extremely entertaining.

Leon Bibb's artistry enhanced all five *Hootenanny* segments in which he appeared.
From the author's collection

Charles Leon Aurthello Bibb was born in Louisville, Kentucky in 1922. He sang in school glee clubs in both high school and at Louisville

Municipal College, where he'd risen to soloist. After graduation he went into the Army, then headed to New York City and Broadway, where he landed a chorus job in Irving Berlin's *Annie Get Your Gun*, starring Ethel Merman. That led to a featured part in a touring company of *Finian's Rainbow*, which in turn led to subsequent stage appearances both on and off Broadway, augmenting these jobs by performing folk songs at various coffee houses. Three *Ed Sullivan Show* appearances later, he'd moved up to clubs such as New York's Village Gate, Chicago's Kelly's. Los Angeles' Ash Grove and San Francisco's the hungry i.

In 1959, he recorded *Leon Bibb Sings Folk Songs* for Vanguard, earning him the respect of the music's gate keepers in New York City. "Typical of Leon Bibb," say the liner notes, "is that whatever song he sings must be one in which he feels complete conviction." He saw himself as an interpreter of each song's "dramatic image [and] the human story it has to tell," and had high hopes for the series: "The college crowd is the best audience for folk music right now. When you perform, they share a musical experience with you. *Hootenanny* will show the strength of this appeal with other groups."

Lester Flatt & Earl Scruggs were well-known to general audiences by this time, having performed the theme song to television's number one program, *The Beverly Hillbillies*. The twosome started out as members of Bill Monroe's Bluegrass Boys in the mid-1940s, then departed near the end of the decade in hopes of earning more than Monroe sidemen were used to being paid. They formed their own band, the Foggy Mountain Boys, and although Monroe's legendary status kept them off the *Grand Ole Opry* for a few years, Flatt & Scruggs built their own following via a long-running syndicated television show sponsored by Martha White Flour.

Bibb, Hester and Flatt & Scruggs would return to *Hootenanny* during season two.

1-12: University of Virginia, Charlottesville #2

Recording Date: April 30, 1963.

Airdate: June 22, 1963. *Repeat*: August 31, 1963.

The Chad Mitchell Trio: "Puttin' On The Style" (*Jack Linkletter opening*), "Where Have All the Flowers Gone?," "Lizzie Borden."

Bud and Travis: "It's the Man," "La Bamba"

Jo Mapes: "San Francisco Bay Blues," "Gold Wedding Ring," "One For the Money" (with *Bud and Travis*).

Josh White Jr.: "Bald Mountain."

FINALE: "Meetin' at the Building" (*Everyone*).

Another completely lost episode, *TV Key* considered this "one of the best of the series. The Chad Mitchell Trio is in top form with [their selections]. Jo Mapes almost steals the show with her distinctive styling…. The versatile team of Bud and Travis and the big voiced Josh White Jr. add to the excellence of the entertainment."

On the other hand, William K. Stevens, a staff writer for the daily *Virginian-Pilot*, was present for the taping and decidedly unimpressed. "A hootenanny ain't really a hootenanny on TV. That is, ABC's half-hour program called 'Hootenanny' doesn't do full justice to folk music…. Network men had packed $1 million worth of electronic gear to Charlottesville. They converted Memorial Gym into one of the biggest TV studios you'd ever want to see, but they ended up cramping the performers' style." Lewine had hoped to make this the first *Hootenanny* to be shot out-of-doors, on the mall in front of the campus rotunda, but typical April weather in Virginia—rain and overcast skies—put the kibosh on that idea.

"It's very difficult to work in this medium," Joe Frazier told Stevens. "You can't build up a mood. It's hard to sustain crowd enthusiasm during cuts away, for one thing." As if by providence, the reporter immediately saw an example of what Frazier was talking about: "On the other side of the bleachers… the cameras at that moment cut away from the onstage duo of Bud and Travis. The young singers stood there strumming away, hesitating, trying to keep the student audience on the string. What the camera cut to… was slick-tongued, clean-cut, well-tailored Jack Linkletter—parroting the biographies of Bud and Travis, and of the song they were about to sing, from a set of idiot cards." Clearly cut from the same cloth as critic Rick DuBrow, Stevens decried "Linkletter's pasted-in commentary, written by someone else and delivered with all the authority of, say, Carol Channing talking about the Common Market."

To be fair, this was one of the drawbacks of the format. We're supposed to believe we're seeing a folk concert as it would happen whether Linkletter was there or not, yet either the strumming, plucking intros go on interminably as he's speaking to us, or worse, he narrates over the singing and we miss the first verse of a song. Probably the most egregious example of the former was in the first U. of Virginia show: for their opening number, The Travelers 3 are strumming the introduction on and on while Linkletter tells us about them, then miss their cue and play it twice more before finally singing.

Still, the series was ultimately intended for home viewers that now numbered in the millions, not the six hundred or so attending each taping. "With it all, though," concluded Stevens, "the *Hootenanny* crew must be given credit. Producer Dick Lewine, Director Garth Dietrick and their men perform an operation of great magnitude in moving their tons of equipment from college to college, creating a studio and working up a show…. Crewmen work long, hard hours. They were up till 1:30 a.m. arranging cameras, lights and cables…. The performers, too, put up with a lot to get some part of their work across to television viewers who can't go to a hootenanny except through the picture tube. However squeezed and dampened the finished product, there are those who say it's better than no product at all."

Moreover, as reported by *Sponsor* magazine on June 17, "ABC-TV's *Hootenanny* is drawing a good chunk of its audience from an unusual quarter: 'light' viewers." This demographic consisted of higher-educated and therefore higher-earning households Nielsen estimated as representing 40% of the entire television audience, yet doing only 19% of its viewing. The rating service had determined the show was drawing

34% of its audience from this group. In other words, if there were no *Hootenanny*, these "light" viewers were more likely to not watch at all than tune in a different show. It was yet another reason why the series would be continuing come September.

1-13: Syracuse University, Syracuse NY

Recording Date: November 18, 1962.

Airdate: June 29, 1963

The Limeliters: "There's A Meetin' Here Tonight," "Wabash Cannonball," "The Hammer Song."

Jo Mapes: "Kisses Sweeter Than Wine," "Buffalo Boy" (with *Glenn Yarbrough*)

Mike Settle: "Shenendoah," "Sing Hallelujah!" (with *The Limeliters*).

Clara Ward and Her Gospel Singers: "Come in the Room."

FINALE: "Down By the Riverside" (*Everyone*).

At long last, the pilot gets on the air. It couldn't have been very cohesive, what with Jack Linkletter intercut in places where Jean Shepherd had been, and no doubt from an entirely different university. Still, *TV Key* enthused, "you can see why the network snapped it up. Jo Mapes, so good on last week's lineup, tops herself with 'Kisses Sweeter Than Wine.' There is a good comedy song, 'Buffalo Boy,' by Jo and one of the Limeliters, Glenn Yarbrough; and Mike Settle and the frantic, frenzied Clara Ward singers round out the entertainment."

At age 11, JoAnn Shanas had moved from Chicago to Los Angeles and attended Thomas Starr King Junior High School with Odetta, who introduced her to folk music. In 1951, now living in San Francisco, she married Paul Mapes; the union lasted long enough to produce a daughter. By mid-decade, she was singing in coffee houses billed as Jo March. In

1958, she recorded an album for Kapp, described by one reviewer as "jazz intermingled with blues for pleasant listening."

A publicity photo of Jo Mapes from around the time of the *Hootenanny* pilot. *From the author's collection*

When the album's sales failed to warrant a follow-up, she returned to her birthplace and began her career in earnest at the Gate of Horn, where Bob Gibson helped her get established (and encouraged her to bill as Jo Mapes, rather than a character from *Little Women*). Although second to air, this was the first of her four *Hootenanny* appearances. The first verse of "Kisses Sweeter than Wine" takes up most of the surviving video, from a network promo overdubbed with Linkletter pitching the series; the rest of the show is among the missing.

Hootenanny had logged 13 successful weeks and a growing audience would tune in eleven weeks of reruns before the start of the new season. On July 17, *Variety* reported, "Show has been running very close to the CBS-TV competition, 'The Defenders,' in the multi-market Nielsens and has pulled way ahead of the 'Joey Bishop Show' on NBC-TV…. The folksing has also developed as a solid lead-in to the 'Lawrence Welk Show,' whose share of audience has climbed since 'Hootenanny' bowed." And, as if anyone ever doubted it, American consumers would be so bombarded by "Hootenanny" merchandise in record shops, magazine stands and even toy stores, there was zero chance the word would ever again be used in place of dingus, thingumajig or whatchamacallit.

Advertisement for the first of several 'Hootenanny' albums to debut during the show's first season.

CHAPTER FOUR

"A Business That Can Pay Off Handsomely"

Hootenanny Flood Is On heralds an article in *Billboard's* June 15 issue announcing the first of "what promises to be a deluge of hootenanny disks." Little did they realize how prophetic that headline would be.

Consider: between May and December, radio stations across the country created disk jockey programs titled "Hootenanny Hits," "Your Weekend Hootenanny," etc. and, in at least one instance, a 24-7 "Hootenanny" format. Three high schoolers from Long Island released a tune called "Hootenanny" on an obscure label and broke into radio and retail's Top 40. Two magazines with "Hootenanny" in the title found their way to the nation's newsstands, while "Hootenanny" toy guitars and "Hootenanny" paper dolls found their way to children. In Hollywood, Metro-Goldwyn-Mayer hired a producer known for low-budget serials and rock 'n' roll exploitation flicks to make a "hootenanny" movie, and a pilot called *The Big Hoot* was taped at a Pasadena nightclub. Amusement parks hosted hootenannies that included stars and local talent. Booking agencies that normally specialized in bands and pop singers assembled touring packages with names like "American Hootenanny Festival," "Hootenanny USA" and "Hootenanny '63." And in Rhode Island, for the first time, the Newport Folk Festival outdrew its prestigious parent, the Jazz Festival.

For '63 was, indeed, the Year of the Hootenanny. Although The Kingston Trio jump-started the genre five years earlier, and vocalists like Joan Baez, groups like Peter, Paul & Mary, and singer-songwriters like Bob Dylan garnered critical hosannas, it was the millions drawn to ABC's fast-tracked mid-season replacement show that fueled a phenomenon. As *Look* magazine put it that August: "Yesterday, it was the esoteric kick of history buffs and music scholars. Today it's show biz… [and TV's] Saturday-night *Hootenanny* is final proof that folk music has gone big-time."

Emenee's Hootenanny Guitar "brings out the folk singer in kids of all ages" and priced for Christmas 1963 at $8.88 in major department stores.

"There hasn't been anything like it since rock and roll exploded on the music scene a decade ago, for the interest it has stirred up on [the] radio, TV, concert, one-nighter and festival level," *Billboard* affirmed, including for coffee houses, "those spirit-less dens that have sprung up in large cities all across the nation [where] the young folk acts have a chance of getting discovered and where the hootenanny scene is hot and fervid." Only slightly tongue-in-cheek, Oscar Brand recalled for Robbie Woliver, "You could walk from the East coast to West coast, from coffee house to coffee house, without putting your foot on the ground. They were being set up all over [and] young people were learning their trade and making a couple of bucks a week, enough to live on."

Fred Weintraub, still talent scouting for *Hootenanny*, was hired to perform the same function for New York City's WINS-AM radio in its own half-hour "Hootenanny" broadcast live from Palisades Park across the Hudson on Wednesday nights. Weintraub brought in name performers—and *Hootenanny* guests—like Brand, The Tarriers, The Rooftop Singers, Mike Settle, Josh White Sr. *and* Jr., and others… even Allen and Grier.

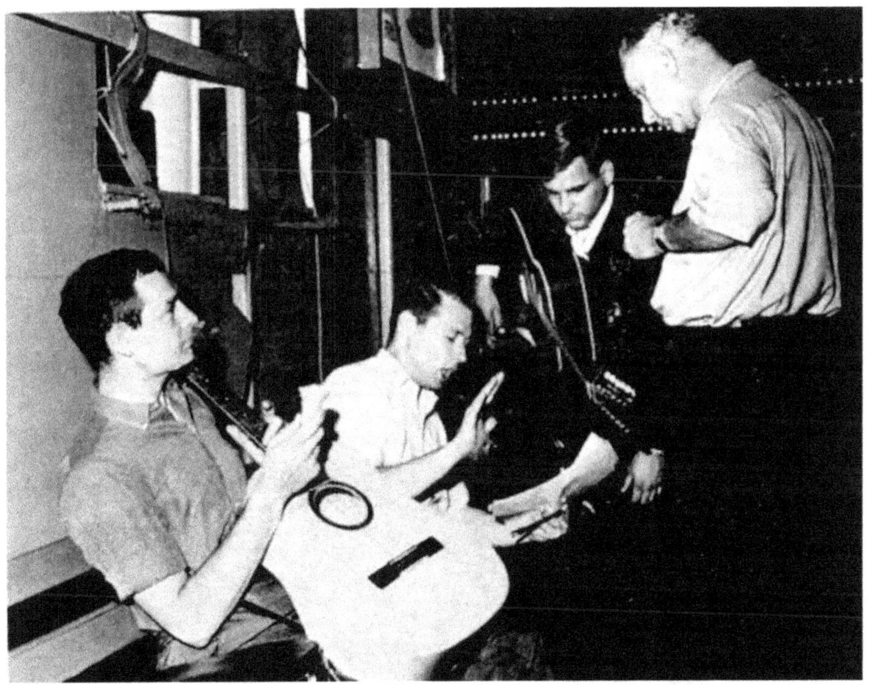

Oscar Brand, far left, and Mike Settle, second-from-right, await the start of the first WINS-AM "Hootenanny" live from Palisades Park, New Jersey.

Other big city stations would broadcast live shows from coffee houses and such, but the vast majority simply played the records. FM radio especially took to folk music as a way of growing audience without succumbing to 100% classical or jazz formats. On July 29, an AM station, Cincinnati's WCPO, abruptly dropped its "good music" lineup in favor of all folk, all the time, at least through the summer months. "The recording industry for several years has undergone a metamorphosis during which time the top selling records in the country seemed to be completely devoid of anything resembling musical taste or talent," the station's program director, Bill Dawes, commented dryly. Clearly no fan of "Surf City," "Judy's Turn to Cry" or "Candy Girl," all of which were in the Top 20 that week, Dawes concluded, "We at WCPO Radio are certainly not going to knock it. We intend to smother it with our 'Summer Hootenanny' idea." Three days later, WCPO-TV aired a live folksing from the Cincinnati Zoo featuring local talent. Naturally, the show was called *Zootenanny*.

WCPO personnel plug their station's new 24-7 Hootenanny format. The bassist in the back is Program Director Bill Dawes; in front, l-r, are disk jockeys Jim Dandy, Bill Burns, Myles Foland and Dick Provost.

The money-losing Pittsburgh Pirates, in union with station KDKA, staged three hootenanny events for the home games. For the first, "with local folk singers and 50-cent price for teenagers as the draw, the station succeeded in attracting 4,622 additional fans to the ball park," wrote *Billboard*. The third event on Friday, July 19 was "the world's first Kazootenanny." Five thousand kazoos were offered; 8,089 teens paid admission in hopes of snagging one. KDKA deejay Rege Cordic led the ad-hoc "orchestra" ahead of the game, after which "the Kazooters hummed the Pirates to a resounding 9-4 victory over the Chicago Cubs."

That same weekend, a heretofore unknown group, The Glencoves, on a tiny label, Select, reached #43 on *Billboard's* Hot 100 in its sixth week on the chart. "Two bright sides by a new group that could make a real dent," according to the venerable trade mag's Pop Spotlight. "First up is a snappy hand-clapper rhythm effort with a catchy sound. It moves." The song, titled "Hootenanny," was cowritten by two veteran composers, George Goehring ("Lipstick on Your Collar") and Eddie Deane ("The Men in My Little Girl's Life"), plus one relative newcomer, Peg Horther, all housed at New York City's Brill Building under the employ of Joy Music, Inc.

Joy Music was founded in 1934 by George Joy; he also owned Select Records, where a handful of artists recorded Joy-published songs. Horther had written a humorous B-side candidate, "It's Sister Ginny's Turn to Throw the Bomb," described by *Cash Box* magazine as "a whacky folk-novelty satire." The off-center tale of an anarchist family never charted, but over ensuing decades occasionally cropped up on Dr. Demento's novelty-record radio show. With songs for a single ready to capitalize on a hot new market, all Joy needed was a group to cover them.

Influenced by The Kingston Trio and The Highwaymen, The Glencoves began as "The Balladeers" in 1961, during their sophomore year at Charminade High School in Mineola, New York. Banjo player Don Connors was the organizer; Billy Byrne and guitarist Jim O'Toole were his companions. By their senior year, O'Toole had moved on and was replaced by Brian Bolger, also attending Charminade: "I had a nylon-string guitar and they found out I played and could sing a little tenor harmony."

Don Connors recalls, "My girlfriend at the time lived in Glen Cove and her mother had been involved in the music business in the late '40s, and knew George Joy. She told him, 'George, why don't you give these boys a chance?' That's how we got the audition [and] went to see George and his crew at the Brill Building."

From left-to-right, Don Connors, Billy Byrne and Brian Bolger are The Glencoves: three high school seniors who reached the Top 40 and, according to Connors, "had some adventures for the summer of '63" even though "our parents were dead set against it." *Photo courtesy of Don Connors*

It was Joy who introduced them to "Hootenanny." "He was a typical tin pan alley character," says Connors. "His cigarette ash was as long as his cigarette. And he was sitting at a piano and he'd say, 'Hey boys, boys, come ovah heah, come ovah heah! I gotta show ya somethin',' and he'd play 'Hootenanny' on the piano. I'd seen some tin pan alley films from the forties and it was really like stepping back in time even then."

None of them were overly excited by "Hootenanny," and Bolger especially didn't care for "Sister Ginny's Turn to Throw the Bomb," but they all recognized this was an amazing break for a trio of highschoolers and were pleased to work with Select's Al Ham. Bolger recalls Ham as "an outstanding arranger. He helped us put together an act," while Connors considered him "the guy with the *real* talent." It was Ham who renamed them "The Glencoves," after the city in Long Island's Nassau county where Connors' girlfriend resided.

Ham sweetened the vocals, Bolger's guitar and Connors' banjo with echo, mixed in some crowd noise and clapping… then touted on the label the disk had been recorded "live" at "Fink University," which was a joke institution concocted by comedian Steve Allen's writers a year earlier. "We recorded in a New York studio and all the background noise and the laughter on 'Ginny' were added later," says Bolger.

On July 27, "Hootenanny" climbed to #38 on the Hot 100, where it peaked for two weeks, while *Cash Box*, which tracked retail sales, placed it at #39. Regionally, it reached #14 in Chicago, #8 in Kansas City, #6 in Columbus, Ohio. In Canada, it was #8 in Montreal, #6 in Vancouver and #4 in Ontario, which was good enough to get The Glencoves invited to appear in a TV pilot called *Junior Hootenanny*, produced in Quebec and presumably aimed at the high school set. That summer they did some touring, the highlights of which were opening for Connie Francis and the New Haven Pops at the Yale Bowl on August 17, and as one of "5 Big Acts" on a "Hootenanny" stage show at Baltimore's Civic Center on September 7, with a lineup that included Ian & Sylvia and Judy Henske. In fact, during the previous Monday through Wednesday, both Henske and the Canadian duo had been rehearsing and taping *Hootenanny* programs for the upcoming season at the University of Pittsburgh.

Which begs the question: why didn't The Glencoves appear? Connors recalls performing at a Bitter End open mic hoot and impressing Fred Weintraub, but it didn't lead to a TV shot. "We would have loved to have done the *Hootenanny* show, but they never invited us," says Bolger. The most likely reason is poor timing: their big hit had been released after the first season had wrapped. Three subsequent releases failed to chart, and by the time production resumed in earnest, they had temporarily set music aside and were attending different colleges full time. The following summer, they added a fourth member, Bluegrass banjoist John Cadley whom Byrne met at College of the Holy Cross, and performed "as the house act in a Long Island bar, the Canoe Place Inn" where, Bolger affirmed, "we warmed up for José Feliciano." After that, The Glencoves parted ways. The original trio went on to graduate and live productive lives, and could look back with pride on what they'd accomplished.

Back on July 13, when The Glencoves were at #47 and climbing, guitarist Al Casey's "Surfin' Hootenanny" entered *Billboard's* Hot 100 at #97. The song was a novelty attempting to capitalize on two crazes simultaneously ("Surf City" and "Wipe Out" were each in the Top 10 that week), but only managed to peak at #48 on August 17 before quickly dropping off the chart. Thanks to a stereo LP release, Casey's recording proved more radio durable, but in all fairness to "Surfin' Hootenanny," it was The Glencoves who caught a wave and rode it with the perfect song at the exact right moment.

Out on the west coast that July, veteran fast-buck producer Sam Katzman oversaw shooting of his first feature for venerable MGM: *Hootenanny Hoot* (1963). The man who'd produced such low-budget musical bonanzas as *Rock Around the Clock* (1956), *Juke Box Rhythm* (1959) and *Twist Around the Clock* (1961), told the AP's Hollywood columnist Bob Thomas, "I keep an eye on all the record charts, hunting for the latest rage. I had a script all ready for the bossa nova—put $15,000 in it. Still, I held back; it didn't seem right to me. So I took the same script and changed it to a hootenanny. MGM called me up and said, 'We want you to do a folk music picture.' I told them I just happened to have a script on my desk."

The Brothers Four flank Johnny Cash as they rehearse for *Hootenanny Hoot*, but the only cash producer Sam Katzman can hear is at the box office. *From the author's collection*

Katzman spent nine days and $280,000 of MGM's money filming the tale of a New York TV director (*Peter Breck*) deciding to televise a hootenanny from Missouri's mythical Norburg College and falling for pretty co-ed Billie Jo (*Pam Austin*), much to the dismay of his producer ex-wife (*Ruta Lee*) who schemes to win him back. All of this drivel was sparked with lip-synch performances by The Brothers Four, The Gateway Trio, Johnny Cash, Sheb Wooley, Joe and Eddie, Cathie Taylor, Judy Henske and George Hamilton IV. Wooley gets the brand-new composition "Hootenanny Hoot" for the opening titles and closing. Everyone else just mimes to their records; in Cash's case, his five-year-old recording of "Frankie's Man, Johnny."

Some of the performances are just embarrassing. For reasons only Katzman could've explained, the televised 'hootenanny' takes place at a circus, and so we get The Gateway Trio singing and playing "Foolish Questions" while they're on a trampoline. For Judy Henske's "Wade in the Water," she's surrounded by "six willowy male dancers dressed in black," as she told Linda Solomon. Earlier in the film, she does "The Ballad of Little Romy" in a bikini. (In Katzman's world, just because you're nowhere near an ocean doesn't mean there aren't any bathing beauties.) Never one to indulge polite society, Henske had no qualms about any of it. "It's a riot," she assured Solomon ahead of the film's release. "I love Hollywood—it's so full of obvious bull."

"Following roughly the same formula utilized for his rock 'n' roll and twist concoctions," began *Variety's* review, Katzman "has taken a related group of musical acts and strung them together via a featherweight romantic plot. In this case, the musical form pursued—folk music of the strictly commercial variety—has a somewhat more widespread appeal." Added *The Hollywood Reporter*, "The exploitation picture lumps country music with folk singing for the purpose of the picture, a combination the purists may resent although it is hardly likely to trouble anyone else. The story is mild and unobtrusive, a peg for getting together some of the top country music and folk-singing acts of the current day." Opening in hundreds of theaters beginning Labor Day weekend, *Hootenanny Hoot* grossed in the neighborhood of $1.2 million. MGM's share of the profit was $94,000, enough for Katzman to have earned the dubious honor of producing Elvis Presley's next two films for the studio: *Kissin' Cousins* (1964) and *Harem Scarum* (1965).

The last weekend in July also saw the return of the Newport Folk Festival after a two-year absence. Three weeks before, the Rhode Island city's Jazz Festival, in its tenth year, tallied a new record of 38,000 attendees. "The upcoming Folk Festival July 26-28 will attract thousands to Newport and will again highlight interest in the city," predicted the *Newport Daily News* on July 8, but even they didn't expect a crowd of 47,000 and a $70,000 gross over the three days. The police department placed fifty extra patrolmen around the city, but the few arrests made were primarily of minors attempting to buy beer. One police official told a *Cash Box* reporter, "These kids are remarkably well-behaved. We don't expect any trouble."

Newspaper advertisement for the 1963 Newport Folk Festival.

The lineup ran the gamut from big names (Peter, Paul & Mary, Joan Baez, Judy Collins, The Tarriers, Theodore Bikel and, of course, Pete Seeger), the specialists (Bill Monroe & His Bluegrass Boys, Jim & Jesse, Mac Wiseman, Jean Ritchie and Maybelle Carter for Bluegrass and old-time country music; John Lee Hooker, Mississippi John Hurt and Dave Van Ronk for black *and* white blues, The Freedom Singers for gospel); newcomers in all genres (Ian & Sylvia, The Rooftop Singers, John Hammond Jr., Mike Settle, The New Lost City Ramblers, Doc Watson, The Dillards).

"However," wrote *Cash Box*, "the acclaimed hero of the fete was a 22-year-old writer-singer-guitarist-harmonica player from Hibbing, Minnesota called Bob Dylan.... Looking something like a displaced Bowery Boy, the sandy-haired, lanky youth, who wore the same pair of bluejeans(*sic*) and mustard-stained workshirt for most of the Festival, ranks as the logical successor to Woody Guthrie as the folk-poet laureate of the nation. [Dylan] completely captured the imagination of the audience and performers alike with his hard-driving talkin' blues style and biting, topical songs of protest."

Newport's opening night closed with the kind of hootenanny finale ABC dreaded: Peter, Paul & Mary, Joan Baez, Bob Dylan, The Freedom Singers, Pete Seeger and Theodore Bikel, hand-in-hand and leading the crowd in the gospel-cum-civil rights anthem "We Shall Overcome."

Between four concerts and 18 panels & workshops, *Cash Box* enthused, there was plenty for attendees "who were, in the main, clean-scrubbed collegiate types" that brought their own instruments, to occupy their attention. "The success of the Festival has an important, far-reaching meaning," their reviewer concluded. "Folk music need no longer take a back seat status. Folk music is a business as well as an art form and it's a business that can pay off handsomely." A handful of East Coast promoters were in full agreement and happy to take advantage.

Those who couldn't travel to Newport were likely to find a folk fest coming to the nearest city. The first touring show, "The American Hootenanny Festival," had launched on July 17. Hosted by Billy Faier and starring The Greenbriar Boys, the Festival "has been playing to capacity in most locations," according to *Variety*, and booked solid through Labor Day. The tour was produced by Fred Hertz, whose Gotham Recording Studio was home to "The World of Folk Music," a 15-minute weekly show underwritten by the Social Security Administration since 1961. "Although the bill doesn't spotlight big names," *Variety's* Mike Gross wrote, "the promoters figure that the package's pick-along contest for amateur guitarists and banjo players is the big draw in addition to the low admissions (average $1.20-$1.80) and the three-to-four hours running time." Among the professionals were Bob Carey, who'd just left The Tarriers, and Joan Meyers, both of whom would be tapped for *Hootenanny's* upcoming season.

Another package, headed by ex-Limeliter Glenn Yarbrough, was "Hootenanny USA," created in August by promoter Tim Gale, and featuring Jo Mapes, The Geezinslaw Brothers, The Journeymen and The Halifax Three, a Canadian group whose members included Denny Doherty; the tour may well have been Doherty's introduction to future collaborator John Phillips. This troupe made news beyond the music when they were booked at Jackson, Mississippi's city auditorium: upon learning the audience would be segregated, the performers opted to cancel the show about three hours before it was to take place.

Still another show, launched in August by promoter Hal Zeiger, was "Hootenanny '63," which presented unknown talent auditioned at various campuses around the country. According the *Tulsa Tribune* of September 12: "Featured on the program will be Dan Cox, who sings in the Harry Belafonte style; the Bilson Brothers, a comic singing duo not unlike the Smothers Brothers; the Villagers Quartet, reminiscent of the Brothers

Four; the Leaders trio; the Blue Grass Playboys; and Margaret Cox, sister of Dan Cox and a singer in the style of the famed Odetta."

In September, one of the big players, International Talent Associates, put together a "Traveling Hootenanny" package also hosted by a former Limeliter: Dr. Lou Gottlieb. This one featured The Modern Folk Quartet, Lynn Gold, The Knob Lick Upper 10,000 (a male trio, in case you were wondering), and Bessie Griffin and the Gospel Pearls.

Ad for the "Traveling Hootenanny" directed at colleges and other likely locales.

Lastly came a relative newcomer to the field: Jack Linkletter. First, he created Link Records, gathered some heretofore unrecorded talent, set up a gig at Pasadena's Ice House nightclub, hired the sole remaining ex-Limeliter, Alex Hassilev, to produce, and recorded an album, *Jack Linkletter Presents a Folk Festival*. The then-unknowns were The

Yachtsmen, a male quartet that performed at Disneyland; Jim and Jean Glover, a husband-wife duet that went on to sign with the Phillips label; soprano Chloe Marsh, a Baez sound-alike who'd appeared on Jack's father's radio program; and Les Baxter's Balladeers, another male quartet best remembered as David Crosby's entry into the music business. Crosby fared much better a year later as co-founder of The Byrds and later still as one-third of Crosby, Stills & Nash. Released in mid-November and distributed by GNP-Crescendo Records, *Billboard's* review was little more than "nice sound throughout."

Ahead of the album's release, though, Linketter put together his own touring package, which included Les Baxter's Balladeers; The Big 3, a trio that also featured a future folk-rock star, Cass Elliot; Joe and Eddie, by then on theater screens in *Hootenanny Hoot*; and 18-year-old Philadelphia native Raun MacKinnon, another Baez-esque soprano whose debut album, *American Folk Songs*, was released earlier in the year. The "Hootenanny: Jack Linkletter Folk Festival" tour was to run 32 days between October 22—November 23, beginning in Sioux Falls, South Dakota and concluding in Flushing, New York.

"This tour is fun and good for me," the mobility-loving Linkletter told *Detroit Free Press* TV columnist Bettelou Peterson after the first week. "It's an education meeting people all over the country and seeing their enthusiasm for what we're doing…. There was a show in Fargo, North Dakota, where we had 4,500 packed into

a space for 3,000 and turned another 1,000 away. That's the great thing about folk music: there is a style for everyone."

Those who couldn't get into a "Hootenanny" touring show could easily find "Hootenanny" long-playing records on practically every label, old *and* new. *Hootenanny Live At The Bitter End* was one of the earliest releases for FM Records, a new company created by Monte Kay and Pete Kameron, managers of jazz artists like Dizzy Gillespie, Herbie Mann and Chris Connor. Weintraub was engaged to oversee FM's folk output; the deal also included exclusive rights to record at his coffee house. The album featured selections by Jo Mapes, Bob Carey, Len Chandler and Fred Neil.

For the discerning enthusiast who enjoyed reading about folk artists and singing their songs as much as listening to them, there were two "Hootenanny" magazines to choose from, each featuring a section of folk tunes in sheet music form, both traditional and modern.

The first, simply titled *Hootenanny*, was published by entrepreneur (and future film producer) Fred B. Tarter and edited by the *New York Times'* folk music critic Robert Shelton. "There is a need for a national newsstand magazine that can keep abreast of the fast-developing trends in the field, the new personalities," Shelton wrote in the opening piece. "There is a need for a type of journalism that relates music to life and life to music…. There will be stimulating debate in these pages about ends and means in folk music, about integrity and expediency, about elevating taste or pandering to it." Which was a tasteful way of saying they'd be knocking the TV series at least some of the time… and they did, as we'll see.

The first issue hit the street near the end of September and featured interviews with Peter, Paul & Mary and Judy Henske, written pieces by Bob Dylan, Lou Gottlieb and Ralph Rinzler, guitar instruction by Erik Darling, regional reports and LP reviews and even a few relevant cartoons, plus music and lyrics for a dozen-and-a-half traditional songs.

Not to be outdone, ABC and Dankar licensed Maurice Murray's SMP Publishing to print its own magazine, *ABC-TV Hootenanny*. They, in turn, hired *Village Voice* music reviewer Linda Solomon (who'd submitted the Henske interview to Shelton's *Hootenanny*) as editor. The first issue, which reached newsstands on October 29, featured an interview with Chad Mitchell, written pieces by Judy Collins, Theodore Bikel and Tommy Makem, banjo

instruction by Eric Weissburg, regional reports and LP reviews and music and lyrics for eight traditional songs, plus articles written by both Jack Linkletter and *Hootenanny's* original host, Jean Shepherd.

There was an expectation among the cognoscenti Shelton's magazine would be an in-depth probe of the music, its artists and the craze, while Solomon's would consist of promotional fluff. Yet while the former couched his intentions in abstract terms, the latter tackled the Seeger controversy head-on in her interview with Mitchell:

Q: *Many performers have been criticized for participating on the* HOOTENANNY *show because of its policy toward Pete Seeger and the Weavers. Have you received such criticism?*

A: *Not directly, no, but I've read articles attacking performers in general for participating in the show and I assume the Chad Mitchell Trio is included. Because of this I would like a chance to comment on this issue.*

First of all, I believe that the arts should be free from political or social discrimination. And, of course, this includes the performing arts. I feel that this freedom is inherent in the basic concept of democracy. If one suspects that a communications medium is discriminating on a social or political basis, then of course he does not have to participate on that medium. This, however, seems to me to be a rather negative approach if one has something positive to offer. In the case of the Chad Mitchell Trio, we approached the HOOTENANNY *people with our "John Birch Society," a satire with a definite political theme, and were allowed to perform it on the show. Also we performed a racially integrated number with Miss Miriam Makeba of South Africa, a combination not often seen on national television. I feel that those contributions were a more positive remedy to suspected discrimination [than] if we had not participated at all.*

Despite this, Lynn Muscrave would write in Shelton's second issue, "Linda Solomon has encountered resistance in getting articles from folk musicians and managers…. Because of the link with the ABC show, Billy Faier, Sam Charters and Dave Van Ronk, to name three, have refused to write for the magazine. Billy James, Columbia Records publicist who touted Bob Dylan within the company long before he became popular, refused to write a 'non-political, non-controversial' article on Bob, saying, 'you can't turn salt into sugar.'" So, while *Hootenanny* #2 had Dylan and Joan Baez on the cover, and a lengthy Shelton-penned article ("The Voice Meets the Poet") about them, *ABC-TV Hootenanny* #2 had two pages of photos of the pair giving an impromptu performance at Gerde's Folk City in the Village and one paragraph describing the event.

On August 7, the board of directors of an extremist right-wing organization, the Fire and Police Research Association of Los Angeles (FI-PO), adopted a resolution that "formally requests the Congress of the United States, through its House Committee of Un-American Activities, to investigate Communist subversive involvement in the folk music field, that the continued, effective misuse of this media may not be made, and that it may not be further used as an unidentified tool of Communist psychological or cybernetic warfare to ensnare and capture youthful minds in the United States...." Among FI-PO's "whereases" in their resolution: "[It] is becoming more and more evident that certain of the hootenannies and other similar youth gatherings and festivals, both in this country and in Europe have been used to brainwash and subvert, in a seemingly innocuous but actually covert and deceptive manner, vast segments of young people's groups." Two weeks later, Karl Thor, president of the board of directors, sent the resolution and a cover letter to Edwin E. Willis, HUAC's current chairman. Thor wrote several paragraphs pointing out Pete Seeger's omnipresence in both concerts and publications and otherwise recapping what the Committee already knew. Copies were sent to F.B.I. head J. Edgar Hoover and seven Congressional Republicans.

One of the latter was Senator Kenneth Keating, R-NY, who on September 26, entered the resolution into the Congressional Record, but not before giving it and the Association a thorough skewering. After admitting he needed to look up the definition of "cybernetic," Sen. Keating professed, "I had always had the impression that if anything was thoroughly American in spirit, it was American folk music. To be sure, I was perfectly aware of certain un-American influences in it, like Elizabethan balladry, English protestant hymns and... native African rhythms. But in my naivete, I never considered these un-American influences to be of a sinister nature and simply passed them off as part and parcel of the melting-pot tradition which has contributed so much in the way of variety and interest to the American cultural heritage."

Having set up his thesis, Sen. Keating went on to cite lyrics to several songs and spirituals that, he was now certain, could be construed as "subversive;" i.e., the following verse from "Copper Kettle":

> *My daddy, he made whiskey*
> *My granddaddy did, too*
> *We ain't paid no whiskey tax*
> *Since 1792*

"If enough people went around singing this at hootenannies, Americans might get the idea that they don't have to pay their taxes," the Senator professed, with tongue firmly in cheek. "After all, the family in the song got away with it for 171 years. And if the Government loses its ability to collect taxes for our defense effort, we would be wide open for a Communist takeover, would we not?" After going along these lines for several minutes, Keating admits, "There is one concern I still have about a congressional investigation of folk music such as proposed by [FI-PO]. What I fear is that such an investigation would stimulate the writing of new folk music making fun of congressional investigations. This shows how devious the Communists really are…. [There] may be no logical stopping place once an investigation of folk music goes forward. Any such investigation would ultimately have to be extended ad infinitum, to take in a study of the folk songs composed in response to the investigation itself, which can go on indefinitely."

Concluded Keating, "It all boils down to a gigantic plot, one that has been brought to our attention before…. And so, now, to the list of subversive individuals, institutions, and ideas, which presently includes the United Nations, the income tax, the Chief Justice of the United States, the Girl Scouts of America, fluoridation of the water supply, the last four Presidents of the United States, beatniks, Harvard University, civil rights demonstrations… we must now add, merciful heavens, American folk music…. This resolution is but another demonstration of the absurd lengths to which the amateur ferrets of the radical right will go in their quixotic sallies against the Communist menace…. With devotion to our freedom, with trust in the American ideal of cultural diversity, with above all a sense of proportion and discernment in meeting the challenges of our times, I for one have every faith that—in the words of that inspiring song—we shall overcome."

Senator Clairborne Pell, D-RI, eloquently added his concurrence: "I wish to congratulate the Senator from New York on his spoof of the charges that folk music is a subversive wing of the Communist conspiracy. This past summer we had the most successful music festival that we have ever had in Newport. More people came to it… and more enjoyment was received by our local citizens than had ever before been the case to any form of public entertainment. When it is suggested, because of political reasons, that we should clamp down on forms of art expression, I think we are treading dangerously close to totalitarianism. This approach is very akin to that of the Kremlin with regard to impressionist artists and jazz musicians. Certainly it is not an approach that we should emulate."

Newspapers reported on the speech—*The New York Times'* headline was "Keating Sings Out for Freedom of Hootenanny"—and Shelton's magazine reprinted the entire Congressional Record entry in its second issue. Alas, ABC didn't take the hint from Republican and Democratic congressmen united through faith in America's diversity and trust in its freedom of expression; aligning instead with FI-PO and similar associations, all of which loudly cried "Foul" on Keating's speech, in fear they and their sponsors would also be targets for backlash.

The banning of Pete Seeger had hung over *Hootenanny's* first season like a spectral threat to its future. As season two got off the ground, with voices still grousing about who was and wasn't "good enough" for the show, the network finally made its position crystal clear.

Norman Keenan accompanies Nancy Ames as they rehearse for *Hootenanny's* second season premiere. *From the author's collection*

CHAPTER FIVE

SEASON TWO: "That Great Sea of Squares"

No question: *Hootenanny* **was a** solid success by anyone's standards, much less ABC's. It was the second-most popular program on the network after *Ben Casey*. There is a downside to having such success, however: network and ad agency executives tend to notice. Now that they knew people were actually watching this show, they had ideas about how it could be "better." The first was obvious: make it longer. And bigger. Let's use the gymnasiums and auditoriums and bring in *thousands* of students instead of hundreds! And since we're making it longer, let's add *more* kinds of folky-type music! Let's bring in some country & western stars, some jazz stars! Maybe even some pop singers that are getting hits with folk material! Let's up the gospel group quota and attract *that* market! And let's have a comedian during the second half, for a respite from all that music!

And, by all means, let's have a theme song; one that can get on a record and promote the show even *more!*

What Lewine thought of all this personally, we'll never know; publicly he put as positive a spin on it as he could. "In our new one-hour format," he wrote for UPI, "the folk singing will be seasoned—spiced, we trust—with other entertainment that has proved good campus fare. There will be young stand-up comedians, a Dixieland group every now and then, gospel singing, and on occasion, a group from the college itself." He personally composed the music for the new theme song, lyrics having come from the pen of young Alfred Uhry. The man who'd one day write the play *Driving Miss Daisy* was then a recent Brown

University graduate who was in New York learning the librettist's craft under the mentorship of Broadway's Frank Loesser.

One who *did* make his feelings known about the changes was Jack Linkletter. "I would have been just as satisfied had the show remained a half-hour," he told reporter Micheline Keating. "I think you take an awful chance when you change a program that has clicked on its first outing. No one can foretell how the hour format will turn out. It is possible that with the addition of comedians and jazz performers, the country flavor of the show will be lost. I think the great popularity of the program this summer has been that its entire appeal stems from devotion to grass roots songfests."

A more reasonable addition was a full-time bassist who could accompany the singers and groups that didn't bring one of their own; for this, Norman Keenan was hired. After some fifteen years of playing for the era's jazz performers, Keenan became house bassist at the Village Vanguard in 1949, worked for Harry Belafonte beginning in 1957 and had played on Miriam Makeba's first and The Chad Mitchell Trio's final Belafonte-produced albums in 1962.

Colleges and universities were requesting to host the show. Petitions were being circulated; campus organizations were offering their services. In at least two cases, advertisers pushed for specific institutions. Lewine's main concerns were a photogenic campus and enough space for the equipment. He kept to the "two shows at each college every other week" modus operandi, but this necessarily meant spending an extra day, since rehearsals and staging precluded recording two hour-long shows back-to-back. With rare exceptions, Tuesdays and Wednesdays were allocated for afternoon dress rehearsals and evening performances. Since the start of the new season mostly coincided with the start of the fall semester, eventually taping weeks caught up with airdates.

Since ABC liked the idea of growing Lawrence Welk's audience, they shifted *Hootenanny* ahead one hour, to 7:30 pm. Welk's hour followed at 8:30, after which came the network's biggest gamble for the season: a live, two-hour talk & variety show hosted by Jerry Lewis, which would be costing them over $1 million per week.

Lastly, they saw fit to send the following memorandum to Dankar Productions:

We understand that with our election to continue the "Hootenanny" series into the 1963-64 season there will be the opportunity for additional artists to be considered for the series and that you are now in process of engaging the talent. We also understand that you have been offered the services of Mr. Pete Seeger for one of the programs in the series.

It is a matter of public knowledge that Mr. Seeger appeared as a witness before a subcommittee of the Committee on Un-American Activities of the House of Representatives on Aug. 18, 1955, during hearings which were being conducted on the subject of Communist infiltration in the field of entertainment in New York. The record will show that Mr. Seeger refused to discuss allegations that he was connected with or had participated in functions allegedly sponsored by the Communist Party.

The Management of ABC has asked me to inform you that it has a long established and firm policy, insofar as entertainment programs are concerned, against allowing the use of its facilities by performers identified with the Communist Party. In case of doubt (for example, where a person has taken a public position before a Congressional committee), it uses best judgement based on all objective data available to it.

In the circumstances, ABC will consider Mr. Seeger's use on the program only if he furnishes a sworn affidavit as to his past and present affiliations, if any, with the Communist Party, and/or with the Communist front organizations. Upon so doing, the company will undertake to consider his statement in relation to all the objective data available to it, and will advise you promptly, under the terms of its agreement with you, whether it will approve the employment of Mr. Seeger.

Seeger, of course, refused to sign anything that smacked of a "loyalty oath" and Harold Leventhal announced as much to the press on September 5, adding, "it is apparent ABC is continuing a blacklisting policy." ABC's terse response was that Seeger "would not be considered for an appearance." Six days later, *Variety* put "ABC Finally Puts Itself on Record Re 'Hootenanny'" on its front page, reminding readers of the network's original position "that Seeger was not the type of talent suitable for the show."

ABC had to know how Seeger would respond. Eight years before, the man had refused to provide the very same information to a Congressional committee. Did they really believe he'd capitulate in order to *maybe* appear on their TV series? For that matter, did they think they could placate the boycotters with, "Hey, we *tried!* It's *his* fault he's not on the show!" If so, they failed to bank on the loyalty he engendered in the folk world. Artists that had appeared during season one, when there was still some question as to whether it was ABC, or Dankar, or Ashley-Steiner, or sponsors calling the shots, would fail to answer the call for season two. Moreover, now that *Hootenanny* was an hour long, giving Joan Baez or Peter, Paul & Mary an uninterrupted fifteen-minute set wasn't out of the question, but after Leventhal's announcement they made it known there was no way they'd appear.

It could've been worse. Prior to making ABC's memorandum public, Leventhal "called a meeting with Pete Seeger, Theo [Bikel] and me to discuss the situation," Judy Collins later wrote. "I was surprised at Pete's response. He said that *Hootenanny* would help to make folk music popular, which was something he had fought for all his life, and urged Theo and me to accept invitations to go on the show again." He also apparently managed to coax The Greenbriar Boys to do the same, although the group's organizer, guitarist John Herald, balked.

Nevertheless, Bikel, who signed with Dankar for two appearances, was irked. "I'll be doing the shows with misgivings," he told *Billboard*. "As an American, I find it distasteful to think that anybody has to bargain for his livelihood on any other basis than talent alone. Beyond that, I have never seen any evidence that Pete Seeger has tried to overthrow the government with his banjo."

"We hope to get Burl Ives, Odetta, Miriam Makeba and others like them. We also hope to get The Smothers Brothers," Lewine told the press. None of that happened… but they *did* get most of the performers from *Hootenanny Hoot*. They also landed the services of commercial folk's latest Grammy-winner: a picking, strumming nine-member chorale assembled like a mosaic from among various soloists and duos, which yielded the classic whole greater than the sum of its parts. A similar conglomeration from the University of Colorado that had spent part of their summer auditioning in New York would sign a management contract with Fred Weintraub in September. Thanks to *Hootenanny*, they'd become just as well-known.

2-01: Boston University, Boston MA #1

Recording Date: August 14, 1963.

Airdate: September 21, 1963

Video 1: UCLA Film & Television Archive: 35mm Safety Storage archival copy, T61259 (reel 1 of 2), T61283 (reel 2 of 2); VHS non-circulating Research & Study Center copy, VA2631_T.

Video 2: 16mm dupe kinescope minus commercials. Licensing: Historic Films Archive, LLC, #V-1019. Viewing: The Library of Congress, catalog # MAVIS 2899690. Excerpted on ***The Best of Hootenanny***.

The Chad Mitchell Trio: "Hootenanny Saturday Night" (*Jack Linkletter intro*)

The Chad Mitchell Trio: "Mighty Day"

Nancy Ames: "Longtime, Boy"

Mike Settle: "What Shall We Do with a Drunken Sailor?"

The Rooftop Singers: "Tom Cat"

The Chad Mitchell Trio: "You Can Tell the World," "The Song of Youth"

Stan Rubin and the Tigertown Five: "Battle Hymn of the Republic"

Albertina Walker & the Caravans: "I Won't Be Back No More"

Mike Settle: "Oleanna" (Commercial bumper)

Nancy Ames: "Raise a Ruckus" (with *The Chad Mitchell Trio*)

Vaughn Meader: Stand-up comedy

The Rooftop Singers: "Mama Don't Allow"

Albertina Walker & the Caravans: "Old Time Religion" (with *Stan Rubin and the Tigertown Five*)

Mike Settle: "Settle Down"

The Rooftop Singers: "R.C. Frog"

The Chad Mitchell Trio: "Nobody Knows You When You're Down and Out," "Last Night I Had the Strangest Dream"

FINALE: "You'd Better Get a Home in That Rock" (*Everyone*)

Thank goodness for the summer semester: it meant a full auditorium for a mid-August taping.

The Chad Mitchell Trio opens with the show's new theme song, "Hootenanny Saturday Night" in an arrangement that has none of them exclusively singing the melody. During the instrumental break, Jack Linkletter tells us about the university's history and locale, while the camera pans along the campus view of the Charles River. He also names some of the cast. At this point, Lewine's thought was to repurpose the same opening performance for both shows, with only Linkletter's narrative changing. That idea would last exactly one more taping session.

After belting out "Mighty Day" at a furious pace that must have tested backing musicians David Ander (guitar) and Paul Prestopino (banjo), the Trio give way to newcomer Nancy Ames. Born Nancy Alfaro in Washington DC, she was the daughter of a physician and granddaughter of Ricardo Alfaro, former President of Panama. A brief marriage to a man named Emes and one vowel change led to her stage name. She signed with Harry Belafonte around the same time as did The

Chad Mitchell Trio ("He was putting together a 'stable of stars,'" she recalled, "and somehow he chose me"), but realized little in the way of work.

The Chad Mitchell Trio (Mike Kobluk, Chad Mitchell, Joe Frazier) gather around the microphone at Boston University. *From the author's collection*

After parting from Belafonte, Ames and her second husband, hypnotist Traian Boyer worked the supper club circuit together, her repertoire consisting mainly of Spanish-language songs and ballads. She signed with Liberty Records who released her first album in January 1963, but the big break took place shortly after this appearance when she was cast as a "singing commentator" for NBC's version of Britain's current event satire program *That Was The Week That Was*, which debuted as a special in late October and a series in January 1964.

Mike Settle, who did the pilot, returns for the first of six appearances this season. Better known as an accomplished songwriter, Settle's career began when he replaced John Montgomery in The Cumberland Three in early 1961, teaming with the group's organizer John Stewart and Gil Robbins. The gig ended that summer when Stewart was invited to replace Dave Guard in The Kingston Trio. He embarked on a solo career, recording many of his own compositions, including "Sing Hallelujah" (performed with The Limeliters on the pilot) and "Settle Down (Goin' Down that Highway)," performed here as well as by Peter, Paul & Mary on both their second album and a single that reached #14 on *Billboard's* Adult Contemporary chart, bringing Settle enough royalties to remain solvent while building his reputation.

For their second *Hootenanny* booking, The Rooftop Singers open with "Tom Cat," their follow-up single to "Walk Right In." Unfortunately, program managers for several top 40 radio stations felt the lyrics were too suggestive and wouldn't play it. ABC's censors either believed otherwise or weren't paying attention: the saucy song is performed here without a lyric change. But the dearth of radio play cost the group all the momentum garnered by their initial success, and they never had another chart hit. The other two tunes would appear on their second LP *Good News*, not released until early the following year.

The Chad Mitchell Trio return with Bob Gibson's "You Can Tell the World" and "Maladyozhenaya," a 19th century folk tune of Russian origin introduced as "The Song of Youth." As during the previous season, when the Trio sings in Russian, Linkletter is compelled to assure us the lyrics are harmless: "The words say, 'How good it is to be young, when the days fly along like a golden whirlwind.'"

Clarinetist Stan Rubin and the Tigertown Five bring a Dixieland swing to "The Battle Hymn of the Republic," the Civil War's anti-slavery anthem, and then gospel returns in the form of The Caravans, led by Albertina Walker. In the coming weeks, the series usually alternated between jazz and spiritual groups, but Lewine and company couldn't resist combining the forms later in this show when Rubin and his combo accompany Walker and The Caravans on "(Give Me That) Old Time Religion." Although each group occupies opposite ends of the stage, it still qualifies as an integrated performance, and a lively one.

If *Hootenanny* had to have comedians, at least Lewine was savvy enough to start with the hottest on the market, one especially appropriate for this university. Abbott Vaughn Meader was born in Waterville, Maine, on March 20, 1936. His father died when he was a year old, his mother went to work as a waitress, and for most of his childhood he lived with aunts and uncles. He attended Winslow High School, played in the band and performed in school plays. After a stint in the Army, during which he was stationed in Germany and occasionally sang self-penned country songs, he made his way into show business as a cocktail lounge pianist and singer. He also possessed a sharp wit, and tried his luck as a stand-up comic in a Greenwich Village club called The Phase Two. Never a celebrity impersonator, Meader was a gifted mimic and as part of his routine he would do President John F. Kennedy holding a press conference. Audience reaction led to an appearance on a summer replacement TV show called *Celebrity Talent Scouts* in July 1962, which led to bookings with Jack Paar and Ed Sullivan.

The night *Hootenanny's* second season premiered was a day shy of eleven months since Meader and a handful of New York actors entered a studio and recorded *The First Family*, an LP of sketches that lampooned the Boston-reared President, his wife and relatives. Only after the performance was over did they and the studio audience learn about a speech the real President had delivered concerning Soviet missiles in Cuba. "Like most of us on *The First Family* album, I did not take the royalties that were offered," Naomi Brossart, who portrayed the First Lady, recalled. "The original recording was made the night of the Cuban missile crisis, October 22, 1962, and except for Vaughn Meader and the sound effects man, the performers felt that if there was going to be a nuclear war, there would be nobody left to buy the album anyway." Meader, too, "would have taken $500 and run. He was broke," his manager, Buddy Allen, remembered in 1975. "I insisted on some kind of royalty. I didn't care how small. We wound up with two percent," or seven cents per disc, which quickly translated into $315,000 when four-and-a-half million copies were sold in a matter of weeks. It was the fastest-selling LP in history up to then, and brought Meader $10,000 per week gigs in places like Las Vegas.

Comedian Vaughn Meader as audiences would always remember him: satirizing a President Kennedy press conference. *From the author's collection*

Already keenly aware of being perceived as a one-trick pony, Meader begins his routine here with some proclamations by the "colorful politicians" in and around Boston, complete with ethnic dialects, followed by humorous political observations on such things as American television going to foreign countries. He gets some decent laughs but everyone knows what's coming. Naturally, his spot concludes with a JFK press conference. He takes questions from the students ("What would Vaughn Meader have done if Richard Nixon had won in '60?" "That's *his* problem. I'm wondering what *I* would've done if Nixon had won in '60!"), and nearly all get hearty laughs and applause.

After The Rooftop Singers' jazz-infused take on "Froggie Went a-Courtin'" the camera cuts to Chad Mitchell sauntering out of the audience toward the stage whistling and singing into a hand-held microphone to kick off an attention-grabbing solo performance on "Nobody Knows You When You're Down and Out." Then he's joined by his partners on one of the Folk Era's greatest anti-war statements: Ed McCurdy's "Last Night I Had the Strangest Dream." Written in 1950, it's a simple, straightforward song with an idealistic message that, had it been taught to grammar school children in all nations when it was new, might have brought us a more peaceful world.

"'Hootenanny' still registers as one of the web's brightest, bounciest hours," wrote 'Tube' for a review in *Variety*. "Although expanded to 60 minutes this season to permit inclusion of other variety elements, the show still retains its basic quality as an enthusiastic folk-sing outing. Once again, the show is originating from various college campuses, which provides an excellent setting for the show's performers and an opportunity for the cameras to pan over the marvelous faces of the students."

Labeling him "the offbeat feature of this stanza," 'Tube' felt Vaughn Meader "came through very well…. Another good departure on the show was the appearance of Stan Rubin & His Tigertown Five in some Dixieland offerings that certainly are part of the American folk heritage. The major portion of the show was carried by the more typical folksingers, such as the excellent Chad Mitchell Trio, the Rooftop Singers, Mike Settle and Nancy Ames, all of whom belted their material to tremendous and authentic audience response. In the gospel idiom, the Caravans also scored with their rousing religioso rhythmics."

Harry Harris of *The Philadelphia Inquirer* thought, "ABC's 'Hootenanny' profited from its expansion to an hour Saturday night. The added time permitted more informative 'program notes' by host Jack Linkletter, a more generous sampling of guest stars' talents and, a questionable blessing, a community-toasting preamble of which Chambers of Commerce, at least, will approve. The Boston University students enthusiastically 'dug' the [performers]."

At least two critics liked the "bigger and better" *Hootenanny*. As far as viewers went, the verdict was still out. According to Trendex, the premiere pulled an 11.5 rating, considerably less than the 27.6 reported at the end of season one. Slated opposite *Hootenanny* were NBC's *The Lieutenant*, a new Gene Roddenberry-produced series about a marine during peacetime that drew a 13.8 rating, and a years-old *Lucy-Desi Comedy Hour* rerun on CBS that won the timeslot with 15.4. It's possible—probable even—that fans, especially among the "light" viewers, weren't yet savvy to the new timeslot. ABC could only hope they'd catch on quick: the following week, *The Jackie Gleason Show* would have its season premiere, and the *real* competition would begin.

2-02: University of Pittsburgh, Pittsburgh PA #1

Recording Date: September 5, 1963.

Airdate: September 28, 1963. *Repeat*: May 16, 1964.

Video: 16mm kinescope of the repeat broadcast. Licensing: Historic Films Archive, LLC, #V-1012. Viewing: The Library of Congress, catalog # MAVIS 2899691. Excerpted on **The Best of Hootenanny**.

The Brothers Four: "Hootenanny Saturday Night" (*Jack Linkletter intro*)

The Brothers Four: "Michael, Row the Boat Ashore"

Judy Henske: "High Flying Bird"

The Dillards: "Reuben's Train"

Leon Bibb: "Rocks and Gravel"

The Rooftop Singers: "I'm On My Way"

Will Holt: "Raspberries, Strawberries"

The Brothers Four: "Island in the Sun"

Marion Williams & the Stars of Faith: "Packin' Up"

The Brothers Four: "If I Had A Hammer" (commercial bumper)

The Rooftop Singers: "Working on the Railroad"

Louis Nye: Stand-up comedy

Judy Henske and The Dillards: "Charlotte Town"

Marion Williams & the Stars of Faith: "I've Got to Live the Life I Sing About in My Song"

BLUES MEDLEY: "Every Night When the Sun Goes In" (*Leon Bibb*), "You Don't Know" (*The Rooftop Singers*), "Low Down Alligator" (*Judy Henske*)

The Brothers Four: "Five Hundred Miles"

FINALE: "He's Got the Whole World in His Hands" (*Everyone*)

According to the student newspaper *The Pitt News*, this was the show taped on the second evening. Why it aired first is a mystery lost to time, especially since it resulted in presenting The Rooftop Singers two weeks in a row.

The Brothers Four were an international success. Bob Flick, Dick Foley, Mike Kirkland and John Paine met at the University of Washington in Seattle after pledging to the Phi Gamma Delta fraternity. All four enjoyed folk music and were clearly gifted, honing their skill at college parties and other social gatherings, eventually invited to perform at local venues for pay. Having completed their junior year in June 1959, they played for 28 weekends at Seattle's Colony Club, moved on to San Francisco and the hungry i, were signed to Columbia and saw their debut single, "Greenfields," reach number one.   Their first year as professionals, the foursome netted a half-million dollars.

The Brothers Four: Dick Foley, Mike Kirkland, Bob Flick and John Paine in rehearsal. *From the author's collection*

Like The Kingston Trio, they toured overseas, scoring especially big in Japan. Like The Limeliters, they made significant residual money doing Coca-Cola commercials. By the time of their appearance here, they'd released nine albums, including a greatest hits package, sang the theme to 20th Century-Fox's *Five Weeks in a Balloon* (1962) and of course appeared in *Hootenanny Hoot*. They open with the show's theme song, which they'd release as a single in November, then move on to "Michael, Row the Boat Ashore" from their most recent LP, *The Big Folk Hits*.

Judy Henske, "that green-eyed wonder" as Linkletter describes her, makes a welcome return with the title track to her new album, *High Flying Bird*. Later, she and The Dillards do another from the LP, "Charlotte Town." Although both acts were signed to Elektra, they didn't work together until this show and the result is another *Hootenanny* highlight; the Bluegrass foursome and the bluesy chanteuse mesh seamlessly.

Thanks to *The Andy Griffith Show*, then the nation's fifth-most popular TV series, America knew The Dillards as "The Darling Boys," the music-making mountaineers who'd drop by Mayberry now and then to shake things up and pick and sing. The group consisted of two brothers, Douglas and Rodney Dillard on banjo and guitar respectively, Dean Webb on mandolin and bassist Mitchell Jayne. All were born and raised in Salem, Missouri deep in Ozark country. Their opener is "Reuben's Train" from their first album, which had also been included on Crestview's initial *Hootenanny* compilation.

Drawing from his theatrical experience, Leon Bibb presents a dramatic interpretation of "Rocks and Gravel," one of folk's mainstays in the sub-genre of chain gang songs. Then The Rooftop Singers return for their final appearance, again with selections from their upcoming second album. The group would continue until 1967, albeit with changes. On June 27, 1964, after a performance at the Utah amusement and water park Lagoon, Lynne Taylor kissed her bandmates goodbye and left the group for permanent wife-and-motherhood in Los Angeles with her radio personality husband, Skip Weshner; reportedly they never saw her again. She was replaced with Mindy Stuart, with whom they recorded a third album, then with Patricia Street. Bill Svanoe left, ending the Rooftop Singers and leaving Erik Darling and Street to work as a duo into the 1970s. Svanoe turned to writing, turning out scripts for several made-for-TV movies into the 1980s, and today is a professor at UNC-Chapel Hill. Darling also moved to North Carolina, where he died of lymphoma in 2008. Sadly, Lynne Taylor Weshner committed suicide on April 29, 1979 at age 43. Astonishingly, there was no press coverage in the *Los Angeles Times* or elsewhere in the county, so respected was her husband by the populace. The circumstances remain private within the family.

The Rooftop Singers: Bill Svanoe, Erik Darling, Lynne Taylor, during their final *Hootenanny* appearance at the University of Pittsburgh. *From the author's collection*

Will Holt returns with his composition "Raspberries, Strawberries," which had been released by both The Kingston Trio and Bud and Travis a few years earlier. The student audience is clearly more familiar with the Kingstons' recording, which substituted half of the refrain's French lyrics with "la-la-la's." Holt gamely harmonizes, but sings the song as written, pointedly slowing them down at the finale.

Gospel singer Marion Williams was born in Miami in 1927 and sang in churches until, at age 20, she joined The Clara Ward Singers. She stayed with Ward for eleven years, then she and three other members formed The Stars of Faith. In 1961, they appeared on Broadway in Langston Hughes' gospel musical *Black Nativity*. Here she performs the rousing "Packin' Up" with her group, then later solos on "I've Got to Live the Life I Sing About;" unable to keep from moving about the stage, she uses the hand-held mic for both numbers. "Packin' Up" prominently features her "octave-leaping high whoops," as described by Jon Pareles in *The New York Times*, which Little Richard affirmed had influenced his singing style on such hits as "Tutti Frutti." The students, presumably raised on that brand of rock 'n' roll, react accordingly. Going solo in 1965, Williams would continue performing faith-based material until her passing in 1994 from vascular disease.

Louis Nye, long-time regular on *The Steve Allen Show*, spontaneously opens his slot with a "high whoop," which of course delights the audience, then moves on to a routine about an Army sergeant welcoming new recruits. Briefly mentioned in the bit is "a sex lecture… and after that, a nice breakfast." The lecture subtopic was to have received more attention but was shut down by ABC's censors.

The final quarter marks the debut of another *Hootenanny* innovation: the multi-artist medley. Leon Bibb tells the students that he, The Rooftop Singers and Judy Henske will present three interpretations of the blues, and starts it off with a wistful "Every Night When the Sun Goes In." Lynne Taylor and Erik Darling go slightly more up-tempo with "You Don't Know," accompanied solely by Darling's guitar. Then Henske belts out "Low Down Alligator," which also proved problematic for the bluenoses at ABC. "They made me sing 'catch you with your socks rolled down' instead of the way the song was written, 'catch you with your britches down,'" she told Linda Solomon a few days later, adding, "It really infuriated me," which is made clear in her performance. When it first comes up, she growls the line and can't resist rolling her eyes in disgust, right when the camera is in close.

According to Trendex, *Hootenanny* began the hour with a 9.2 rating, but by the finale it had fallen to 7.9. All of the viewers who dropped switched to the second half of *The Lieutenant*, which had begun with 11.5 but finished with 15.0. *The Jackie Gleason Show's* premiere handily won with 17.7 and 17.2 respectively, with only a half-point lost to *The Lieutenant*. The message was clear, at least to ABC: figure out a way to keep viewers tuned in.

2-03: Southern Methodist University, Dallas TX #1

Recording Date: October 1, 1963.

Airdate: October 5, 1963.

The Highwaymen: "Hootenanny Saturday Night" (*Jack Linkletter intro*)

The Highwaymen: "March on Brothers"

Joan Toliver: "Black is the Color (of My True Love's Hair)"

Bud and Travis: "Ah, Nora, War is Over"

Theodore Bikel: Medley of Drinking Songs: "The Charlady's Ball" (*Ireland*), "Nancy Whiskey" (*Scotland*), "When I'm Drunk, and I'm Always Drunk" (*Russia*).

Johnny Cash: "Going to Memphis"

Tommy & Diane: "This Little Light of Mine"

Bob Gibson: "I'm Going to Leave Old Texas Now"

Pete Fountain and the Mardi Gras Strutters: "Marchin' 'Round the Mountain."

Bud and Travis: "Vamos al Baile"

Johnny Cash: "Pickin' Time"

The Highwaymen: "I'll Fly Away"

Dave Astor: Stand-up comedy

Pete Fountain & the Mardi Gras Strutters: "After You've Gone"

MEDLEY - SAME SONG, DIFFERENT VERSIONS: "The Unfortunate Rake" (*Theodore Bikel*), "Streets of Laredo" (*Johnny Cash*), "Laredo (Parody)" (*Bud and Travis*)

Bob Gibson and Joan Toliver: "I'm Gonna Tell God How You Treat Me"

Theodore Bikel: "Come Away, Melinda"

FINALE: "Joy, Joy, Joy" (*Everyone*)

With this segment, the production team set a precedent. "The show taped here Tuesday will have the quickest airing of the program's history," wrote Fairfax Nisbet of the *Dallas Morning News* on October 2. "It will be shown on ABC-TV [this] Saturday. Immediately after Tuesday's performance, the tape was edited by the staff, then air-mailed to New York." The hasty post-production notwithstanding, what emerged is an entertaining hour with top-notch talent, but at present, only the audio is known to exist of everything except the commercial bumper and the finale.

The Highwaymen take a fling at the theme song, then return from commercial break with the title track of their most recent album, *March On, Brothers*. Like The Brothers Four, they came together as fellow undergraduates, specifically at Connecticut's Wesleyan University: Bob Burnett, Steve Butts, Chan Daniels, Dave Fisher and Steve Trott were asked to play professionally after being heard at various school gatherings. Unlike The Brothers Four, they opted not to leave college, even after their debut single, "Michael (Row the Boat Ashore)," went to number one. All five graduated in 1962, by which time they'd logged two additional hit records, "Cotton Fields" and "The Gypsy Rover." After a year of unencumbered performances, Trott elected to attend Harvard Law School; he was replaced by Gil Robbins, who'd briefly teamed with Tom Paxton after The Cumberland Three disbanded. The group sings the spiritual "I'll Fly Away" from the same album, their first with Robbins, during the show's second half.

Joan Toliver makes the first of five *Hootenanny* appearances. Born Joan Moore Scrivner in Berea, Kentucky, the 31-year-old contralto was another of Harry Belafonte's discoveries, touring with him through Canada and the northern U.S. during the previous summer. Then the wife of actor Josef Sommer, it was feared that 'Joan Sommer' would cause confusion with pop singer Joanie Sommers, so the name Toliver was chosen; "picked out of a hat," according to a relative. Her version of "Black is the Color" is a haunting one, and so impressed Fred Weintraub that he became her manager, booking her for steady appearances at The Bitter End.

Bud and Travis were folk music's Martin and Lewis: a team that had great difficulty getting along offstage, yet capable of unquestioned magic and witty comic repartee when on it. They'd already split once in December 1960 after nearly two years of solid success. Bud Dashiell formed his own group, The Kinsmen, while Travis Edmonson, who'd been a founding member of The Gateway Singers back in the fifties, tried for a solo career. In September 1962, they again cast their lot together and almost literally picked up where they'd left off, profitable enough to hire their own bassist, ex-Whiskeyhill Singer "Buck" Wheat. Having appeared twice during *Hootenanny's* first season, this is the first of two for the second; they opt for two high-energy pieces, the calypso "Ah Nora, War is Over" and the Latino "Vamos al Baile" or "Come to the Dance."

Although The Highwaymen opened the show, Theodore Bikel is the unquestioned headliner, granted time and freedom to joke about his upcoming medley: "I wanted to sing some drinking songs, and then somebody remembered that this is a Methodist university, so we talked to the dean about it. And he said, 'Can't you sing about something else?' And I said, 'All right. I'll sing about love.' So, he went away and thought it over and came back and said, 'Sing about drinking!'" Methodist or no, the appreciative students were at least familiar enough with "Nancy Whiskey" to accompany Bikel on its chorus.

Johnny Cash rehearses at SMU. *From the author's collection*

Johnny Cash makes his *Hootenanny* bow with his backing group, The Tennessee Three: Marshall Grant on bass, Luther Perkins on lead guitar and W.S. "Fluke" Holland on snare drum. Cash's first selection, "Goin' to Memphis," is drawn from his 1960 concept album *Ride This Train*. It's fascinating to hear this son of an Arkansas cotton farmer interpret a black chain gang song, but Cash was never one to let racial or class distinctions get in the way of performing a number he liked. Later in the program, he does what was his then-favorite of all the songs he'd written: an ode to his family's day-to-day life, "Pickin' Time."

Cash is followed by a local duet act making their network TV debut: Tommy Tiemann and Diane Decker, both students at the University of Texas. Two years' earlier, while studying pre-law, Tiemann had formed a folk duo with classmate Sandra Ewell, who left to get married prior to their senior year. Undaunted, he discovered and teamed with Decker, a sophomore, and together they'd spent the 1962 Christmas holidays in the east appearing on Arthur Godfrey's radio program in New York, getting signed by the famous William Morris talent agency, and performing at Toronto's version of The Purple Onion. The reception was enough to encourage Tiemann to take a break from his studies and pursue folk singing as a career; it took some persuasion on Decker's part to get her parents to agree, which they did in April. "We figure the first year is an investment," Tiemann said at the time, "and will be lucky to make any money. This television show is our biggest break. You can establish a national reputation this way that used to take years." Their performance of "This Little Light of Mine" is respectable, although lacking the bridge that accompanied The Kingston Trio's and others' recordings, but Weintraub was impressed with their ability, not to mention their youthful appearance. What he had in mind for them, though, wasn't duet stardom, but a chance to capitalize on the music's hottest new trend.

Tommy Tiemann's father snapped this photo of his son and Diane Decker making their TV debut on *Hootenanny*. *Photo courtesy of Eugene Tiemann*

Bob Gibson and his banjo make a welcome, low-key return with one of folk's best "echo" sing-alongs: "I'm Going to Leave Old Texas Now." The plaintive performance by Gibson and students is delightful. It's followed by New Orleans native Pierre Dewey LaFontaine, better known as Pete Fountain, and his Mardi Gras Strutters. Strut they do in a lively, Dixieland-infused take on "She'll Be Comin' 'Round the Mountain." Jazz snobs liked to thumb their noses at the unabashedly commercial Fountain, but his home city embraced him as their official musical ambassador. When Diane Decker called home during rehearsals to let them know she'd arrived safely, her mother asked her not to hang up. "She wanted to hear more of Pete and his group performing," Decker told Fairfax Nisbet. "It was good the call was local and not long distance!"

Posterity remembers Dave Astor as the first stand-up comedian to break in new material at the initial Improv nightclub in New York City, which owner Budd Friedman conceived as a place where current Broadway performers could come by after hours and sing what they pleased. Astor's material eventually led to television appearances and a comedy album on Columbia, not to mention a new theme for Friedman's club. Here he panders to his audience by poking fun at literature, Shakespeare and especially poetry. Among the latter is a swipe at "beatnik poets [that] are just a bit too uncomfortably realistic," backed up with the following:

> *My hope is a hollow skull*
>
> *Of rotted grin that's bleaching*
>
> *In this morturary of tortured towers,*
>
> *Reaching clotted course in aura*
>
> *Of stone to hollow jaws,*
>
> *Of broken bone and splintered spine,*
>
> *So won't you be my Valentine?*

The multi-artist medley is introduced by Bikel as a look at a single song's metamorphosis. "A song can have a lot of different versions…. We'll show you how differently you can treat them," he says and launches into a verse of "The Unfortunate Rake," a traditional Irish lament that came to America and evolved into the cowboy ballad "The Streets of Laredo," which Johnny Cash handles with aplomb. Then Bud and Travis take over with a parody version that The Smothers Brothers had done on their first album. This must have rankled the pair a bit; Tom Smothers had been strongly influenced by the comedic elements of Dashiell and Edmonson's act when honing his and Dick's own.

Gibson returns with his 12-string and Joan Toliver; together they belt out a rousing rendition of "I'm Gonna Tell God How You Treat Me." The result is another fine example of artist pairing in the *Hootenanny* canon. Then Bikel closes with Fred Hellerman's anti-war statement, "Come Away, Melinda." As the story of a little girl who's made a curious discovery and has lots of questions unfolds, its message becomes frighteningly clear: if we keep making war, all mankind will cease to exist. Bikel's rendition of this Folk Era classic is both tasteful and ominous, and puts the lie to the assertion that *Hootenanny* never presented any meaningful music.

2-04: United States Naval Academy, Annapolis MD #1

Recording Date: September 21, 1963.

Airdate: October 12, 1963. *Repeat*: July 25, 1964.

Video 1: UCLA Film & Television Archive: Type C, 1-inch Videoreel Archival copy T70022; 35mm Safety Storage archival dupe negative T61258 (reels 1 and 2); ¾-inch videocassette non-circulating Safety Storage copy T70023.

Video 2: The Paley Center, NYC: 8mm video tape containing Milt Kamen's performance. Catalog # B-37188.

The Gaslight Singers and Joe Frazier: "Hootenanny Saturday Night" (*Jack Linkletter intro*)

The Chad Mitchell Trio: "Leave Me if You Want To."

Judy Collins: "John Riley."

Eddy Arnold: "Cowpoke."

The Gaslight Singers: "Mary, Don't You Weep."

The Tarriers: "Bile Them Cabbage Down."

Glenn Yarbrough & The Tarriers: "Times Are Gettin' Hard."

Judy Collins & Mike Kobluk: "Boatman."

The Chad Mitchell Trio: "Rum By Gum."

Glenn Yarbrough: "I Wish I Was Single Again." (*commercial bumper*)

LOST LOVE MEDLEY: "The Girls in Their Summer Dresses" (*Glenn Yarbrough*), "All The Good Times" (*The Gaslight Singers*), "Careless Love" (*Eddy Arnold*).

Milt Kamen: Stand-up comedy

Alex Bradford and His Gospel Singers: "I Wasn't Gonna Tell Nobody."

The Tarriers: "Take This Hammer."

Eddy Arnold & Grier Reynolds: "Rovin' Gambler."

The Chad Mitchell Trio: "Paddy West," "Blues Around My Head."

FINALE: "Old Joe Clark" (*Everyone*).

The first of four military academy *Hoots*, this was the second one taped at Annapolis, which must have caused some confusion when the following week's guest lineup didn't match Linkletter's closing.

A relatively new group, The Gaslight Singers, take the theme song chore, assisted by The Chad Mitchell Trio's Joe Frazier. No one remembers why Frazier accompanied the quartet, but both groups had a common bond: arranger Milt Okun, who worked with several folk artists, including Leon Bibb, The Highwaymen and most famously, Peter, Paul

& Mary. After the opening, during which Linkletter shows us around the Naval Academy grounds, the Trio officially start the show with "Leave Me if You Want To," adapted from "Columbus Stockade Blues" and performed at a pace that feels about 20% faster than the one on the group's *In Action* album.

Judy Collins follows with another song brought to the U.S. from Ireland: "John Riley." The ballad of a sailor who's been away at sea for so long his betrothed doesn't recognize him originally ran to six verses, but the producers cut two "just to speed things up," a distraught Collins informed Robert Shelton, adding, "It took all the sense out of the song." It isn't quite *that* damaging, but the complete version, as heard on her debut album, more fully expresses the devotion of both lovers. Musically, the performance is sparkling. As a guitarist, Collins can clearly hold her own against anyone, and Eric Weissburg provides more than able support on bass.

Next up is *Hootenanny's* first foray into country music of the Nashville variety. Eddy Arnold began his career in the late 1930s as vocalist for Pee Wee King and His Golden West Cowboys, a troupe already comfortably ensconced on radio's *Grand Ole Opry*. After a few years, he struck out on his own and his gentle, almost crooning approach to the genre brought tremendous success. In 1948, an Arnold record sat atop the #1 spot on the country & western charts for all but two weeks, a feat that of course has never been matched since. Fifteen years later, though, he'd been eclipsed by many other innovators and was somewhat at sea musically. Unafraid to experiment, he tried emphasizing the "western" half of what was still termed "country-and-western" to capture the folk market, and here gives us "Cowpoke," complete with lonesome cowboy yodel.

Following what had become a template for folk success, the four Gaslight Singers came together as juniors at Long Island University in 1962, and officially launched their professional career at Washington D.C.'s folk club The Shadows the following April. The group consisted of Jeffrey Hyman, Alfonse Alcabes, Earl Zimmerman and Martha Velez; their first album for Mercury reached store shelves around the time this show aired. A lively performance of "Mary, Don't You Weep" gives each member a solo verse and has a lot of punch.

As for the group, their run was brief and essentially ended with 1964's British Invasion. "I wanted to combine the folk genre with the changes to rock and roll that The Beatles were creating," Hyman recalled in 2004. "The Mamas and The Papas… and others were doing the same thing, but my partners were not convinced and wanted to keep the sound and the look the same." Hyman opted to return to school and get his degree; the others replaced him and released a second album, but failed to make further inroads and ultimately split before year's end. Of the original foursome, only Velez made a career in music, on Broadway and recordings with Eric Clapton and others, including collaborating with Bob Marley on a reggae solo album, *Escape From Babylon*.

Now a trio again, The Tarriers return to the show with a Bluegrass-infused, yet decidedly off-kilter rendition of "Bile [Boil] Them Cabbage Down" that differs from the more traditional version heard on the group's 1959 LP *Tell the World About This*. The audience of midshipmen and their dates are especially cheered by a verse that thankfully made it past network censors:

Out behind the henhouse on my knees

Thought I heard a chicken sneeze.

Only the rooster sayin' his prayers,

Thankin' the Lord for the hens upstairs.

Two weeks after *Hootenanny's* first season ended, the Limeliters went their separate ways. "I never intended to entertain after [we] broke up," Glenn Yarbrough wrote five years later. "I just thought I would like to take a crack at sailing around the world. No more group decisions and lots of time to be alone [but] it didn't work out that way. A record offer came along, and almost before I knew it there were albums, nightclub and television dates, extensive concert appearances across the country." As we've seen, Yarbrough went on the road with "Hootenanny USA" a mere month after completing the final Limeliters tour. He's joined here by The Tarriers for a number drawn from his former group's very first album: Lee Hays' "Times Are Gettin' Hard." His ex-partners also forged individual careers, but would complete a contractual obligation to RCA-Victor with a surprising choice, singer-songwriter Ernie Sheldon who'd also been an editor for *Sing Out!* During this time, Sheldon penned the lyric for Yarbrough's greatest solo success: the theme to *Baby, The Rain Must Fall* (1965), starring Steve McQueen and Lee Remick.

Judy Collins and Mike Kobluk from The Chad Mitchell Trio combine on "Boatman," for which Mr. Kobluk was decidedly uncomfortable, as evidenced by a slight tongue-tripping while soloing on verse three. "The producers suggested the duet," he explained in a 2005 email to the author. "She'd done it before, I hadn't, [as] you can tell right off from my flubbed verse. The words just came too quickly." Even given an hour's running time, producer Lewine couldn't resist keeping things "fast and snappy." Paul Prestopino's driving banjo and Collins' guitar chops sustain the pace, while she and Kobluk harmonize perfectly. When it's over, he joins his usual partners for a tune he endorses as "a particular favorite of ours." It's "Rum By Gum," a satiric anthem directed at the Women's Christian Temperance Union, still hoping to outlaw liquor despite the colossal failure of the 18th Amendment.

Yarbrough introduces the love songs that comprise the multi-artist medley. It begins with his gentle take on Belafonte's "The Girls in Their Summer Dresses," which suits his tenor to a 'T,' but he didn't record it until five years later. The Gaslight Singers give us a verse and two choruses of "All The Good Times" and "the great lover" (as Yarbrough terms him) Eddy Arnold sings the classic "Careless Love" in typical *Hootenanny* up-tempo fashion.

Comedian Milt Kamen, who comes across as a bargain basement Milton Berle, does one of his movie review routines, in this case a new science fiction release about a genetically engineered tomato that grows "eighty stories high" and threatens the nation. Whether it ultimately inspired the cult classic *Attack of the Killer Tomatoes* (1978) is anybody's guess, but the bit gets its share of laughs, as well as thunderous applause when he makes a gratuitous dig at the Army. At the end of the show, as the singers are hooting "Old Joe Clark," Kamen obnoxiously wanders about, pretending to conduct, prompting the audience, eavesdropping on the others and mouthing along to the chorus, until Eric Weissburg pulls him toward a microphone. He brays something that is thankfully obscured by the "*Hootenanny* was brought to you by…" blurb.

A scene from above: Glenn Yarbrough and The Tarriers, backed by Norman Keenan and David Ander, finish up "Times Are Gettin' Hard," while at stage right Judy Collins, Mike Kobluk and Paul Prestopino await their turn. *From the author's collection*

The third-quarter hour closes with Professor Alex Bradford and His Gospel Singers, the only male-led gospel choir to appear on the series. Bradford, an Alabama native, was ordained a minister of the Baptist Church in 1950, toured with Mahalia Jackson during that decade, wrote music for *Black Nativity* and would later write for and appear on Broadway, earning a Tony nomination for *Don't Bother Me, I Can't Cope* (1973). His flamboyant style, like that of Marion Williams, influenced Little Richard and serves him in good stead here. Perhaps best remembered for one of his last works, music for the play *Your Arms Too Short to Box with God* (1976), Bradford died in February 1978 at age 51, two weeks after suffering a massive stroke.

Clarence Cooper's stirring baritone on Leadbelly's "Take This Hammer," highlights The Tarriers' third performance of the show. Cooper was the polar opposite of Professor Bradford, infusing his vocals with quiet dignity and poise that compels listeners to pay attention. Sixty years later, it seems impossible that this versatile threesome would have any difficulty reaching the upper echelon of folk stardom, but in 1963 the adverse stigma of a black man, no matter how talented, performing with two whites still sadly pervaded, and it's to *Hootenanny's* (and its sponsors') credit that they set that mentality aside and granted the group, who would appear twice more this season, a place to be heard.

Grier Reynolds, formerly half of Allen and Grier and normally a soprano, was slated to perform only in the previous day's taping, but shared her enthusiasm for "Roving Gambler" with Eddy Arnold during rehearsals and he invited her to sing it with him, presumably after getting the okay from Lewine. She accepted even though the song wasn't in her key; after all, it meant a paycheck for *two* shows instead of one. After this, The Chad Mitchell Trio wrap up the festivities with two: "Paddy West," which came from their debut album when Mike Pugh was still a member, and the plaintive Bob Gibson composition, "Blues Around My Head."

The A.C. Nielsen company would soon release its "new-season-to-date" ratings figures, which covered the period from premiere week through this show. Within that span they judged *Hootenanny* the nation's 67th-most popular regularly scheduled series, with a 14.0 rating. Of its timeslot companions, NBC's *The Lieutenant* was number 56, its rating 16.5, and *The Jackie Gleason Show* on CBS was sitting comfortably at number 31, with a 19.9 rating.

During the season, Gallup & Robinson, which specialized in media advertising research, conducted a study among 1,400 metropolitan Philadelphia area adult viewers—700 male, 700 female—who were interviewed in person about the shows they'd watched the day before and specifically which commercials they remembered and what they liked or disliked about them. Each week covered a different evening's viewing. This Saturday night was the first for their Total Prime Time (TPT) study, and the basic numbers are in line with what Nielsen and Trendex were reporting. The details, however, bring additional perspective.

Between 7:30 and 8:00 PM, 219 men were tuned to *The Jackie Gleason Show*, 149 to *The Lieutenant* and 104 to *Hootenanny*. For the show's second half-hour, *Hootenanny* picked up 22 additional male viewers, including four from *Gleason*, but lost six, including two to *Gleason* and one to *The Lieutenant*. The other two shows also picked up viewers proportionate to their popularity, and the second half hour came in with *Gleason* at 232, *Lieutenant* at 162 and *Hoot* at 120.

The story was similar among women: the first half hour began with 200 watching *Gleason*, 129 tuned to *Lieutenant*, and 104 watching *Hoot*. Twelve women dropped *Hootenanny* by 8:00 PM, of which three switched to *Gleason*; the other nine turned off their sets. But sixteen women joined the program at 8, including three from *Gleason*. The second half-hour finished with 216 *Gleason*, 139 *Lieutenant* and 106 *Hootenanny*.

2-05: University of Arizona, Tucson #1

Recording Date: October 15, 1963.

Airdate: October 19, 1963. *Repeat*: September 5, 1964.

Video: 16mm incomplete kinescope. Licensing: Historic Films Archive, LLC, ##VM-1546. Viewing: The Library of Congress, catalog # MAVIS 2899692. Excerpted on ***The Best of Hootenanny***.

"Hootenanny Saturday Night" (*Everyone*) (*Jack Linkletter intro*)

The New Christy Minstrels: "Walk the Road"

Mike Settle: "Aunt Rhody"

Joe and Eddie: "Jerry"

Addiss & Crofut: "Back Band," "Arison De Tunga"

The New Christy Minstrels: "Green Green," Bits and Pieces: ("Temperance and the Gutter Set" & "Animal Husbandry"), "The Last Farewell"

Mike Settle: "Judy Drownded" (*commercial bumper*)

Dian & The Greenbriar Boys: "Browns Ferry Blues," "He Was a Friend of Mine"

Pat Harrington Jr. (in character as "Guido Panzini"): Stand-up comedy

Joe and Eddie: "Cindy Jane"

Stu Ramsay and Ray Tate: "Soft Blues"

Mike Settle: "Hills of Shiloh"

The New Christy Minstrels: "Beaucatcher Mountain," "Saints Train"

FINALE: "Pay Me My Money Down" (*Everyone*)

ABC's immediate solution to keep viewers from switching out began with this show. Instead of throwing a random group or two on stage to handle the theme song while Linkletter named a few of the evening's guests in his opening spiel, he now introduced (off-camera) the entire lineup, each of whom would join the headliner on stage in singing the theme. This had the effect of having to repeat what was basically a one-verse song two or three times before the instrumental break, but at least showed the complete cast at the start.

The headline act is The New Christy Minstrels, making the first of eight appearances. The Christies, as they were known informally, were no strangers to television: during the 1962-63 season, they were regulars on NBC's *The Andy Williams Show*. Their first album, *Presenting The New Christy Minstrels*, had won a Grammy for Best Choral Performance earlier in the year, although only three of the musicians on it were still around for this *Hootenanny*.

The ensemble was the brainchild of folksinger Randy Sparks, who began as a soloist in San Francisco about the time The Kingston Trio made its debut. Shortly afterwards he formed his own trio, The Randy Sparks Three featuring himself, his then-wife Jackie Miller, and Paul Sykes, who would soon be replaced by smooth baritone Nick Woods. After hearing such long-established conglomerations as The Norman Luboff Choir adding traditional material to their repertoires, in 1961 Sparks merged his group with two others: The Fairmont Singers, a quartet from Eugene, Oregon and The Inn Group, a Los Angeles-based trio, plus four other soloists: Billy Cudmore, Dolan Ellis, Art Podell and Terry Wadsworth (who also contributed a couple of original compositions). When the time came to make their debut disc, The Fairmont Singers had to opt out owing to a previous engagement. Luckily, the ten remaining voices were enough to get the job done.

Sparks' intent was for recordings only, but was pressured by Columbia Records' Irving Townsend, head of West Coast A&R, to make the Christies a performing unit that could promote the record, which led to the loss of The Inn Group, Cudmore and Wadsworth. Sparks quickly replaced them with a duo, Barry (Kane) & Barry (McGuire), singer/banjoist Larry Ramos from Hawaii, bassist Clarence Treat of Arkansas, and vocalist Peggy Connolly. This lineup joined Williams' variety show, polished its act at Doug Weston's Troubadour nightclub in L.A., and made a second album, *The New Christy Minstrels In Person*. By the time of this *Hoot* appearance, the Christies had recorded five albums with four in release and had a hit record smash with "Green, Green." Connolly and Ellis had departed, replaced by Gayle Caldwell and Gene Clark, and Sparks had stopped performing, opting to focus on recording, songwriting and opening his own coffee house, Ledbetter's, situated near the UCLA campus. He envisioned it as a place for new folk talent to strut (and strum) their stuff, with an eye toward creating a Christy Minstrel pipeline.

The New Christy Minstrels lineup that appeared on six *Hootenanny* shows. Top row, left-to-right: Barry Kane, Larry Ramos. Middle row: Nick Woods, Art Podell, Gene Clark, Clarence Treat. Bottom row: Gayle Caldwell, Barry McGuire, Jackie Miller.

Topical and controversial material was never an issue for the Christies because they purposefully avoided it. "This extroverted group of unmixed-up performers," reads one of their publicity releases, "happily point out that they have no political connections and no psychological problems that anybody would be interested in." Their selections here prove the point. From the gospel-tinged "Walk the Road," to their big success "Green, Green" (which reached #14 on *Billboard's* Hot 100), to the comedic "Bits and Pieces," to the melancholy "Last Farewell" (set to the tune of "The Water is Wide"), to the frolicky "Beaucatcher Mountain," to the driving "Saints Train" (a mashup of "This Train is Bound for Glory" and "When the Saints Go Marching In"), it's all high-spirited froth.

Which wasn't to everyone's taste. "Hailed by critics less than two years ago as the freshest new musical group to appear in years," *Tucson Daily Citizen* reporter Gene Brooks reminded readers in his write-up of the taping, "subsequent commercial success on TV and in nightclubs has turned the Minstrels into another glib group of ersatz folk singers. Everything short of stylized choreography is used to add pizzaz to what once was grass roots music. But they were crowd pleasers, with applause swelling beautifully on cue…. Whenever the audience grew restless or applause lagged, the New Christies were trotted out for a reprise."

Little did Mike Settle know that in about two years he'd be one of the New Christies. For now, though, with 12-string guitar in hand he assumes the "younger, handsomer Pete Seeger" role and leads the students in the traditional "Go Tell Aunt Rhody." After that comes Joe and Eddie, an exciting duo that livened up *Hootenanny Hoot* with a blazing rendition of Bob Gibson's rewrite of an old gospel tune, "Meetin' Here Tonight." As Linkletter summarizes in his intro, Joe Gilbert and Eddie Brown, friends and students at Willard Junior High in Berkeley, California, signed up individually for a talent contest. Since they didn't want to compete with each other, they joined forces… and took first prize. Over the next seven-plus years, they trod the folksinger's standard path of sorority parties, local nightclubs, talent agent discovery, recording contract, network television, etc. For their first spot, they pick one from Josh White's and Harry Belafonte's repertoires: "Did You Hear About Jerry," concerning an onery mule who looks out for the laborers in a lumber camp. Belafonte's rendition was lively, but Joe and Eddie infuse it with dramatic flair, including handclaps, stomps and, toward the end, whispers.

Similarly, Steve Addiss and Bill Crofut were buddies while attending high school in Putney, Vermont. They attended music college, but their paths diverged when Crofut went into the Army and was stationed in peacetime Korea. Doing "everything from ditch-digging to singing," Crofut voluntarily assisted at clinics, orphanages and schools for both the locals and children of GI's. Discharged in 1959, he went directly to Japan to assist Prince Mikasa, the Emperor's youngest son, in establishing recreation and rehabilitation programs for Japanese citizens. After that, the U.S. State Department called, offering a Far East tour under a Cultural Exchange Program. Since music was to be a major part, Crofut contacted Addiss; they met up in Hong Kong and set out on an 18-month journey that took them through both China and Africa.

The pair's first selection, the upbeat "Tighten the Back Band," is introduced by Linkletter as "a Native American tune," but the second, "Arison De Tunga," has Addiss playing a 12-stringed Ch'ung, "an ancient harp-toned, zither-like instrument from Taiwan," while Crofut sings in Cantonese. Concluded Gene Brooks, "Their performance… produced the evening's most genuine folk music."

"A word about Dian and the Greenbriar Boys," begins a lengthy Linkletter intro that obscures the first verse of "Browns Ferry Blues." "Dian's an ex-movie actress, now a housewife, who takes occasional time off from raising a family to sing with the Greenbriar Boys." In fact, the statuesque brunette born Dian Evelyn Newman in New York City wed her third husband, Travis Edmonson of Bud and Travis, in Tucson just seven weeks before the taping of this show. The liner notes on the Elektra album *Dian and the Greenbriar Boys* state she "played a featured role" in *The Bachelor and the Bobby Soxer* (1947), then turned to singing on southern California's country music programs *Hometown Jamboree* and *Town Hall Party*. Her prior marriages, to service station manager Robert James at age 17 and furniture dealer Irwin W. Belsky at age 24, produced one child each and ended in divorce after less than four years. Dian would have a child by Edmonson as well, but their union ended after a mere seven months, when she sued for separate maintenance ("because she does not believe in divorce" said the *Los Angeles Citizen-News*), alleging physical abuse, which had also been cited in the complaint against her first ex-husband. The request was granted on April 4, 1964. Eight years later, a divorce was finalized; by then she'd left the public eye. In 1974, she applied for Social Security Disability, which was denied. Having never married again, Dian settled in northern California near Tahoe National Forest, where she passed away in May 2006.

Two of the three Greenbriar Boys join her here: banjoist Bob Yellin and mandolinist Ralph Rinzler. The group's lead singer, guitarist John Herald opted not to end his boycott of the show and is replaced by an anonymous young man who for the most part remains off-camera. Rinzler takes lead guitar on the second number, "He Was a Friend of Mine." After this, comedian Pat Harrington, Jr. comes on as "Dr. Guido Panzini," a character he'd created back in the late 1950s that used to drop by Jack Paar's *Tonight Show*. In this and most subsequent *Hootenanny* appearances, Panzini poses as a folk music authority, one whose credentials, like Harrington's material, leave much to be desired.

Joe and Eddie return with their finger-snapping indictment of two-timing "Cindy Jane" and then Darsono "Stu" Ramsay, nineteen-year-old multi-instrumentalist, plays his own guitar piece "Soft Blues" with a buddy, guitarist Ray Tate; sadly, the performance is missing from the only known kinescope. Born in the Chicago suburb of Elmhurst, Ramsay studied at the city's Old Town School of Folk Music and was briefly tutored on guitar by folk musician Frank Hamilton. His talent, though, developed naturally; at seventeen he took up banjo and mastered it, then moved on to the dobro. Chad Mitchell helped produce his first LP for Mercury, recorded shortly before this show aired. He would record only one more album, a collaboration with Daniel Ivankovich, better known as "Chicago Slim," in 1969. Eventually Ramsay returned to the Old Town School of Folk Music to teach other progenies and aspiring talents.

Mike Settle covers the haunting "The Hills of Shiloh," cowritten by Jim Friedman and Shel Silverstein, which tells the story of Amanda Blaine, a bride-to-be whose betrothed never returned from the Civil War... but forty years later she still waits for him. Unfortunately, Settle only gets to sing two of its four verses because Lewine and crew wanted to bring on the Christies for a dual-song rousing finale. Before too long, *Hootenanny* would give the group half the program's running time.

In a tempo that races like a rocket, the ensemble piece over which the credits ran, "Pay Me My Money Down," was a Georgia Sea Islands song that black laborers—still largely exploited by white employers—sang while working on shipboard. Pete Seeger learned it and The Weavers recorded it at their 1955 Carnegie Hall concert. It's almost laughable that Lewine and ABC okayed this political, pro-worker, anti-management number for the show while willfully excluding the artist that brought it to prominence because of his pro-worker, anti-management politics.

Gene Brooks' write-up told of a lone protester, "a sad-faced young man… ignored by the chattering students. He carried a pencil-lettered indictment of ABC on a cardboard boxtop. It read 'Censoring is Anti-Freedome. ABC Censores Folk Music.' Queried on his cause, he said he was picketing in the interest of Pete Seeger…. A fatherly member of the campus police asked the youth if he had a dictionary and was told, 'I have a perfectly adequate one, thank you.' After additional counseling, the young man disappeared."

2-06: Boston University, Boston MA #2

Recording Date: August 15, 1963.

Airdate: October 26, 1963

The Chad Mitchell Trio: "Hootenanny Saturday Night" (*Jack Linkletter intro*)

Mike Settle: "Sylvie"

The Chad Mitchell Trio: "I Feel So Good About It," "The Great Historical Bum"

Jo Mapes: "Red Clay Country"

The Big 3: "Come Along"

Leon Bibb: "The Song of the Ox Drivers"

The Chad Mitchell Trio: "Ballad of the Greenland Whalers"

Richard & Jim: "Feast Here Tonight"

Richard & Jim: "Jimmy Crack Corn" (*commercial bumper*)

Mike Settle & Jo Mapes: "Cottonfields"

Woody Allen: Stand-up comedy

Richard & Jim: "Turkey in the Straw"

The Big 3: "Rider"

Leon Bibb: "The Water is Wide"

The Chad Mitchell Trio: "Vaichazkem," "Four Strong Winds."

FINALE: "Cindy" (*Everyone*)

The Big 3 sing "Rider." From left: Tim Rose, Cass Elliot, Jim Hendricks.

Mike Settle starts off the second Boston U. show with "(Bring a Little Water) Sylvie," a "lovely, tender ballad" per Linkletter's intro, recorded by Harry Belafonte. The Chad Mitchell Trio follow with two upbeat numbers; the first, "I Feel So Good About It," a recent composition by Roy Inman also known as "Sin Bound Train," is in the same gospel vein as their "You Can Tell the World" from the season premiere. The second is an adaptation of Woody Guthrie's "Biggest Thing That Man Has Ever Done," initially recorded by him in 1945. Then it's the welcome return of Jo Mapes, who sings her own "Red Clay Country," which, according to Linkletter, she'd heard only as a fragment and expanded by adding lyrics from another traditional song, "Chilly Winds."

The Big 3 began as The Triumvirate in Washington DC at the start of 1963, consisting of Tim Rose, Cass Elliott and John Brown. Arriving in Omaha to play at The Third Man Coffee House, they met Nebraska native Jim Hendricks who played several stringed instruments. Rose and Elliot asked Hendricks to accompany them to New York City where they'd be playing The Bitter End. Sometime after arriving, Brown dropped out and the group changed its name. Weintraub got them signed to FM Records; the two songs performed here are from their debut album, which sold so many copies so quickly that the young company ran out of custom-designed disc labels and had to print up a generic variant.

After Leon Bibb's stirring "Song of the Ox Driver" and an encore from The Chad Mitchell Trio, Richard Lockmiller and Jim Connor, two of the high spots of the previous season, return with their Alabama-flavored take on old-time music. Since that first appearance, they'd signed with Capitol Records, who were about to release the result. The duo outran the end of the folk boom, remaining together until 1966. The parting was amicable: Lockmiller, who'd studied acting prior to teaming with Connor, wanted to return to that, while Connor wished to hone his songwriting, although he briefly kept his hand in performing when he joined The New Kingston Trio in 1969. As a writer, Connor is best remembered for "Grandma's Feather Bed," recorded by John Denver. During the 1980s, he and Lockmiller re-teamed for a few successful engagements, most back home in Alabama. "We knew it would never go away," said Connor in 1984. "The energy and the flow of playing together was still there. We could get together when we're 70 and still have it."

After the commercial break, Mike Settle and Jo Mapes team uncomfortably on "Cotton Fields." The arrangement, which favors Settle's tenor on melody, assigns harmony to Mapes, and she struggles vainly to come up with something that fits her range. She livens up the refrain with an occasional growl, but for the most part is stuck on a single note with nowhere to go.

Neither of the audio sources for this segment include the *Hootenanny* debut of Woody Allen. The quirky comedian had been writing comedy since the latter days of Sid Caeser's TV reign during the previous decade. As a stand-up performer whose routines were always about his bizarre life experiences, Allen was definitely an acquired taste. If Linkletter's introduction for his next appearance is to be believed, at least one letter came in after this show asking the producers, "Is he for real?"

Since both the jazz and gospel acts had appeared on the first Boston U. show, the final quarter of this one ends with "Rider" by The Big 3, Leon Bibb's beautiful rendering of "The Water is Wide," and two from The Chad Mitchell Trio, including an equally beautiful "Four Strong Winds." Ian Tyson's ode to the fading romance of a Canadian drifter was fast becoming a folk standard, and the Trio's arrangement, featuring a sensitive lead vocal by Tyson's fellow countryman Mike Kobluk, is perfect.

2-07: University of California, Los Angeles (UCLA) #1

Recording Date: October 29, 1963.

Airdate: November 2, 1963.

"Hootenanny Saturday Night" (*Everyone*) (*Jack Linkletter intro*)

The Brothers Four: "Vive L'Amour"

Anita Carter: "I'll Be All Smiles Tonight"

The Good Time Singers: "John Peel and the Fox"

Hoyt Axton: "Young Man"

Max Morath: "Leave Before Suppertime"

The Brothers Four: "Seven Daffodils," Foreign Phrase Song (satire)

Hoyt Axton: "Banks of the Ohio" (*commercial bumper*)

The Dalton Boys: "Silver Dollar," Ethnic Folk Medley (parody)

Louis Nye: Stand-up comedy

The Good Time Singers: "Goin' Away From Here," "Freedom Calling (What's That I Hear?)"

Hoyt Axton: "Greenback Dollar," Children's Song Medley (with *Anita Carter*)

Brothers Four: "Run Come See Jerusalem," "This Land is Your Land" (with 65 UCLA students on guitar and banjo)

FINALE: "Done Laid Around" (*Everyone*)

At the time this show was taped, ABC publicly announced it would extend *Hootenanny* through March for a full 26-week season, despite the "bigger, better" format's failure to crack Nielsen's top 40. The network glossed over that inconvenient tidbit in its announcement, instead proclaiming the series had become "a weekly viewing habit for close to 20 million Americans." Recent ratings figures pointed to an audience that was roughly half of ABC's estimate, but although such sponsors as Ford Motor Company and Lady Clairol moved on, others like Chevrolet and Muriel Cigars leapt into the breach. The network had a much bigger problem with Saturday nights: *The Jerry Lewis Show* was doing far worse and they were scrambling behind the scenes to get out of their $35 million deal with the comedian.

The Brothers Four and Louis Nye return from the Pittsburgh show, but nearly everyone else is a *Hootenanny* first-timer. Anita Carter had appeared the previous season with her mother and older sisters as part of The Carter Family; she'd recently recorded a solo album for Mercury and was promoting it. Although possessing the most pleasing voice of Maybelle Carter's daughters, as a performer she lacked the charisma to hold an audience's attention. Her album did little in the way of sales and her next appearance would be with the rest of the family.

Hoyt Axton, on the other hand, had charisma to spare. A rough-hewn Oklahoma native, Axton made his TV debut that summer in "The Story of a Folk Singer," an episode of David Wolper's syndicated *The Story of...* series. By then he'd written and recorded "Greenback Dollar," which The Kingston Trio took into the upper reaches of the Hot 100. He growls it out here, minus the "damn" in the refrain that was too profane for the sensitive souls in ABC's censorship department. Opting to be extra-cautious, the producers also didn't mic the audience singing along.

The debut album by the hastily assembled Good Time Singers. *From the author's collection*

When The New Christy Minstrels left *The Andy Williams Show* to pursue more lucrative engagements, a replacement troupe was sought. Tom Drake, a Los Angeles high school teacher who spent some of his free evenings performing at local folk clubs and coffee houses, heard about the opening and spent a weekend reaching out to fellow full- and part-time folksingers, including Doug Brookins, who'd been with the Christies for a few weeks, just long enough to work on their Christmas album, before being replaced by Gene Clark. They rehearsed for three days, auditioned on a Thursday and one week later got the job. Along with this appearance, the group would appear in *The Big Hoot*, a pilot for Revue Productions, Universal's TV arm, taped at The Ice House in Pasadena.

The pilot didn't sell, but The Good Time Singers, with various members coming and going, remained with Andy Williams for three seasons. Unlike the Christies, they didn't shy away from topical songs and turn in a fine rendition of Phil Ochs' "Freedom Calling (What's That I Hear?)," an uplifting civil rights piece that predicts equality and freedom for all via the changing of hearts. This is their lone *Hootenanny*, partly due to their commitment to Williams but mostly because the show didn't need them: they had the Christies signed to one appearance per month, and a brand new folk nonet, currently in rehearsals at The Bitter End, would be making its national debut on the series the first Saturday in December.

Max Morath offers a mini-symposium on ragtime in his all-too-brief segment that *The Record* of Hackensack, NJ, termed "a welcome novelty… full of talent, charm and style." Morath was already well-known to viewers of what was then called educational television for a series titled *The Ragtime Era* that ran on 53 stations during 1961. His song here, which dates to 1907, has a refrain that anyone who's ever dealt with guests that stay too long can appreciate:

Come after breakfast, bring your own lunch, and leave before suppertime.

If you do that, I feel positive that we'll all get along just fine!

Now everybody's welcome at my house, whether rain or shine,

If you'll come after breakfast, bring your own lunch, and leave before suppertime.

After this, The Brothers Four slow things down with the romantic ballad "Seven Daffodils," accompanied by pretty much all co-eds in the audience.

The Dalton Boys consisted of two brothers, Jack and Danny Dalton on banjo and guitar, respectively, and John Ziga on bass. Picking up where Max Morath left off, they begin with a ragtime-era tune, "Silver Dollar," which would be completely forgotten if not for its long-time use in a commercial touting Aunt Jemima pancakes and syrup. Their next offering, a series of one-verse folk parodies sung by Jack Dalton, is set up by Danny as follows: "You people have heard of Allan Sherman: 'My Son the Folksinger,' 'My Son the Celebrity,' 'My Son the Nut.' President Kennedy's father is putting out an album. It's entitled, 'My Son's the Government.'" He then introduces "My brother the folksinger, Smilin' Jack," who offers brief ditties like this one to the tune of "Camptown Races":

I have a younger brother, he says "Doo-dah, doo-dah."

That's all that he can say, and he'll be 28 next May.

Louis Nye's second visit consists of "a routine about an Arab student at Princeton and his revealing letter home," according to *TV Key* since it's not included in the surviving audio. After two more from The Good Time Singers, Hoyt Axton offers a medley of children's songs ("Yeah, isn't that out of character?" he jokes), and invites Anita Carter to join him. As the students sing "Row, Row, Row Your Boat" as an underscore, Axton and Carter trade off other children's standards like "Mary Had a Little Lamb" and "London Bridge is Falling Down," which makes for a sweet presentation. The quarter-hour's grand finale has The Brothers Four leading 65 guitar- and banjo-playing students in Woody Guthrie's

"This Land is Your Land," which hopefully looked more impressive than it sounds.

Audio for roughly three-quarters of the show survives in the author's collection.

2-08: Southern Methodist University, Dallas TX #2

Recording Date: October 2, 1963.

Airdate: November 9, 1963. *Repeat*: May 2, 1964.

Video: 16mm kinescope of the repeat broadcast. Licensing: Historic Films Archive, LLC, #V-1017. Viewing: The Library of Congress, catalog # MAVIS 2899693. Excerpted on **The Best of Hootenanny**.

The Journeymen & The Wanderers Three: "Hootenanny Saturday Night" (*Jack Linkletter intro*)

The Wanderers Three: "Roll Along"

Ian & Sylvia: "Jesus Met the Woman at the Well"

Judy Collins: "Anathea"

Theodore Bikel: "Follow the Drinking Gourd," "When I Go Down to Bimini"

The Journeymen: "Stakolee"

SOUTHWESTERN MEDLEY: "Spanish is a Loving Tongue" (*Ian & Sylvia*), "Skyball Paint" (*Judy Collins*), "Cryderville Jail" (*The Journeymen*).

Bob Gibson: "Marching to Pretoria"

Clara Ward and Her Gospel Singers: "Swing Low, Sweet Chariot"

Bob Gibson: "Long John" (commercial bumper)

The Journeymen: "Someone to Talk My Troubles To"

Sylvia Fricker (backed by *Ian Tyson, Red Shea, Bob Gibson,* and members of *The Wanderers Three* and *The Journeymen*): "Salty Dog Blues"

The Carolina Kloggers: Clog Dance

Judy Collins & Theodore Bikel: "Kisses Sweeter Than Wine"

Freddie Powers & His Powerhouse Four: "Bill Bailey."

Bob Gibson: "Telling Those Lies About Me"

Ian & Sylvia: "The Greenwood Sidie"

Theodore Bikel: "Sissu Vesimchu"

FINALE: "Kumbaya" (*Everyone*)

The second SMU *Hoot* is a compilation of mostly memorable and a few cringe-worthy moments that thankfully survives in full. The close-cropped Wanderers Three, whose sole LP on Liberty Records' budget-line Dolton label was titled *We Sing Folk Songs* (just in case there was any doubt), team with The Journeymen on the theme song, take the opening number "Roll Along," and then all but vanish, just like their career. What little is known about them comes from the album sleeve: "Shortly after their meeting at the University of Houston's Sigma Chi fraternity house, the three tall young Texans made the decision to give up the reliable business careers for which they had been preparing in favor of the more hazardous but more exciting career of becoming a really top-flight folk trio." Ultimately, that decision didn't work out.

Ian & Sylvia charge forward with a spiritual they "learned from Mahalia Jackson," according to Linkletter's narration, accompanied by Ian's and Red Shea's driving 12-string rhythm. Judy Collins is on next and "she brings us 'Anathea.' This is an international collaboration," says Linkletter, who spells it out while she gamely strums until he's finished. The "flamenco overtones," as Linkletter describes the meter, prove a challenge for Norman Keenan, one he doesn't quite master; at times her guitar and his bass seem to be playing at different tempos.

The Wanderers Three, who seemingly came and went in a heartbeat. From top: Tim Evans, Ernie Mills, John James. *From the author's collection*

But what made this performance the final straw for Collins were the lyric changes she was handed, so when Dankar asked her to sign for another appearance, she told them forget it, then unloaded to Robert Shelton. "The New York censor—I don't know who she is, just a voice on the other end of the phone—objected to certain words in my singing of 'Anathea.'" The song told the story of a young man, jailed for theft and due to be executed, and his sister, who tries to win her brother's freedom by sacrificing her virginity to the judge, a cruel man who accepts her offer but orders her brother hung anyway, at the very moment she's in bed with him.

"I had to change the girl's giving her 'flower' to 'honor' and going to [the judge's] 'gold bed' to 'righteous arms.'" Still fuming days later, she assured Shelton, "I will not appear again on 'Hootenanny' as it is currently constituted," and made it clear that "my quitting has nothing to do with the Pete Seeger issue. As of now, I would suggest an artistic boycott of the 'Hootenanny' show…. I knew the people running the show had very little aesthetic concept of feeling for folk music. The producers… have created a monster that threatens to destroy popular folk music. They have no perception of the people they are working with nor of the music they are working with…. The show will destroy its own money-making capacity. It won't destroy folk music and it won't destroy the artists but it is certainly doing harm."

Theodore Bikel, accompanied by The Journeymen's Dick Weissman, sings the freed slave classic "Follow the Drinking Gourd" and then teaches "Bimini" to the student audience, assigning each gender a separate part and adding, "I do a third part, because I'm entitled." The result is sweet, especially as the camera periodically cuts to the singing student body.

After a commercial break, The Journeymen are up with "Stackolee" from what would be their final album, *New Directions in Folk Music*. Once again, Linkletter gives us a lengthy history of the song, an adaptation of "Stagg" Lee Shelton's fatal shooting of William "Billy" Lyons in 1895; throughout, the group is playing away on camera as Scott McKenzie is watching the floor manager, waiting for the cue to start singing. But after several bars, he and John Phillips face each other and exchange grins, silently passing judgement on this ludicrous arrangement. After a nice, Ian Tyson-introduced medley of folk songs from the southwest, featuring himself and Sylvia, Judy Collins and The Journeymen, Bob Gibson comes on to perform "Marching to Pretoria" and *again* Linkletter's narration goes on for several bars. Since he's alone on stage except for bassist Keenan, Gibson silently shares his own frustration and discomfort with the students.

Clara Ward and Her Gospel Singers, last seen in the pilot, return with a mashup of "Swing Low, Sweet Chariot" and "Swing Down, Chariot." It's a lively performance, given the limitations of the stage and camera blocking, but in a savage write-up of the series for Shelton's *Hootenanny* magazine, Nat Hentoff took exception. While admitting "Ward and her singers are an explosively mobile crew, it was on 'Hootenanny' that for the first time I watched them praise the Lord while simultaneously executing a lumbering buck-and-wing" that put him to mind of "a chorus line in a third-rate burlesque house on a slow night." The group, later renamed The Clara Ward Singers, toured almost up to Ward's untimely passing at age 48, a victim of several strokes, nearly ten years later.

A much better moment for The Journeymen comes later with Weissman's "Someone to Talk My Troubles To." This is also drawn from the *New Directions* album, and for once a *Hootenanny* performance is slower and more moving than the disc version. It's a beautiful, definitive rendition, with McKenzie's lead vocal bringing out the song's gentle pathos.

Next, the portable camera makes its way along a row of six male instrumentalists: Tyson, McKenzie and Gibson on guitar; Shea, Weissman and The Wanderers Three's Ernie Mills on banjo; all there, along with Keenan, to accompany Sylvia Fricker on "Salty Dog Blues." No one would've ever accused Fricker of having an overpowering voice, hence the hand-held microphone she uses. She's at the end of the line singing the first verse and refrain, then makes her way to center stage as the males intone the refrain again. It *looks* like it should be musical overkill, but as a TV performance it works… unless you're Nat Hentoff: "Only on 'Hootenanny' have I seen Sylvia… break into a contrived and self-conscious shimmy which had nothing to do with the piece she was singing but was apparently motivated by the dictum that 'you have to *move* when you're on television, baby.'"

In what was usually the comedian's spot, there's a nice change-of-pace: a square dance troupe, The Carolina Kloggers. Accompanied primarily by one fiddler, the audience had to be instructed *not* to clap along, so the dancers could hear the music. This is followed by a Bikel-Collins duet on "Kisses Sweeter than Wine," which was written by Pete Seeger and Lee Hays and first recorded by The Weavers. Somehow, ABC was convinced that it was okay to *hear* songs written by these suspected Communists, but only if others performed them. After this, Linkletter introduces Freddie Powers & His Powerhouse Four, a group with four banjos and a tuba, doing "Bill Bailey" in a sort of Dixieland-ragtime fusion. Raised in Seminole, Texas, Powers' parents both played musical instruments. He traveled the nightclub circuit with his combo for twenty-some years of relative obscurity until finally coming into his own as a country songwriter in the 1980s. His best-known composition, "I Always Get Lucky With You" was recorded by both George Jones and Merle Haggard. Powers died at age 84 in 2016.

Ian & Sylvia had their own problem with the network and Lewine over "The Greenwood Sidie," an acapella variation on "The Cruel Mother"—a young woman who seduces her father's clerk, gets pregnant, gets rejected and ends up stabbing her illegitimate twin babies to death. The producer unsurprisingly felt the subject matter was not fit for television. Fred Weintraub intervened, cannily assuring Lewine it was simply a retelling of Euripides' *Medea*. The song remained, albeit with its own lyric change: "She loved him up, she loved him down" was deemed too graphic, so they were told to sing "She loved him long, she loved him well," which got messed up when Ian sang "strong" while Sylvia sang "well."

Lastly, there was the finale, the legendary "Kumbaya." Anyone who ever sang around a campfire knows this is done at a gentle, plaintive pace. It's intended to be sung prayer (the original lyric was "Oh, Lord, come by here"), but the network now wanted every show to have a rollicking finish, so up-tempo was the new bylaw. "Kumbaya" has never been performed so rapidly, not even by Bluegrass musicians, as it is here. Whatever objections were made during rehearsal, and there had to have been plenty, were ignored, so Bob Gibson spoke for everyone during the performance. As he wrote in his autobiography: "They were doing [the song] in a terrible key and doing it too fast. They would shoot somebody doing a verse and then they'd back off and show a whole shot of the assembled cast singing it. They'd roll the credits over it, then they'd zoom back in again. I got to my verse and didn't think they were zoomed in, so I sang, 'Someone's kidding, Lord, Kumbaya…' Well, that's what made the final cut. The producer saw it and I didn't work there again."

That last was probably wishful thinking. Lewine may have been angry, he may have even used threatening words, but he didn't fire Gibson. He couldn't, not with Collins firmly rejecting another appearance and with Bikel, The Journeymen and Ian & Sylvia[2] also electing never to return. Bob Gibson would be back four more times, including on the very last *Hootenanny* to air, which is fitting since he'd been on the very first.

2-09: Fordham University, Bronx NY #1

Recording Date: November 12, 1963.

Airdate: November 16, 1963.

"Hootenanny Saturday Night" (*Everyone*) (*Jack Linkletter intro*)

The New Christy Minstrels: "Californi-o"

Joan Toliver: "Nothing More to Look Forward To"

Leon Bibb: "John Hardy," "The Bulgine Run"

Will Holt: "The Erie"

Th*e New Christy Minstrels*: "Wheeler Dealers," Bits and Pieces: ("Chocolate Ice Cream Cone"), "The Invalids," "Glory, Glory"

Will Holt: "Clementine" (commercial bumper)

The Big 3: "Nora's Dove"

Woody Allen: Stand-up comedy

---

[2] Their future appearance on the November 30 broadcast had been taped in early September.

The Dukes of Dixieland: "Wreck of the Old 97"

CHILDREN'S SONGS MEDLEY: "There's a Hole in the Bucket" (*Will Holt*), "Can Ye Sew Cushions?" (*Joan Toliver*), "The Ladybug and the Centipede" (*Leon Bibb*)

The New Christy Minstrels: "Sacramento," "Beautiful City"

FINALE: "The Old Ark's A-Moverin'" (*Everyone*)

This broadcast exists solely on audio in the author's collection, but it needn't have been so. Once upon a time there was a 16mm kinescope that some misguided eBay seller got hold of, extracted Woody Allen's stand-up bit and threw the rest away without a second thought. No one would have known had the seller not bragged about it in the subsequent listing.

The show also holds an interesting distinction: none of its performers were destined to remain in folk music. A few weren't particularly thrilled with being there in the first place.

The Christies, as would become customary, perform in three of the show's four roughly quarter-hour segments. By now the group, seemingly becoming more showbiz slick by the hour, were at work with boss Randy Sparks on a sixth album, *Land of Giants*. Since it was close to Christmas and they were performing at a Catholic university, they included a number from their soon-to-be-released *Merry Christmas* album in each show, little realizing the second one wouldn't air until the following February. They also perform the B-side of their newest single: the theme song to MGM's *The Wheeler Dealers* (1963), a comedy starring James Garner and Lee Remick. The studio must have liked it: after completing *Land of Giants*, the group's next assignment would be *all* the songs for another MGM comedy: *Advance to the Rear* (1964).

Joan Toliver's contralto is a fascinating contrast to the sopranos that were dominating the women's folk scene, such as Baez, Collins and Hester. There weren't many like her… and yet, she wasn't comfortable in the role of folk singer, drawn instead to pop and jazz but limited by the realities of a small-town upbringing. "A pop singer needs arrangements, accompaniment and money," she told *The New York Times*. "If you're poor, you're a folk singer."

Leon Bibb belts out one of his songs.

As mentioned previously, Leon Bibb ventured into singing between theatrical engagements, much as Theo Bikel and The Clancy Brothers and Tommy Makem had done. And like those men, Bibb added a theatrical sensibility to the music. His baritone, professionally schooled in New York during the 1940s, brings the material to life: suitably explosive for driving work and story songs; wistfully tender for blues and ballads. His performance here of "John Hardy" is a case in point. Bibb adjusts tempo to the facets of the story, introducing the lead character a capella at a measured pace, which suddenly accelerates with the line, "You ought to see John Hardy gettin' away!" as guitar and bass join in, musically insisting the "desperate little man" is on the run. This faster approach, which continues through three more verses, comes to a near-full stop for a verse concerning Hardy's wife. Bibb takes us through this part tenderly and the slower tempo continues into the next verse, where the remorseful Hardy awaits the gallows, then resumes full speed as he declares, "I've been the death of many a poor man, and now I'm ready to die!"

Will Holt rehearsing at Fordham. Seated on the edge of the stage is a cameraman holding the portable "creepy peepie." *From the author's collection*

Likewise, Will Holt was drawn to the theater, although as composer of "Raspberries, Strawberries" and "Lemon Tree" he certainly had contemporary folk bona fides. Still, from the start of his career, Holt and his wife Dolly Jonah were creating musical-comedy revues such as *All in Fun* and *Signs Along the Cynic Route*, and at the time of this taping, he and Martha Schlamme had recently embarked on their *World of Kurt Weill* program at the Village's cellar theater, 1 Sheridan Square.

Holt was born in Portland, Maine in 1929. His father was a doctor; it was his piano-playing mother, Marjorie, who inspired his future. He attended Williams College in Massachusetts; studied voice under folk singer Richard Dyer-Bennet; traveled Europe in 1950 to learn folk songs; served in the Air Force during the Korean War. But Holt's heart was always in writing and his reaction to the first royalty check for "Lemon Tree" was, "Oh, I guess this means I don't have to keep doing four shows a night."

Still touring with Linkletter's Folk Festival when this show aired, The Big 3 sing "Nora's Dove," a.k.a. "Dink's Song." After that, they were pushed to record a follow-up for what had been FM Records' biggest seller to date. The result was the oddly-titled *Live At The Recording Studio*, an uneven effort that included grade school chestnuts like "Grandfather's Clock" and "Down in the Valley." The trio hung on for a few more months, then split up, with Hendricks and Elliot forming The Mugwumps, a more rock-oriented group, with Canadians Denny Doherty and Zalman Yanovski, both late of The Halifax Three. Tim Rose eventually signed with Columbia as a solo act, while The Mugwumps barely lasted beyond a recording session. Yanovski formed The Lovin' Spoonful with John Sebastian (who appeared in the second Fordham *Hootenanny*), and Elliot and Doherty became half of The Mamas and the Papas with ex-Journeymen leader John Phillips and his wife Michelle Gilliam. Hendricks went to Nashville and embarked on an enduring Bluegrass career.

Thirty-five seconds of thunderous applause greets Woody Allen as he takes the stage to offer "more penetrating revelations about himself," per Linkletter's intro. He begins with a story about attending an art house movie theater, where the "bouncing ball" sing-along is Gregorian chant (the Fordhamites, in what was a university run by Jesuit priests, enjoy this one a lot). Then he veers into a typically Allendian tale about winning a cigarette lighter at an auction, which draws the attention of a woman with "great blonde hair and an upturned nose and high cheekbones… and she's got on a trenchcoat, and an eyepatch." She eventually lures him and his cigarette lighter to her hotel room, and while he's kissing her ("Kissing her great, though. Top kissing"), he's confronted by "a tall man with a blonde crew haircut and a black turtleneck sweater, and he's got in his hand a knife with a silencer on it." His escape plan is twofold: a swift judo move followed immediately by a dead faint.

The nuclei of The Dukes of Dixieland were brothers Fred and Frank Assunto and their father "Papa Jac." The troupe originated in New Orleans in 1949 and included Pete Fountain, who went out on his own six years later. By 1960, the septet had taken a reliably lucrative residence in Las Vegas. For their sole appearance here, they chose the melodic inspiration for The Kingston Trio hit "M.T.A." namely, "Wreck of the Old 97," which was the closing track of their—wait for it—*Dixieland Hootenanny!* album.

The multi-artist medley consists of three children's songs. Will Holt starts it off with "There's a Hole in the Bucket," which is sped up and carved up to such a ludicrous degree that it loses all its humor. Probably because of the tempo, Holt flubs a line ("The ax is too long, dear Eliza, dear Eliza") but recovers nicely ("The ax is too dull, too, dear Eliza, too dull") garnering the tune's only genuine laugh. Joan Toliver's "Can Ye Sew Cushions" is a wistful Scottish lullaby, and Leon Bibb's "The Ladybug and the Centipede" is, as he says in his intro, "a post-graduate course" on insect romance that, being complete and properly paced, is quite humorous.

Writing for the school's paper, *The Fordham Ram*, J. Brendan Ryan described a non-student protest outside the campus entrance consisting of thirty members of the Ad-Hoc Committee Against the Blacklist. The pickets were led by Danny Kalb, a singer-guitarist that would later go on to accompany Judy Collins and Phil Ochs at Elektra before forming his own group, The Blues Project, in 1965. Contacted for comment, an ABC spokesman "denied the charge of a 'blacklist,' but said that some performers who had been 'identified with the Communist Party' had been kept off ABC variety shows." (It must have been challenging for the network to keep track of such performers while not maintaining a list of some kind.)

Ryan also elaborated on what was likely a standard scenario for taping day: "On Tuesday evening, the lines started forming outside the Campus Center about 6:30. By the time 7:15 rolled around the crowd had swelled to several hundred 'spectators-to-be.' The doors were opened and the mob surged up the stairs in a rush for the prime exposure front rows. Within a few minutes, every available location, both on the floor and in the recently constructed stands was over-occupied. After some reshuffling of males and females to provide a more balanced 'normal looking' background, the show was ready to roll. Emcee Jack Linkletter immediately won back the somewhat hostile, chilly crowd and even the most annoyed was completely overcome by the New Christy Minstrels' opening rendition of 'California'(*sic*). In the course of Tuesday evening's performance [the group] sang a total of six numbers and were extremely well received."

The day before this segment aired, Alan Patureau, TV writer for the Long Island-based *Newsday*, informed his readers "'Hootenanny' has the lowest cost-per-thousand viewers of any one-hour show in TV prime-time—which means it can be staged for a paltry $60,000 a week, whereas its opposition, [Jackie] Gleason, costs $130,000. This warms the heart of ABC president Tom Moore," who was then consumed with buying out Jerry Lewis' contract and closing down his show after 13 weeks. Once that headache had passed, the network wound up with an open Saturday night timeslot and a newly-refurbished theater, both of which they'd fill in January with a vaudeville-sytled variety show, *The Hollywood Palace*.

Now that word was out about Pete Seeger and ABC's requirement of a "loyalty oath," Patureau asked Lewine about it. "A TV network is merely a brokerage," the producer stated, "selling time to sponsors whose main goal is to sell goods. You can't blame them for not wanting to be associated with a performer who might lose some customers. If I think it's wrong to bar Pete Seeger from performing, I ought to hire a Broadway hall and put him on… and maybe I will." As there is no hard evidence linking Seeger with Lewine apart from the recurring *Hootenanny* news stories, it's safe to assume no such hall hiring took place. The man pretty much had his fill of folk singers while producing the series.

Especially with ABC breathing down his neck, ordering him "to schmaltz up the program a bit in an effort to lure a bigger audience," wrote Patureau. Lewine defended this as well. "No doubt the purists would welcome a full hour of Josh White, the undisputed granddaddy of folk singers, or Flatt and Scruggs, the Bluegrass specialists. We schedule them as often as possible. But we also hope to tap that great sea of squares that enjoys Ed Sullivan and Lawrence Welk, so we program acts with more universal appeal: the Smothers Brothers, the New Christy Minstrels, Dixieland, gospel music, comedians…. But I insist on one thing: maintaining the folk atmosphere. This is no place for a sophisticated Alan King routine."

Gallup & Robinson's TPT survey covered this evening and likely speaks more to the Christies' popularity than the show's. Among male viewers between 7:30 and 8:00 PM, 228 were watching *Jackie Gleason*, 134 were tuned to *Hootenanny* and 130 to *The Lieutenant*. By eight o'clock, *Hootenanny* had lost 14, including seven to *Gleason* and one to *Lieutenant*, but picked up 19, including four from *Gleason* and two from *Lieutenant*. The second half hour came in with *Gleason* at 243, *Hoot* at 140 and *Lieutenant* at 129.

Among women: the first half hour began with 230 watching *Gleason*, 134 tuned to *Lieutenant*, and 114 watching *Hoot*. Seventeen switched off *Hootenanny* by 8:00 PM, four switching to *Gleason* and one to *Lieutenant*, while 23 other women tuned in *Hootenanny*, including four from *Gleason*. The second half-hour finished with 248 *Gleason*, 139 *Lieutenant* and 120 *Hootenanny*.

It was clear to everyone except, apparently, Lewine and ABC that any attempt to please "purists" *and* "squares" would result in a mishmash that pleased neither.

2-10: University of Pittsburgh, Pittsburgh PA #2

Recording Date: September 4, 1963.

Airdate: November 30, 1963. *Repeat*: August 1, 1964.

The Brothers Four: "Hootenanny Saturday Night" (*Jack Linkletter intro*); "Brady, Brady;" "Tie Me Kangaroo Down, Sport;" "Rock Island Line/This Train"

The Tarriers: "Come on in This House," "San Francisco Bay Blues"

Josh White: "Good Morning Blues," "Apples, Peaches and Cherries," "Molly Malone," "Crawdad Song" (with *The Tarriers*)

Elan Stuart: "I Never Will Marry," "Pastures of Plenty" (with *The Brothers Four*)

Ian & Sylvia: "Poor Lazarus," "Every Time I Feel the Spirit"

Jean ("John") Carignan: "Devil's Dream," "Hangman's Reel"

Will Holt: "Down in the Valley"

Woody Allen: Stand-up comedy

FINALE: "Skip to My Lou" (*Everyone*)

The second Naval Academy show had been slotted for the week before, but a national tragedy in Dallas the afternoon of Friday, November 22, pre-empted that and all commercial television for the entire weekend.

Sheet music for *Hootenanny's* theme song. The single release sold so poorly it never made it onto a Brothers Four LP.

While The Brothers Four, The Tarriers and Josh White are the main attraction in this second (actually first in performance order) Pittsburgh *Hoot*, this show placed a heavier emphasis than usual on Canadian performers, with natives Ian & Sylvia and Jean Carignan, plus transplant Elan Stuart, all on the bill.

The Brothers Four's version of "Hootenanny Saturday Night" is the same performance as on the September 28 broadcast as well as the A-side of the group's latest single, released the week this show aired. *Billboard's* Pop Spotlight reviewer appears not to have known it was a TV series theme: "Here's a big sounding folk-type item that has high spirits and dubbed track of stomping and clapping that adds the real hoot sound. The side should get much play and could go a long way." In fact, the clapping was the U-Pitt student audience; it might have been sweetened a little, but the only true overdub is a bluegrass banjo that sounds suspiciously like Eric Weissburg. The prediction of "much play" turned out false: "Hootenanny Saturday Night" entered the *Billboard* Hot 100 on December 14 at #97, made it to #89 two weeks later, then vanished. In *Cash Box*, it never charted at all. If ABC—and for that matter, Columbia Records, the group's label—were hoping to better or at least equal The Glencoves' success, they were sadly disappointed.

The Tarriers kick off the show proper with "Come On In This House," followed by Elan Stuart. Although born and raised in Dundee, Scotland, she moved to Canada in 1956 and made herself known as a café singer and frequent performer on the nation's TV variety shows; while there, she also dabbled in acting. As Linkletter tells us, she made her American TV debut on *Hootenanny* the prior season. On this, her second and last appearance, she sings the classic ballad "I Never Will Marry," with students enthusiastically joining in, and later accompanies The Brothers Four on Woody Guthrie's "Pastures of Plenty." Having just concluded a "Hootenanny" package tour with Bob Gibson and The Highwaymen when this program was taped, she returned to her adopted country and continued performing in nightclubs and on Canadian television until at least 1975.

Based on both the applause heard in the surviving audio, which threatens to drown out Jack Linkletter's introduction of him, and

Matthew Swetonic, student reviewer for *The Pitt News*, Josh White is "the obvious student favorite." "The Big Daddy of them all," in Linkletter's words, opens his set with "Good Morning, Blues." Later, he and The Tarriers combine on "Crawdad," although not as a duet performance: White simply starts the song, and The Tarriers finish it, which at least makes for an interesting study of contrasting performance styles.

"The Big Daddy of them all," the legendary and influential Josh White.
From the author's collection

When the Folk Era began to recede, Ian & Sylvia transitioned to country music, and then, with a band called The Great Speckled Bird, to country-rock. By 1975, though, their professional and personal unions came to an end. Mirroring his own "Four Strong Winds," Ian moved to a farm in Alberta where he raised and trained horses and recorded sporadically, usually latter-day cowboy music. Sylvia maintained a music career, recording both as a soloist and with a group called Quartette. Although no longer married, the two would occasionally appear together over the ensuing decades, most recently in 2010 at the 50th Mariposa Folk Festival; the two had performed at the first one in 1961. Ian Tyson passed away at age 89 in December 2022.

Quebec-born Jean Carignan, termed "one of Canada's greatest folk fiddlers" in one obituary, was, in 1963, one of the non-professionals that many predicted *Hootenanny* would never showcase. Although he'd played The Newport Folk Festival and Carnegie Hall in 1960 (introduced to both stages by Pete Seeger), Carignan was unable to make a living at music and labored as a shoemaker, factory worker and taxi driver in his home province until 1973, when he was finally able to enter the business full time. He continued until deafness overtook him a mere five years later. "I am deaf because I live in Quebec and had to earn my living in the shop with machines and steam-hammers," he told a reporter in 1978, adding, "On the other hand, I am not dead and that's what counts." Carignan's final public performance was in 1983. He suffered a stroke in November 1987, was hospitalized and passed away three months later.

Unfortunately, Carignan's two numbers aren't in the surviving audio, nor are Ian & Sylvia's performances or Woody Allen's routine. None are referenced in Swetonic's scathing review, which was mainly concerned with a snafu in opening up the Field House for students who'd been on line since 5:00 p.m. ("They waited past 6:30 p.m. when the doors were to be flung open; past 7 p.m. when the doors were to be shut for good; they waited, in fact, until someone opened a minor entrance and started letting in people from the end of the line first"), and the downside of what was foremost a television production ("True to the tradition of the magic mirror—the sponsor comes first—[performers] sang directly into the assembled cameras and ignored the live audience [which] became bored. Like the small boy who discovers that his grandmother peddles bootleg hootch out of her flower stand, the audience grew disillusioned with *Hootenanny*. It became obvious even to the dullest that all their clapping and hooting was merely being employed to dupe the American public into believing that the students were enjoying a great show").

2-11: University of Maryland, College Park #1

Recording Date: December 3, 1963.

Airdate: December 7, 1963.

"Hootenanny Saturday Night" (*Everyone*) (*Jack Linkletter intro*)

The Chad Mitchell Trio: "James, James Morrison, Morrison," "The John Birch Society," "The Sinking of the Reuben James," unknown others.

Brock Peters: "St. James Infirmary"

The Village Stompers: "Washington Square"

Joan Toliver: "Over Yonder"

Don Elliot: "Hold On to That Plow"

The Serendipity Singers: "Sinner Man," unknown others

Joe and Eddie: "Joshua Fit the Battle of Jericho," unknown others.

MEDLEY: Songs unknown (*Joan Toliver, Don Elliot, Brock Peters*)

Charlie Manna: Stand-up comedy

FINALE: "Down By the Riverside" (*Everyone*)

NOTE: Don Elliot is mentioned in a *Baltimore Sun* Sunday magazine article about the taping; no other published source lists him, so it is possible he doesn't appear in the final edit. It is unclear if this was Don Elliot the jazz xylophonist, or a different artist.

The two shows at UMCP are among the missing as of this writing. What remains consists of incomplete audio from each show. TV listings mentioned little more than the artists' names. The surviving audio for this segment consists of "James, James Morrison, Morrison" (an off-kilter children's poem by A.A. Milne set to music by Chad Mitchell), "St. James Infirmary," "Washington Square" and an incomplete "Over Yonder." The university itself has nothing informative archived, despite being the home of the Library of American Broadcasting. *The Diamondback*, the university's student-run newspaper wrote up only the second show. An article by Helen Henry of *The Baltimore Sun*, who attended the taping, provided additional details. Readers possessing either audio or first-hand knowledge of what was performed here are encouraged to contact the author.

Taping was originally scheduled for November 25 and 26, but was postponed a week due to President Kennedy's assassination, which impacted the show in other ways: artists, especially comedians, had to retool some of their material, and programs that included joking references to the late President could not be rerun in the summer.

Those who know Brock Peters the actor, whether as Tom Robinson in *To Kill a Mockingbird* (1962) or as Admiral Cartwright in *Star Trek IV* and *VI*—or in dozens of roles in between—may be surprised to find him guesting on this show. Peters' professional career began in music with *Porgy and Bess*, both the stage and film versions. He also sang backup on Harry Belafonte's early albums and made a few of his own on the United Artists label. His rendition of "St. James Infirmary" is suitably dramatic, but Brock's bass-baritone lacks the subtlety and range that characterizes a Leon Bibb performance.

The Village Stompers' "Washington Square" was riding high on the pop charts at the time of this show, having entered *Billboard's* top 40 on October 5 and remaining for twelve weeks. The seven-member instrumental combo sought to combine folk with Dixieland, which made them ideal *Hootenanny* guests, but after a handful of less-successful releases, the group disbanded four years later.

The always-exciting Joe and Eddie returned for what was presumably another highly-charged set. Their career came to a sudden end in the early morning hours of August 6, 1966 while booked at the Cosmos Club in Seal Beach, California. The wire services reported Joe Gilbert was driving a "German made compact car" onto a transition road between the Santa Monica and Long Beach freeways; the auto overturned and exploded into flames. A passenger, twenty-year-old Karen Joy Miller, suffered major injuries and the 23-year-old Gilbert was killed. Eddie Brown worked briefly as a solo, then went behind the scenes as producer and arranger.

According to *TV Key*, Charlie Manna "does his astronaut-crayon routine" and "steals the show." The bit, concerning an astronaut who has a coloring book in the rocket but can't find the crayons ("I ain't going anywhere without my crayons!"), appeared on his 1961 *Manna Overboard* album and became so popular that when Alan Shepard prepared to enter the Mercury craft for the nation's first manned space mission, his doctor gave him a box of crayons. When the flight ended, John Glenn presented him with another box.

But the big story of this broadcast, and in many ways of *Hootenanny's* entire second season, belongs to The Serendipity Singers. It begins with two groups formed two years apart at Delta Tau Delta House at the University of Colorado. The Harlan Trio consisted of Tom Merrill, Bryan Sennett and Brooks Hatch, three Delts that had taken time off from studies to try their hand at emulating The Kingston Trio. They landed gigs both locally and along the west coast: performing on a 1959 album recorded at a Denver bar, *Folk Song Festival at Exodus*, along with a very young Judy Collins; observing the equally nascent Brothers Four in Washington state. They gave it a good whirl and returned to the university in 1962.

The previous year, sorority brothers Jon Arbenz, Johnny Madden and Mike Brovsky had formed the Mark III Trio and were playing the fraternity house party circuit. Having been down that road, and aware of the splash caused by quartets, quintets and more, Sennett offered to merge his trio with theirs. It worked for a while, but Merrill soon wearied of the grind and departed. It was at that point they thought about adding a female voice. Before long, Lynne Weintraub came aboard. "I think Mike Brovsky found her," Madden recalls. "We were recording radio commercials for an ad agency in Denver and the sound engineer called Bryan and me in and says, 'You know, that girl you've got has a helluva voice.' He plays back just her part and the two of us looked at each other and said, 'Wow, she *is* great.'" In rapid succession, they took the name The Newport Singers and used their radio money to pay for a six-song demo disc. "Bob Young came in to play bass," says Madden. "We pressed 100 copies, then got the Yellow Pages for New York and Los Angeles and went through it for every agency and management name we recognized. We put in a one-page bio, a glossy photo and the album, and sent it out in the spring of '63."

"We should have put it together earlier," Sennett later opined for *Colorado Music Experience*, but in fact it was the exact right time. *Hootenanny* was gaining traction on ABC, the craze was about to explode and agencies were seeking folk talent. "Pretty quickly we had a lot of calls," Madden remembers. "One was William Morris." According to Sennett, the venerable agency didn't even need a live audition. "I had signed [us] with William Morris when we were still in Colorado. Seven of us borrowed $1,500 and we took it all to New York in the summer of '63, hoping to land a recording contract." In *Variety's* May 29 issue, an article about the launching of FM Records mentions "a new group called The Newport Singers" are among the acts "on tap" to record for the label, which suggests Fred Weintraub heard the demo.

Madden's recollection was auditioning for Weintraub during the summer. "William Morris had us audition at a lot of places, every day for three weeks. One I remember was the Copacabana. They said, 'You guys are too clean-cut. This is more of a sophisticated audience.' We also auditioned for Fred at William Morris." Madden had interrupted his first year of law school, but most of the others were graduating in August. They returned to Boulder for that and planned on launching their career in September. "We had to pass a test," Madden remembers. "Lynne's family was in Dallas, and this was out of left field for them. They owned a commercial wholesale carpet and flooring company; her dad was the president. The father flew up and met us, and we wore suits and met with them. He thought we were great guys and would protect his daughter. He agreed to front our airfare to NY."

Once they arrived in late September, Fred Weintraub, who was no relation to Lynne, took them under his wing. "Weintraub wants to manage us and he makes a proposal. We were already formed as a group. He got us to a law firm and we incorporated as 'Shawbym.' The name was one letter of each group member's [last] name." The corporation signed him as manager; unlike the situation with the Christies, where Randy Sparks owned everything down to the last tuning peg, Weintraub had no ownership stake. Madden insists, "Fred was very generous. He was very reasonable with us."

Which didn't mean he wouldn't make changes. "Two things Fred did. First, he said, 'I know The Newport Singers is for Newport, Rhode Island, but we need something different. I'm gonna suggest Serendipity.' There's a New York shop called Serendipity 3, and he told us how it was inspired by Horace Walpole and *The Three Princes of Serendip*. Well, if he thinks it's a good idea, okay, but we talked it over and told him, 'We don't want to be just Serendipity, we want to be The Serendipity Singers.' He said okay."

The second thing he told them was equally conflicting. "I'm trying to get you guys on as semi-regulars of the *Hootenanny* show, but the other management people want a nine-person group like The New Christy Minstrels. So, I've got a duo, a girl and a guy, that would fit in with you." These were Tommy Tiemann and Diane Decker, who'd auditioned for the show during the summer and were lined up for the SMU taping, which was just days away.

The weekend Tommy & Diane's *Hootenanny* aired, they were already in New York meeting the others. "Diane and I came to realize that just the two of us wouldn't get very far in the entertainment field," Tiemann later told the *New York Daily News*. "We saw that our chances of advancement would be much better with the help of [the others'] talent." Madden, who up to then had been doing The Newport Singers' arrangements, was told by Weintraub, "Take Tommy and Diane, and Bryan and Lynne, and just pick out part of a song and play around with their voices." After thirty minutes, "we came out and we did the song, and we could just tell, it was a match. Fred said, 'What do you think?' I said, 'They give us something we don't have.'" The duo were made full corporation members, which became T.D. Shawbym Corp.

The Serendipity Singers, although perceived as a New Christy Minstrels rip-off, had more freedom in selecting material and were more charming in performance. Top row, from left: Bob Young, Bryan Sennett, Mike Brovsky. Middle row: Tommy Tiemann, Diane Decker, Lynne Weintraub, Brooks Hatch. Bottom: Johnny Madden, Jon Arbenz. *From the author's collection*

Several weeks of rehearsals followed before their official debut at The Bitter End on November 13, opening for Woody Allen (the day after his Fordham performance). *Cash Box's* Jack Maher was on hand and kicked off a very favorable review with "Record companies on the lookout for strong new folk talent can take the Serendipity Singers at their name value. The word means, in essence, making fortunate discoveries when searching for none at all. Any record executive who stumbles on Greenwich Village's Bitter End these nights will find something most fortunate." *Variety* was equally impressed: "Displaying an amazing commercial maturity in stride with their collegiate freshness and bounce, the Serendipity Singers blast a nine-voice set backed by five guitars, banjo, bass and tambourine self-accomp that rocks the joint.... All solo lustily and most all take a turn at emcee chores, a gimmick that adds nicely to the lively pace. [Their repertoire] includes 'Sing Out,' 'Goin' Home,' and 'Sunshine Special,' all upbeat and belted straightaway with little or no arranging bric-a-brac. They frankly dip into the ersatz folk catalog for 'Boots & Stetsons' and 'Don't Let the Rain Come Through'(*sic*), the latter a bright takeoff on a nursery rhyme. Of special interest is a folklike original based on the Negro rights battle, 'Freedom Star,' done in the sock style of the other upbeaters."

The last hurdle: in order to become *Hootenanny* regulars, the group needed to be represented by Ashley-Steiner. That meant getting everyone out of their respective deals with William Morris. Incredibly, the agency was amenable. Says Madden, "The guy at William Morris says, 'I'm not going to hold you kids back. I'll release you.' I got a kick out that, 'kids.' I'm 26 and married; so is Mike!" With that done, Dankar signed the newly-constituted Serendipity Singers for a minimum of six appearances, which ended up being eight. By this time, FM Records was dealing with financial contraints; luckily, the better-established Phillips label made an attractive offer.

The group members voted to make Sennett their nominal leader. At the time, Brovsky joked it was because "at six-foot-one and 185 pounds, he's bigger than everyone else." Madden's recollection is that none of the others wanted the responsibility. But perhaps Sennett was the appropriate choice. He and Hatch had been at it for over four years, and it had been his idea to move beyond the stereotypical all-male trio. "It was my last go-round," he remembered. "We were at the Bitter End night and day [rehearsing, and] I thought, 'If something doesn't happen, I'm going to law school.'"

2-12: University of Arizona, Tucson #2

Recording Date: October 16, 1963.

Airdate: December 14, 1963. *Repeat*: June 6, 1964.

Video: 16mm kinescope of the repeat broadcast. Licensing: Historic Films Archive, LLC, #V-1016. Viewing: The Library of Congress, catalog # MAVIS 2899694. Excerpted on ***The Best of Hootenanny***.

"Hootenanny Saturday Night" (*Everyone*) (*Jack Linkletter intro*)

The New Christy Minstrels: "Denver"

Eddy Arnold: "Cool Water"

Cathie Taylor: "Tarrytown"

Mike Settle: "We Shall Not Be Moved"

The Clancy Brothers and Tommy Makem: "I'll Tell Me Ma," "Will Ye Go, Lassie, Go?"

The New Christy Minstrels: "Saturday Night," "Julianne," "Song of the Pious Itinerant (Hallelujah, I'm a Bum)"

Eddy Arnold: "Red River Valley" (commercial bumper)

Cathie Taylor and Mike Settle: "Land of Odin"

Robert MacGimsey: "Shadrack"

Woody Allen: Stand-up comedy

Bessie Griffin & the Gospel Pearls: "Goin' Up to Meet Him"

LOVE AND COURTSHIP SONGS: "I Wanna Play House With You" (*Eddy Arnold*), "Reilly's Daughter" (*The Clancy Brothers & Tommy Makem*)

The New Christy Minstrels: "Down the Ohio," "Michael, Row the Boat Ashore"

FINALE: "Goodnight, Irene" (*Everyone*)

The Perils of Jack Linkletter: after showing us the Santa Catalina mountains during his opening spiel, he's seen cradling a tethered young wildcat that is enthusiastically nibbling the cuff of his suit jacket, presumably in hopes of breaking free of restraint. "My furry friend here eating me is the mascot namesake of Arizona's Wildcats," he nervously tells us. "About a year-and-a-half old; weighs twelve pounds, about six months away from full growth. Comes from those mountains you saw over there." In truth the animal, named Diablo, wasn't the school's mascot but a loaner from the Arizona-Sonoma Desert Museum.

Musically, the show is another mixed bag. Those who like The New Christy Minstrels will revel in the cheerful nonet's six selections, including their latest single's A-side, "Saturday Night," during which Barry McGuire blows the first verse by starting with the wrong lyric. Along with the single are songs drawn from three albums plus a take on "Michael, Row the Boat Ashore" that, according to McGuire, they were "just kinda funnin' with" during rehearsal. He encourages the students to join in, playfully adding, "We *know* you know the words" to much laughter. In true Christies fashion, the normally-plaintive South Carolina slave-era spiritual is belted out to a rollicking beat. It also features a shockingly *un*-P.C. moment as Hawaii native Larry Ramos takes center stage and croons, "Char-ree, row the junk ashore" and the others respond "Har-ray-ROOO-yah," putting to mind the Chinese restaurant employees that sing "Deck the Halls" in *A Christmas Story* (1983).

For his second *Hoot*, Eddy Arnold takes advantage of the piano that would later accompany the show's gospel group. His first selection is another western tale, "Cool Water," originally written and performed by The Sons of the Pioneers, a troupe formed in the early '30s that included Roy Rogers. The piano arrangement smooths out what is otherwise a tragic tale of a man lost and hallucinating in the desert, destined to die of dehydration.

Next up is 19-year-old Cathie Taylor, last seen in *Hootenanny Hoot*. Born in Winnipeg, her father died when she was three, and a year later her mother packed up the family and settled in northern California. During high school, it became clear Taylor was a gifted vocalist. She entered—and won—several talent shows, scored a guest appearance on *The Lawrence Welk Show*, was signed to Capitol Records and as a regular on 'Tennessee' Ernie Ford's variety show, all before her sixteenth birthday. By then she'd moved to Hollywood with her mother and was studying acting, but *Hootenanny Hoot* would remain her lone film appearance. Here she sings "Tarrytown" from her third album and first for the Reprise label. In the early 1970s she switched from folk-pop to Christian music as both writer and performer.

Cathie Taylor in a publicity still for *Hootenanny Hoot*. *From the author's collection*

Mike Settle sings the spiritual-turned-union anthem "We Shall Not Be Moved," with the enthusiastic accompaniment of the students. After that, it's the welcome return of those lusty Irishmen, The Clancy Brothers and Tommy Makem. The sweater-clad foursome give out with the supposed children's ditty, "I'll Tell Me Ma," as Linkletter's narration obscures the first verse. It's followed by "Will Ye Go, Lassie, Go," which Tom Clancy tells us "came by way of Scotland to Ireland." It must have been someone's favorite, as it would return twice more this season by other artists.

The second half begins with Norman Keenan's bass intro for "Land of Odin," which leads to a gorgeously arranged duet between Cathie Taylor and Mike Settle. Perhaps having learned from his prior experience with Jo Mapes to not carry the melody, Settle adds tenor harmony to Taylor's lead and the blend is perfect; unfortunately, the two never performed it together in a recording studio.

They're followed by Robert MacGimsey, a Louisiana-born lawyer who, beginning in 1928, provided a unique three-toned whistling accompaniment for Gene Austin, a Texas-born crooner, for the latter's records as a sideline. Austin's label, Victor, was impressed enough to schedule solo sessions for him the following year. Around the same time, MacGimsey started collecting spirituals. "I began collecting the songs from some old Negro friends, who were former slaves," he told a reporter. From there, he composed his own, most famously the one he performs here, "Shadrack." Written in 1930, the song was introduced two years later by Willard Robinson; thirty years after that, Brook Benton took it to #19 on *Billboard's* Hot 100. In between were countless other interpretations, including one by Louis Armstrong and the Lyn Murray Singers in 1939. MacGimsey, who'd retired to Phoenix in 1960, was never a vocalist and the lyrics were originally crafted in the once-acceptable "colored" dialect; thankfully, he doesn't sing it that way, although he does add an occasional growl and braying laugh for questionable effect. MacGimsey passed away in Phoenix in March 1979.

Woody Allen makes his fourth and final appearance (although, in taping order, this was actually his third). He begins by telling the audience how impressed he is by their presence, given he was "thrown out of New York University" after ten months. "When my friends were in college, I was in analysis," which leads to a story about Allen in group analysis, which leads to a story about dating a Bennington girl "studying to be a woman male nurse," and her bohemian roommates who "tried to make opium out of poppies given out by veterans on street corners." This pseudo-stream of consciousness monologue runs longer than expected and an off-camera floor manager has to prompt Allen to wrap it up, which he does: "They're signaling me for time, so I'm going to browse around the campus and see if I can fall in love." Arguably, Allen's cinematic future was based on that premise.

Publicity still of Woody Allen during his pre-cinema auteur days.

Bessie Griffin and the Gospel Pearls, along with pianist Charles Barnett, took a quick break from ITA's "Traveling Hootenanny" tour to do this lively spot on the show. Born in New Orleans, Griffin was given her start in the gospel world by Mahalia Jackson, who helped her get established in Chicago. In 1953, she joined The Caravans, then left to form her own group, The Gospel Pearls, six years later. Not a screamer like Clara Ward or Marion Williams, Griffin and the Pearls manage to capture the students' fancy with their high-spirited performance and they're easily given the biggest ovation of the program. Despite recurring health issues that began toward the close of the 1960s, Griffin continued entertaining until shortly before her 1989 passing from cancer at age 67.

The multi-artist medley is actually two songs introduced by Pat Clancy as a look at folk music's treatment of love in America and Ireland. Eddy Arnold's contribution is his 1951 success, "I Wanna Play House With You," then the Clancys and Makem give us "Reilly's Daughter," an off-color dirge the group cleaned up lyrically and set to a swift pace. (For a hint of how the song originally went, take the line "I'd like to marry old Reilly's daughter" and substitute 'marry' with a word prominent in the *Austin Powers* movies.)

After the Christies and the last commercial break, we get the finale, "Goodnight Irene." Unlike the first season rendition at Penn State, this one has been accelerated for that "socko" windup the network so dearly enjoyed. About two verses in, Woody Allen appears on stage with a chair, which he places in front of the performers, takes a seat and proceeds to read a paperback novel. In lieu of a verse, Eddy Arnold does his "Cowpoke" yodel to the song's melody as Robert MacGimsey performs his three-toned whistle. It could've been a nice moment for posterity, but unfortunately, just as they begin, they're drowned out by the "brought to you by" announcement.

2-13: University of California, Los Angeles (UCLA) #2

Recording Date: October 30, 1963.

Airdate: December 21, 1963. *Repeat*: June 13, 1964

Video: 16mm kinescope of the repeat broadcast. Licensing: Historic Films Archive, LLC, #V-1013. Viewing: The Library of Congress, catalog # MAVIS 1882240. Excerpted on *The Best of Hootenanny*.

"Hootenanny Saturday Night" (*Everyone*) (*Jack Linkletter intro*)

The Travelers 3: "Bowling Green"

Nancy Ames: "Should I Follow?"

Jimmie Rodgers: "Waterboy," "If I Had My Way"

The Brothers Four: "The Ox Driver's Song"

Beverly Wright: "I Will Love You"

Bud and Travis: "Angelico," "Fiesta in Guadalajara"

The Brothers Four: "Hard Travelin'" (commercial bumper)

Stan Wilson (w/guitarist Lenin Castro): "Ghost Riders in the Sky"

Bill Cosby: Stand-up comedy ("Toss of the Coin," "The Locker Room")

Trini Lopez: "Lonesome Traveler," "If I Had a Hammer"

The Travelers 3: "Good Morning, Captain"

The Brothers Four: "Four Strong Winds"

FINALE: "Tell Old Bill" (*Everyone*)

The all-polish, no-spit version of folk music takes center stage in this one. It's not the worst in the surviving *Hootenanny* canon, but there's very little that would impress the discerning aficionado. When Trini Lopez is as close as you get to an ethnic folk musician, you haven't done a proper job to balance the lineup. Then again, there weren't many ethnic performers left that would do the show. Lewine and crew would be genuinely stretching the genre's boundaries in the months to come.

The Travelers 3 return with two fast ones, each nearly identical in tempo and arrangement, from their debut Elektra album nearly two years old. The Brothers Four, headliners on the first UCLA show, give us only two this time around, and both were performed by others in the second Boston U show two months earlier. First, "The Ox-Driver's Song," which sounds like what it is: a white man's interpretation of Leon Bibb's more dramatic rendition. They close out the show with "Four Strong Winds" in an arrangement that pales compared to The Chad Mitchell Trio's, although in fairness the students are just as happy to sing along on the refrain. Bud and Travis also serve up two, one of which is Tom Lehrer's hysterical "Fiesta in Guadalajara," probably the show's high point.

Among the women soloists, who only get one song apiece, there's the return of Nancy Ames, soon to be seen weekly on NBC's *That Was the Week That Was*, singing her own composition, which is quite good. And there's newcomer Beverly Wright of Cresskill, New Jersey, singing a six-year-old pop tune, the cloying "I Will Love You," originally written and recorded by Shelby Flint. More surprising than the idea of Wright being judged suitable for any network show is the fact that she'd been singing professionally since age five, recording since the mid-1950s and hitting the club circuit since 1961. In its "New Acts" column, *Variety* termed her "one of the better femmes to appear in recent months.

Attractively gowned, she draws plenty of response with a well-chosen selection of standards, showtunes, a rock 'n' roll number, a couple of folksongs and the novelty 'He Taught Me How To Yodel,'" which she might've done well to showcase here. For the syrupy ballad, her voice is ordinary at best, and given *Variety's* rave plus the singing lessons taken since early childhood, her performance sure sounds like she's giving her nose a workout.

Although Stan Wilson claimed Josh White as inspiration, about the only similarity is the open-button shirt. Wilson, who'd been performing for nearly a decade, was better suited for nightclubs than coffee houses; his rendition of "Ghost Riders in the Sky" lacks the subtlety of a White or the dramatic flair of a Bibb. More interesting is his accompanist, a guitarist whose name, believe it or not, is Lenin Castro. It's tempting to speculate if he was required to sign ABC's "loyalty oath" in order to appear.

Why Lewine thought two pop performers in a single show was a good idea is a head-scratcher, but he opted for it and so we get Jimmie Rodgers during the first half and Trini Lopez in the second. Rodgers was originally marketed as a teen idol in the wake of Elvis Presley, along with Fabian, Bobby Rydell and others of that ilk. His delightfully cheesy "Honeycomb" still makes the rounds on satellite radio services that program "the Fabulous '50s" and he even recorded The Weavers' "Kisses Sweeter Than Wine" in 1957 and scored a top ten hit. Having switched exclusively to folk material two years earlier, at the time of taping he was about to launch a Hollywood-produced series, *The Folk World of Jimmie Rodgers*, which ran for two seasons in syndication and featured guests that did and those that wouldn't appear on *Hootenanny*. Here, backed by The Fairmont Singers—the same group that quit The New Christy Minstrels at the last minute—he brings a Vegas showroom panache to "Waterboy" and "If I Had My Way" that looks embarrassingly out of place.

Trini Lopez employs his combo, Dick Brant on electric bass and Mickey Jones on drums, and his own Gibson electric; together they rock out on "Lonesome Traveler" and his #3 pop chart smash "If I Had a Hammer." Lopez, born in Dallas, Texas to native Mexican parents, learned music from his father, who bought him a $12 guitar from a pawn shop. As an adult, he set folk music to a Latino beat, making it suitable for dancing, which, he said in 2014, "helped me a lot. Discotheques back in those days were not only playing my songs, they were playing my album all the way through."

At last, Trini Lopez has a hammer, but as you can tell by the placement of his fingers, he's more at home with an axe. *From the author's collection*

Bill Cosby's reputation has been considerably tarnished in recent years owing to accusations of sexual misconduct, but in December 1963 he was a rising star making his third-ever appearance on network prime time; his first two having come earlier in the season on *The Jack Paar Show*. Paar was a huge fan, as would be Johnny Carson, Ed Sullivan and others over the coming weeks. Cosby was still a few months from signing a record deal with Warner Brothers as he performs two routines that would appear on his first album, to the hearty enjoyment of the students. Between the two, he receives a thunderous ovation and needs to quiet the audience: "Don't have much time here; gotta get off... or else some folksingers will come and get me."

Off-camera, a few students were agitating for a boycott, according to the *UCLA Daily Bruin*. The president of the college's Folk Song Club, Dave Cohen, told them, "It is unfortunate that the only national medium of folk music on television is concerned only with commercial, non-traditional folk music." Cohen was backed up by the club's sponsor, Dr. D. K. Wilgus, professor of Anglo-American Folklore: "It is very rarely folk music that is presented [on *Hootenanny*]. The music is an improvement over some popular music of the past, but to parade it as folk music is an untruth."

Rather than picket, though, the Club sponsored an alternative show in a separate auditorium the afternoon of the first taping and dress rehearsal, featuring prominent boycotter Barbara Dane, along with The Chambers Brothers, Rita Weill, Bill Cunningham and Jackie DeShannon, among others.

The *Bruin's* classified section published some calls for protest in its Personal column, including: "HOOTENANNY won't let Pete Seeger sing for refusing to testify for HUAC. Joan Baez boycotted in sympathy. Will you?" Underneath this plea was a related submission: "ATTENTION Hootenanny Boycott: Are you the same group that boycotts soap, water and razor blades?"

The cast hoots "Tell Old Bill" at the close.

2-14: University of Maryland, College Park #2

Recording Date: December 4, 1963.

Airdate: December 28, 1963. *Repeat*: May 9, 1964

"Hootenanny Saturday Night" (*Everyone*) (*Jack Linkletter intro*)

The Modern Folk Quartet: "Yes, I See," "Sassafras"

The Chad Mitchell Trio: "Super Skier," "The Tarriers Song," "An Irish Song," "Johnny," "Whistling Gypsy"

The Serendipity Singers: "Don't Let the Rain Come Down (Crooked Little Man)," "Freedom's Star"

Josh White: "John Henry," "One Meat Ball," "Foggy, Foggy Dew"

Enid Mosier: "Jordan"

Carolyn Hester: "Can't Help but Wonder Where I'm Bound"

Charlie Manna: Stand-up comedy

FINALE: "Down by the Riverside" (*Everyone*)

NOTE: Network publicity lists Johnny Cash as a guest, but he is not mentioned in TV listings nor in the show introduction that survives on audio tape.

Surviving audio for this program consists of the opening, The Modern Folk Quartet's arrangement of Bob Gibson's "Yes I See," Josh White's three performances, all of the listed Chad Mitchell Trio numbers except "Super Skier," and The Serendipity Singers' first hit "Don't Let the Rain Come Down (Crooked Little Man)."

Formed in Hawaii in 1962, The Modern Folk Quartet consisted of Henry "Tad" Diltz, Chip Douglas, Cyrus Faryar (formerly of The Whiskeyhill Singers) and Jerry Yester (formerly one of The Inn Group). Their debut album on the Warner Bros. label had been released in August and at taping time they could be seen on theater screens in the studio's teen comedy *Palm Springs Weekend* (1963). They were among the stars of the "Traveling Hootenanny" tour and when this show aired, they were opening for Bud and Travis at the Hootenanny Club in Canoga Park, California. The MFQ, as they liked to call themselves, specialized in intricate four-part vocal arrangements and were touted as bringing a fresh approach to the traditional genre, which was a publicist's way of saying they were another slick batch of folk song interpreters. Although the troupe turned to folk-rock upon the advent of The Byrds, and even became the Modern Folk Quintet with the addition of drummer Eddie Hoh in 1965, they failed to chart a big success. Its members would make their most significant contributions to music lore separately: Diltz as photographer of several pop-rock groups, Douglas as producer for The Turtles and The Monkees, and Yester as a member of The Lovin' Spoonful.

The Chad Mitchell Trio wait between songs while taping their final *Hootenanny* appearances. *From the author's collection*

With this, their ninth appearance (although the eighth to air), The Chad Mitchell Trio would bid farewell to *Hootenanny*. They make the most of it, with tunes culled from three of their albums, including "The Tarriers Song" from their latest release, *Reflecting*. The highlight, though, is "Johnny," their poignant combination of the uplifting "When Johnny Comes Marching Home" and the somber "Johnny, I Hardly Knew Ye" from Ireland. The result is, as Chad says in his intro, "a contrast that we feel makes its own point."

"Not long ago, we presented for their television debut a *Hootenanny* discovery, a group known as The Serendipity Singers," Linkletter tells us in his introduction. "These nine very young and attractive singers have been delighted that so many of you have wanted to hear them again at the earliest possible opportunity. Well, this is it!" It's a surprising statement, considering it was taped the day after their debut show, which obviously hadn't yet aired. Given the reception the Serendipities received during their Bitter End booking, however, it's possible Linkletter (or rather, writer David Greggory) had been prescient rather than misleading.

What's *more* surprising, though, is that the student audience already knows the refrain of the group's opener and happily joins in right at the start. "Don't Let the Rain Come Down" not only hadn't been released yet (that would come the following February), it hadn't even been *recorded*. Granted, the song is something of an earworm, and no doubt many in the audience were present during dress rehearsal and may have even been taught the lyrics just ahead of the taping. The catchy record, for which the arrangement is identical to this performance, would eventually peak at number six on *Billboard's* Hot 100 in May, at number two on its Adult Contemporary chart, and be nominated for a Grammy in the Best Performance by a Chorus category.

Once again, Josh White receives an enthusiastic ovation when he follows the Serendipities for his first selection, "John Henry." He also performs two of his long-time standards, "Foggy, Foggy Dew" and "One Meat Ball," the latter during a prolonged commercial bumper. White's career ended prematurely on June 5, 1969, when he died while undergoing valve replacement surgery at Northshore Hospital in Manhasset, New York. He was only 61 years old. "What Josh did [was] brought to its fullest in Harry Belafonte," wrote music historian Ralph J. Gleason shortly after White's passing. "His style of presentation, with the open shirt unbuttoned almost to the belt, his only accompaniment a guitar, became the style of presentation of a whole generation of singers…. Had he been born a generation later, it is quite possible that he would have become a really big star. He played many well-known clubs in the '40s in addition to Café Society and he was above all else a superb showman. But history, which is governed mysteriously by time, does not wait. It goes by its own pace and it was Josh White's fate to be before his time."

Chad Mitchell and Carolyn Hester take a break together during rehearsals.

Carolyn Hester makes her second and final appearance with one of Tom Paxton's best rambling songs, "Can't Help But Wonder Where I'm

Bound," which might've been a question she was asking herself. By now, Columbia had let her go after two albums, and she'd signed with the less-prestigious Dot Records; her song here would be included on her first for the label the following year. She did three for Dot, including a live recording at New York's Town Hall in 1965.

By the latter half of the decade, she tried forming a rock group, The Carolyn Hester Coalition; their one album, produced by David Blume, tanked ("You can only get it on eBay," she told *Washington Post* reporter Bob Thompson in 2005). She wed Blume in 1969 and had two daughters. Except for annual appearances at the Kerrville Folk Festival in Texas (where she mentored newcomers like Nanci Griffith), Hester focused on wife-and-motherhood for several years. In 1992 she seemingly came out of nowhere to appear at the star-studded 30th Anniversary Tribute to Bob Dylan from Madison Square Garden. Hester continues to make appearances, usually with her daughters, and dazzle audiences with the purity of her voice.

Enid Mosier had been singing calypso before Belafonte, appearing on Broadway with Pearl Bailey in the 1954 musical *House of Flowers*. Born in the British West Indies in 1924, she started out as a dancer, also on Broadway. A three-year European tour as a vocalist led to *House of Flowers*, which led to working the nightclub circuit for the remainder of the decade with a trio of steel drummers. By 1962, Mosier had whittled down to a single accompanist: her husband, Trinidadian Alfonso Marshall.

Charlie Manna wasn't supposed to perform at both U of Maryland shows. Originally scheduled for one was the return of Vaughn Meader, but after the President's assassination, Dankar cancelled his appearance. They also tried to abrogate the contract entirely under the "Act of God" clause, according to *Variety*. Meader's manager Buddy Allen fought them on it and eventually won.

"A capacity crowd at Ritchie Coliseum welcomed the performers," read an article published two days later in the campus paper *The Diamondback*. "Cameras 'snooping,' red lights, cramped knees and warnings of 'no smoking, no drinking, no pictures, and if you're here with someone you shouldn't be seen with, better leave,' did nothing to dampen spirits of the taping." The same issue, in its letter column, printed a lengthy call to boycott the tapings by a student named George B. McCeney, citing the Seeger issue. Unfortunately, his plea didn't reach print until it was all over, but the young man could presumably take comfort in Carolyn Hester's promise to a *Diamondback* journalist that she would not be returning to the show. "I had a commitment to do one more… and now that I have completed the tape, I'm leaving the series. We in the business consider Pete the greatest folksinger in the country today…. It's a pity that the leading person in folk music cannot appear on the show."

Hester did have some charitable words for Jack Linkletter: "[He] is really trying to keep the show going. He knows considerably more about folk music now than he did when he first began emceeing the show." ABC though, still concerned about ratings, was poised to deliver new format changes that would give Linkletter fewer opportunities to demonstrate his knowledge.

2-15: West Point Academy, West Point, NY #1

Recording Date: December 21, 1963.

Airdate: January 4, 1964. *Repeat*: July 4, 1964.

"Hootenanny Saturday Night" (*Everyone*) (*Jack Linkletter intro*)

The Brothers Four: "Brady," "Springhill Disaster," "Take This Hammer," "Yellow Bird," "Tomorrow is a Long Time"

The Dalton Boys: "Oh, Freedom," "San Francisco Bay Blues"

The Brandywine Singers: "Quit Kickin' My Dog Around," "Wabash Cannonball"

Anita Sheer: "Linstead Market"

Bob Carey: "I Got A Woman"

The Paul Winter Jazz Sextet: "John Henry"

The Serendipity Singers: "Sing Out," "Cotton Mill Girls"

Second City: Comedy troupe

FINALE: "Mountain Dew" (Everyone)

The by-now veteran Brothers Four and The Serendipity Singers, along with a host of mostly newcomers, entertain at the show's second visit to a military academy in the first of a pair of *Hootenannies* that aren't known to survive in any format. As with Annapolis, taping had to be done on weekend days to not conflict with the weekday regimen. There is some confusion, based on the newspaper listings, whether this show or the second (listed under March 28, 1964) aired on this date. *TV Key* touted them under the dates found in this book, as did *TV Guide*. These and other wire service listings flesh out what is currently lost:

"Aside from young Anita Sheer and Bob Carey, it's all groups tonight. The folksinging contingent ranges from the huge mob called the Serendipity Singers, down to such smaller combos as the Brothers Four, the Dalton Boys and the Brandywine Singers. The Brothers Four get the longest showing and make the most of it, though the Dalton Boys register the strongest with a couple of bluegrass-styled selections." This was the second of two appearances for The Daltons and first of two for The Brandywine Singers, a group formed at the University of New Hampshire. The quintet, consisting of twin brothers Ron and Rick Shaw, Dave Craig, Fred Corbett and Hal Brown, debuted at Dartmouth College's 1963 Winter Carnival as The Tradewinds, but changed their name prior to graduating that year and turning professional. Their recordings were produced by Al Ham under the auspices of George Joy, the same duo that launched The Glencoves. Now keenly aware of what sells in the folk world, at the time this show aired Joy released an entire album by the group. They would return to the Winter Carnival for their second *Hoot* appearance the following month.

Flamenco guitar was Anita Sheer's specialty, having studied in Spain under Carlos Montoya for two years. It was enough to have her eventually declared the greatest female flamenco guitarist in the world. Presumably she put a Spanish spin upon "Linstead Market," a traditional

Jamaican number. It appears on her debut album released by MGM Records the following year. After settling in San José California in 1981, she founded the city's Flamenco Society, which continues to this day. Sheer passed away in July 1996, a cancer victim at age 61.

Bob Carey had been one of the founders of The Tarriers in 1956 and had gone solo not long after their first season appearance. As discussed earlier, he was a member of the touring show "The American Hootenanny Festival," and recently signed with 20th Century-Fox Records after they'd recorded portions of the tour for an album. Presumably his selection, "I Got a Woman," was performed at the Festival although it would not appear on his forthcoming album.

"The Paul Winter Jazz Sextet interprets 'John Henry.'" It would be surprising if Linkletter's narration didn't mention the combo's goodwill tour of 23 Latin American countries for the State Department, or that they introduced modern jazz to the White House East Room; both events taking place in 1962, a year after their professional debut. In 1967, Winter formed The Paul Winter Consort and gradually steered his talents toward environmental concerns, originating what he calls a World of Living Music. He would go on to win seven Grammy awards; still active as of this writing, his website is *paulwinter.com*.

"The comedy spot that interrupts the 'hoot' is really special here. It's got that well-known troupe of sophisticated satirists, 'From the Second City,' filling the air with their barbs." At the time, Second City members included another founding Tarrier, Alan Arkin, future comedy team Jack Burns and Avery Schreiber, plus Dick Schaal, Barbara Harris, Ann Elder and Paul Dooley. Whether any or all of these appeared here is an open question. *"Among [their] vignettes is the military instruction of a Vietnamese and a visit of a father to his son at an army training base,"* which must have gone over big with the cadets.

2-16: University of Florida, Gainesville #1

Recording Date: January 7, 1964.

Airdate: January 11, 1964.

Video: 16mm kinescope minus commercials. Licensing: Historic Films Archive, LLC, #V-1015. Viewing: The Library of Congress, catalog # MAVIS 2275848. Excerpted on ***The Best of Hootenanny***.

"Hootenanny Saturday Night" (*Everyone*) (*Jack Linkletter intro*)

The Coventry Singers: "Bowling Green"

Jo Mapes: "Me and My Friend," "Someday Soon"

Bob Gibson: "Train to Morrow," "There's a Meetin' Here Tonight"

Johnny Cash: "Busted," "Five Feet High and Rising"

Leon Bibb: "Adieu, Madras," "Little Boxes"

"You Are My Sunshine" (*Audience sing-along*) (*commercial bumper*)

The Johnson Family Singers: "Little Old Pine Log Cabin," "Keep On the Sunny Side"

Adam Keefe: Comedy impressionist

The Coventry Singers: "Little Tyke"

MEDLEY - THE FOLK HIT PARADE OF 1963: "If I Had a Hammer" (*Leon Bibb*), "Green, Green" (*Jo Mapes*), "Abilene" (*Bob Gibson*), "Blowin' in the Wind" (*all three*)

Johnny Cash: "Ring of Fire"

FINALE: "Paul and Silas" (*Everyone*)

The new year brought, along with falling ratings, a new approach to both the show's introduction and staging: the entire cast would remain on stage throughout, singing the opening theme together, then seated in a row behind whichever artist or group was performing. They slowed the program down, allowing artists to perform two songs before yielding the stage. More emphasis was placed on the previous act introducing the next one (a task that required them to either learn lines or read cue cards), leaving Jack Linkletter to do little more than welcome the TV audience at the start, narrate the commercial bumper, introduce the comedian and close out the program. Gospel all but vanished, although jazz and country performers remained.

For most of 1963, The Coventry Singers were a trio—Vic Burnham on guitar and banjo, Bob Shuttleworth on bass, Kerry Clark on lead guitar—that spent several months at the Bayou Room on New Orleans' famous Bourbon Street. Then Gene Marshall joined just before their sole LP, the privately-pressed *Run Come See The Coventry Singers*, was released. At that point, with Marshall also a guitarist, Clark took over on banjo, playing in the old-time flailing manor. Burnham kicks off their opening number, "Bowling Green," then takes tenor parts while Marshall sings lead the rest of the way. Marshall didn't last long; by May 1964 he'd left and was replaced by Dick Bradly who could play genuine Bluegrass banjo. The foursome did a minor Hootenanny '64 tour in August of that year, then went their separate ways.

With some help from Norman Keenan's bass, Leon Bibb's guitarist and Johnny Cash's drummer, Jo Mapes gives us an original composition, "Me and My Friend," as well as Ian Tyson's "Someday Soon," which would someday soon be a hit for Judy Collins. Mapes' rendition races a bit, which might've been Lewine's doing, but the irony of having been among the first female folksingers on the scene yet regularly eclipsed by newbies was not lost on her. Although Kapp Records had just reissued her 1958 album under the title *Jo Mapes: The Hootenanny Star*, thanks to bad breaks and poor business decisions, she never rose to that level.

"Me and My Friend," was from Mapes' second LP, *And You Were On My Mind*, recorded for FM Records and which barely saw the distribution of promo copies before the label went bankrupt. Not long after this latest in a long string of disappointments, she gave up full-time performing and for many years the only singing she did was for a series of animated commercials for Kellogg's Raisin Bran. At the suggestion of Bob Gibson, she joined the teaching staff of Chicago's Old Town School of Folk Music, an association that lasted until the mid-1980s. During these and subsequent years, she would perform at the occasional school or civic fund raiser and folk festival, until her health began to fail. She passed away in 2017.

With fulsome praise and admiration on full display, Mapes introduces Gibson, who gives us the clever "Train to Morrow" ("you cannot go to Morrow anymore today") and one of his signature tunes, "There's a Meetin' Here Tonight," accompanied by full student participation, not to mention the artists seated behind him. After that, it's Johnny Cash with his cotton farmer rewrite of Harlan Howard's "Busted" (the original was about a destitute coal miner) and his own "Five Feet High and Rising." In a piece that decried country stars who masqueraded as folk singers, Boyce Davis, music columnist for the *Northwest Arkansas Times*, would write a couple of months later about Cash's appearances on this series: "He always has a good time when he's working, even if he does look half-loaded once in a while." He's looking half-loaded here; at one point during 'Busted,' he accidentally hits the microphone stand with his guitar. "S'cuse me, mike," he drawls, a line Dean Martin would use when deliberately bumping into a mic stand while *pretending* to be half-loaded.

Cash, of course, wasn't a masquerade folkie but the real deal, one whose original songs, like "Five Feet High and Rising," were drawn from real life experience. The minimal backing of The Tennessee Three only enhanced his folk sensibility, even when interpreting standards like "Cotton Fields" and "Take This Hammer." And rewriting Harlan Howard was nothing compared to rewriting Bob Dylan's "Don't Think

Twice (It's Alright)" as "Understand Your Man," which soon became a crossover pop hit. Cash was an early Dylan enthusiast and close friend of Seeger's, and he and his combo would be given a hero's welcome at Newport that July. (When Dylan was criticized by *Sing Out!* and elsewhere for moving away from topical material and plugging in his guitar, Cash's response was swift and direct: "Shut up and let him sing!") His records sold in the millions; his third song here was one of the biggest of his career. The only disconcerting issue was his escalating use of chemical stimulants, the same problem that plagued Bob Gibson. This was their second *Hootenanny* together; one can only imagine how much carousing the pair did after taping concluded.

Cash brings on Leon Bibb, who sings both sides of his newest single, the lovely, lilting "Adieu, Madras" and Malvina Reynolds' ode to bland suburbia, "Little Boxes." The latter was targeted as the A-side, despite Pete Seeger's version having appeared on the lower reaches of *Billboard's* Hot 100 a few months earlier. Released that week, Bibb's record got lost in the wake of the about-to-explode British Invasion and failed to chart.

The Johnson Family Singers, who'd been singing together since the Depression, had pretty much retired twelve years earlier. Jesse ("Pa") and Lydia ("Ma") Johnson, and their three sons and one daughter, had been literally singing for their supper since leaving Greensboro, North Carolina, for Charlotte and WBT radio in 1940. They stayed for nine years, mixing in church and fair appearances, until eldest son Kenneth headed to college in 1951, eventually becoming a Methodist minister. The group's lead singer, daughter Betty, opted to remain in show business, making her way to New York and the musical stage. Except for occasional appearances on *The Ed Sullivan Show*, the rest of the family remained inactive, so it's a rare treat to have this true old-time ensemble's performances for posterity... even if the first is partially obscured by Linkletter's lengthy introduction.

Adam Keefe's routine centers on old movies and includes his best-remembered bit: an impression of a worn, splice-laden print of *Call Northside 777* (1948). He follows up with a depiction of John Barrymore in the silent *Dr. Jekyll & Mr. Hyde* (1920) that uses a blackout effect: the house lights cut out and return with the comic in a new pose.

From left, The Coventry Singers, Johnny Cash, Leon Bibb, Jo Mapes and Bob Gibson close out another *Hootenanny*.

"The cooperation here at Gainesville has been really something," Lewine told the *Tampa Tribune's* Bernie McGovern. "The school officials have really been a big help." As evidence, he cited being permitted to do something he'd wanted since the previous season: shoot at least some of the program outdoors on campus grounds. "We set up outside and in a few minutes we had about a thousand students for our audience," said Lewine. The crew taped one number for each of the two programs under the Florida sunshine; for this show, it's "Little Tyke" by The Coventry Singers.

The last multi-artist medley ever taped for the series is a look back at folk's biggest successes of the prior year. Leon Bibb covers "If I Had a Hammer," charted by both Peter, Paul & Mary and Trini Lopez; Jo Mapes takes on the Christies' "Green, Green;" Bob Gibson performs his own "Abilene," which had been a big country-western crossover hit for George Hamilton IV, who synched to it in *Hootenanny Hoot*; and all three sing "Blowin' in the Wind" along with the students. As an addendum, Bibb introduces Johnny Cash and "Ring of Fire," and by now the Man in Black is so wired that, in what appears to have been a post-production decision, the record is played on top of his performance. Presumably this was a one-time format violation, but with so many *Hootenannies* missing, including Cash's final one, it's impossible to know.

2-17: Salem College, Salem WV #1

Recording Date: December 10, 1963.

Airdate: January 18, 1964.

"Hootenanny Saturday Night" (*Everyone*) (*Jack Linkletter intro*)

The New Christy Minstrels: "Pick A Bale O' Cotton," "When They Ring Those Golden Bells"

Beverly Wright: "Lonesome Traveler/This Train" (Medley)

The Four Preps: "We Don't Give a Hootenanny" (Parody)

The New Christy Minstrels: "Jamie," "Suzianna," "Stormy," "A Natural Man"

The Four Preps: "Swing Down, Chariot" (commercial bumper)

The Geezinslaw Brothers: "Sweet, Sweet Home," "Charming Betsy"

Stiller & Meara: Comedy routine

Nina Simone: "Israeli Chant"

Beverly Wright and The Four Preps: "Their Hearts Were Full of Spring"

The New Christy Minstrels: "Casey Jones," "Saturday Night"

FINALE: "What Shall We Do with a Drunken Sailor?" (*Everyone*)

"Salem is an outstanding example of the special services small colleges provide," says Jack Linkletter in the preamble. "The president of Salem points out that small colleges 'take the pressure off our larger institutions and keep our big universities from becoming unwieldy.'" Small is right: In 1963, the student body of Salem College, split between two campuses in Salem and Clarksburg, West Virginia, numbered just under a thousand. Neither campus had a facility large enough to accommodate the two-to-four-thousand-plus student audience that ABC expected. Why would such a minor institution be selected for a *Hootenanny*?

The answer is, O. G. "Red" Kennedy, President of Miles Laboratories, whose Alka-Seltzer had been a sponsor since season one, was an alumnus as well as Chairman of the college's Board of Trustees. Additionally, ABC's radio network had done programming with the cooperation of the Council for the Advancement of Small Colleges, founded in 1955 by K. Duane Hurley, President of Salem. Both Kennedy and Hurley had a vested interest and considerable sway in seeing the school selected. Never underestimate the influence of guys who pay the bills.

In order to make it work, Lewine and crew went off-campus for the first time and arranged for the use of a National Guard facility, the General Nathan Goff Armory in Clarksburg, constructed in 1961. In addition to Salem students, over 700 tickets were distributed to West Virginia Wesleyan College in Buckhannon for the first taping, and the same number split between Alderson-Broaddus University in Philippi and Davis & Elkins College in Elkins for the second. High school students and local residents also helped pack the Armory to capacity.

The cover of Miles Laboratories' house organ captures Salem alumnus O.G. "Red" Kennedy greeting the audience prior to the *Hootenanny* taping. Note the considerably-older-than-college-age attendees in the upper section.

What they saw in both cases was "The New Christy Minstrels Show" plus a handful of others. The Christies were given literally half the program, including the entire second quarter-hour segment. Three of the tunes ("Stormy," "A Natural Man" and "Casey Jones") derived from their latest release, the American folk heroes concept album *Land of Giants*. Additional highlights include Jackie Miller's plaintive solo on "Jamie," which appears to have never been recorded by her, and another shot at "Saturday Night," with McGuire singing the correct lyric this time.

Beverly Wright returns with a medley of "Lonesome Traveler" and "This Train (is Bound for Glory)." At UCLA, her performance at least had the virtue of subtlety; here, all restraint goes by the boards as she belts and growls out the lyrics, accompanied by Larry Ramos on banjo, Norman Keenan's bass and the drummer for The Four Preps. At one point on "This Train," her vocal suddenly rises about an octave-and-a-half above the melody, and comes out sounding like she's mixing singing with bird calls. The tempo escalates as she returns to "Lonesome Traveler," and holds the final "I've been a-travelin' on-n-n-n-n-n" to such a ludicrous degree, she literally outlasts her accompanists.

She's followed by The Four Preps, a vocal group known for taking musical shots at contemporaries such as The Platters, Dion and the Belmonts, The Four Aces and even The Kingston Trio. Here they debut a similar series of mock impressions as part of a satiric folk music composition, set up with such lines as:

We don't give a hoot-enanny about this folky scene.

We're saving ourselves for better things,

like a tribute to Jan & Dean

Along with a playful jibe at the "Surf City" duo, the troupe lampoons The New Christy Minstrels (with a take on McGuire's gravelly voice that puts the audience into hysterics) and The Limeliters. Formed in 1957 at Hollywood High School, Bruce Belland, Ed Cobb, Marvin Ingram and Glen Larson became the youngest vocal group signed to a major label when Capitol inked them that year. After disbanding in 1969, three of the foursome remained in show business: Belland as a producer (for Ralph Edwards Productions) and network executive; Cobb as a songwriter (his "Tainted Love," written for Gloria Jones, became a monster hit for the new wave group Soft Cell in 1982) and Larson as creator of such hit TV shows as *Battlestar Galactica* and *Knight Rider*.

The Geezinslaw Brothers made their television debut on an Austin, Texas station owned by Mrs. Lyndon Johnson. After her enthusiastic endorsement, the then-Vice President invited the foursome to entertain a gathering of United Nations diplomats at his LBJ Texas ranch that by all accounts pleased everyone. Next came appearances on Arthur Godfrey's radio show and an album for Columbia. Three of the "brothers" were friends who played at parties and schools around Austin: Sammy Allred on mandolin, Mickey Rumsey on bass and Johnny Deison on banjo. When they were joined by guitarist Dewayne Smith, fresh from high school, the quartet was complete. "We thought we made up the name 'Geezinslaw,'" Allred told the *Chicago Tribune's* Walter Olesky, "but then a reporter in Austin found a big family of cattle ranchers in Snook, Texas, named Giesenshag, and they pronounced their name Geezinslaw." To compound the lunacy, Sammy gave the others new first names: Smith became "Son," Deison was rechristened "Orville," and Rumsey, barefoot, clad in a striped T-shirt and scarecrow sombrero, playing a "bass" that was nothing more than a single string tied to a broom fastened to an upside-down washtub, was naturally called "Elvis."

"Their music has been described as a purely satirical blend of corn mash and vinegar," Linkletter tells us, and they go on to prove it with their twisted take on "Sweet, Sweet Home." When it ends, spokesman Allred assures the audience, "It is for our group a financial pleasure to be workin' here tonight on the *Hootenanny* show. Actually, for our group it's a pleasure to be workin' anywhere." Due to the vagaries of network scheduling, they'd be workin' the following week in a show taped six weeks after this one.

Following the cornpone humor of the Geezinslaws is the sketch comedy of Jerry Stiller and Anne Meara. The pair met as actors in the New York Shakespeare Festival, then went on to an off-Broadway comedy review, "Three Times Three" in 1956 with Charles Nelson Reilly. The two married that year and traded acting for stand-up comedy in 1962. Stiller wrote their material; what we're given here is a brief parody of TV commercials and an on-the-spot interview of a man on the California coast who'd been swallowed by a whale. Meara is the pretentious commentator, fiercely determined to get this exhausted and overtly Jewish man's story. When she asks his name, naturally it's Jonah. "Strange, ironic twist," she tells the viewing audience, "that this man sitting before us should bear the same name as one who long ago endured a similar fate!" The man is incredulous. "Somebody else this happened to here, before me? This is some place, this California…. They should rope it off!" The pair worked together and separately for nearly sixty years, remaining married up to Meara's 2015 passing.

In the jazz spot, Nina Simone accompanies herself on piano with "Israeli Chant," which doesn't appear on the surviving audio tape. Simone, born Eunice Waymon in North Carolina in 1933, was then on the cusp of a lengthy career as both soul stylist and civil rights activist. Always outspoken about racial matters, over the years Simone settled in and departed from various corners of the globe: from the U.S. to Barbados, to Liberia, to Switzerland, to the Netherlands, to France, where she died of breast cancer in 2003.

Before the Christies close out the final quarter hour, The Four Preps and Beverly Wright team up for "Their Hearts Were Full of Spring," written by jazz musician Bobby Troup and first released by Jimmie Rodgers as the flip side of his "Honeycomb" in 1957. But for the absence of an orchestra, the arrangement here would be a perfect fit for *The Lawrence Welk Show* that followed on ABC a few minutes later.

2-18: University of Tennessee, Knoxville #1

Recording Date: January 21, 1964.

Airdate: January 25, 1964. *Repeat*: August 8, 1964.

Video: Approximately 27 minutes from 16mm kinescope, mostly from the show's first half. Licensing: Historic Films Archive, LLC, #VM-236. Viewing: The Library of Congress, catalog # MAVIS 2899700. Excerpted on ***The Best of Hootenanny***.

Housed at University of North Carolina Libraries, Eugene Earle Collection: Digitized open-reel audiotape of the complete January 25 broadcast.

"Hootenanny Saturday Night" (*Everyone*) (*Jack Linkletter intro*)

The Serendipity Singers: "Fast Freight"

Joan Toliver: "The Flowers Are Forever Blooming"

The Geezinslaw Brothers: "Ain't Gonna Rain No More," "Cowboy Boots"

The GoldeBriars: "Saro Jane"

Doc Watson: "Deep River Blues"

Homer & Jethro: "Tennessee, Tennessee"

Pete Fountain: "Basin Street Blues"

Bill Monroe & the Bluegrass Boys: "Done Laid Around" (*Commercial bumper*)

The Cumberland Trio: "Ride Up"

Joan Toliver: "The West Wind"

The Serendipity Singers: "Mud," "Let Me Fly"

Homer & Jethro: "Jam-bowl-liar (Jambalaya)," "Sixteen Tons"

Bill Monroe & the Bluegrass Boys: "Uncle Pen"

Pete Fountain: "Old Gray Bonnet"

FINALE: "So Long, It's Been Good to Know You" (*Everyone*)

On December 12, the *Knoxville News-Sentinel* announced *Hootenanny* would be taping there on January 21 and 22. "Nine executives were here last weekend to begin preparations for the show

[that] will originate from the arena of the C.E. Brehm Animal Sciences Building on the U-T College of Agriculture campus…. Officials of the show expect to have the U-T arena floor covered with straw, with students sitting on the floor for a real homespun atmosphere."

This little bit of speculation about straw escalated into a series of rumors that led to a student protest. The *News-Sentinel* reported on January 14 that "several petitions were being circulated around the campus by a few U-T students today charging ABC television wants to create a 'hillbilly' image of U-T next week…. According to [the student newspaper] *The Orange and White*, the 'hillbilly' controversy came up when students heard that ABC wanted them to wear blue jeans, checked shirts, calico dresses and sit on bales of hay for the filming(*sic*)."

From day one at Syracuse University, *Hootenanny* had employed a student dress code that wasn't much more than "no jackets and ties or evening gowns." The show's format required the students to look casual (but not sloppy) and to dress as they would for classes; the only exceptions being the military academies where cadets and midshipmen wore dress uniforms. "A University spokesman… says ABC never planned to ask the students to wear any kind of 'hillbilly' clothes [and that] some students apparently heard rumors that ABC planned to do this and started the petition."

Although there was no attempt to turn the Animal Sciences arena into a makeshift barn, lineups for both tapings emphasized country music, including Grand Ole Opry veterans: Bill Monroe and the Bluegrass Boys on the first; Eddy Arnold and The Carter Family on the second. More troubling is that, Norman Keenan excepted, not a single black performer appears on either show, despite the University having desegregated three years earlier. Nearly all of the second show is on kinescope, while this one survives in full only on audiotape. The sole video for the broadcast, a grainy dupe, consists of the first half minus Joan Toliver's song and all sponsor references.

This broadcast had the distinction of showcasing two homegrown acts: one veteran, one brand new. The veteran act, Homer & Jethro, were known for their take-offs on hit songs that had crossed over from country to pop; two of their three performances here qualify. Henry "Homer"

Haynes Jr. and Kenneth "Jethro" Burns had been boyhood musical chums in Knoxville and entered radio there as adolescents in 1932, eventually progressing to WNOX's famous *Midday Merry-Go-Round* program. After seventeen years of proficient playing and straight singing on various country music shows, they decided to try parodies when their new label, RCA, asked for something different. Burns once explained their philosophy in selecting a hit record for satiric treatment: "Ideally, you look for a hit ballad, the prettier, the better. You wait 'til everybody gets pretty sick of it, then you give it what everybody's beginning to think it deserves."

The University of Tennessee's own Cumberland Trio. At far left, Jim Shuptrine plays bass while Jerre Haskew, Andy Gaverick and Tom Kilpatrick handle the vocals. *Photo courtesy of cumberlandtrio.com*

The newcomers were The Cumberland Trio, all current U-T students, and the prolonged ovation they received after Burns introduced them literally stopped the taping. Their leader, Jerre Haskew, was a senior at the university's law school; Andy Garverick and Tom Kilpatrick were juniors, with another junior, Jim Shuptrine, playing stand-up bass.

The group had won the National Collegiate Folk-Singing Contest in Jacksonville, Florida just one month earlier. Although they wrote original material, here they perform "Ride Up" with an arrangement that is note-for-note a precise copy of The Tarriers' version from last season's Rutgers appearance.

On the strength of a recommendation by Burns, RCA producer Chet Atkins made them an offer, which included the industry standard 2% royalty. An album's worth of tracks were recorded in Nashville. Then, a new label in New York City, Recording Industries Corporation (RIC), offered an unheard-of 10% royalty that the group eagerly accepted, especially since established artists Bobby Darin and Brenda Lee were on the roster as well. Another session was recorded, but RIC folded before anything could be released. Darin and Lee found other suitors; The Cumberland Trio did not, and they disbanded in 1965. Near the end of the decade, Haskew located one of RIC's founders and purchased the Nashville tapes for $100, but nothing else happened until November 2001, when the three, sans Shuptrine, reunited for a concert to benefit U-T's School of Music Scholarship Fund. The group continued performing locally for a few years, and today Haskew runs a website, *cumberlandtrio.com*, in tribute and from which their CDs may be purchased. The site includes Haskew's memories of the *Hootenanny* experience that is worth a read.

When it came to Bluegrass music, Kentucky's Bill Monroe was the originator, which is why the genre was named after his band. He debuted on the Opry in 1939 and stopped the show with his high-energy spin on the country string band sound; here he does his own "Uncle Pen," which became a big hit for Monroe disciple Ricky Skaggs in 1984. Although various Bluegrass Boys, including Flatt & Scruggs, came and went over the years, Monroe's music remained constant, and after hosting so many that followed in his footsteps, it's nice to know *Hootenanny* also made room for the trailblazer.

We may recall that, back in the spring of '63, Pete Seeger wrote Doc Watson "will not stand a chance of being considered" for *Hootenanny*. Of course, at the time Watson was just developing a reputation outside of his home state of North Carolina; ten months later, he'd been signed to

Vanguard Records and touring extensively after a groundbreaking appearance at the Newport Folk Festival in July. An eye infection at age one cost him his sight, and he learned his first guitar chords at the North Carolina Morehead School for the Blind in Raleigh. The song he sings here, "Deep River Blues," was his own composition. Watson's career, boosted by his contributions to The Nitty Gritty Dirt Band's 1972 three-disc tribute to vintage country music, *Will The Circle Be Unbroken*, continued up to his 2012 passing from complications after abdominal surgery at age 89.

Joan Toliver when managed by Fred Weintraub and still seeking "my own style." *From the author's collection*

The Geezinslaw Brothers return with more countrified comedy of a type that makes Homer & Jethro look austere. Somewhere between 1964-66, Mickey "Elvis" Rumsey and Johnny "Orville" Deison departed, leaving Sammy Allred and Dewayne "Son" Smith as the crux of the act, which was later renamed simply "The Geezinslaws." The pair signed with Capitol Records and recorded four albums up to 1969. They remained semi-active from the 1970s to 2005, making three appearances on their hometown's music showcase for PBS, *Austin City Limits*, as well as occasional visits to The Nashville Network. In between gigs, Allred worked on-air for radio station KVET in Austin. He died in 2018; Smith passed away the following year.

Kentucky native Joan Toliver debuts as a songwriter with "The Flowers Are Forever Blooming." Its structure is 16-bar blues and she puts heart and soul into her vocal. Despite the simple guitar and bass accompaniment, Toliver was veering away from traditional songs and arrangements. "Folk dancing and singing were part of my heritage that I rebelled against," she told the *Louisville Courier-Journal* that year, freely admitting she was "still searching for my own style and kind of music."

Lest the lineup lean too far south for average viewers, four Minnesotans, The GoldeBriars, make their first TV appearance. The quartet consisted of Curt Boettcher, age 20, and Ron Neilson, 17, on guitar, and sisters Sheri (20) and Dotti (18) Holmberg. They'd formed in early 1963 and had only recently progressed from playing private parties to nightclub appearances, with a recording session for Epic in between. Boettcher and Neilson, clad in black turtleneck sweaters and with hair just beginning to fringe upon their foreheads, were ahead of the curve in fashion. Their arrangement of "Saro Jane" is also modern, with Neilson infusing a danceable rhythm to the old sea chanty as Boettcher and the Holmberg sisters vocalize. The group ultimately recorded three albums; only two were released and they disbanded in 1966. Boettcher remained in the music business, producing and arranging for The Association and Tommy Roe, among others, dying in 1987 while hospitalized for a lung infection. Dotti Holmberg-Waddell tells the GoldeBriars' story in a digital book based on a diary she kept during her years with the group; it can be ordered at *thegoldebriars.com*.

News-Sentinel reporter Kaye Franklin Veal attended the taping and assured readers, "From the first lines of the theme song… an audience of over 3,000 students, faculty members and off-campus persons sat dazzled, enraptured, and entertained. A little over an hour-and-a-half later, with the music of the final song, 'So Long, It's Been Good to Know You,' still rattling the rafters in the minds of many, a most delighted audience went home, sorry that it was over."

As for home viewers, this was the final Saturday night for Gallup & Robinson's TPT survey and the results are dismal, especially among female viewers. Between 7:30 and 8:00 PM, 231 women were tuned to *The Jackie Gleason Show*, 123 to *The Lieutenant* and a mere 87 to *Hootenanny*. At eight o'clock, ten women switched off or away, three opting for *Gleason*, and 13 tuned in the *Hoot*, including three from *Gleason*. The second half hour came in with *Gleason* at 234, *Lieutenant* at 129 and *Hoot* at 90.

Among males, 235 were watching *Gleason* at 7:30 PM, with 127 tuned to *Lieutenant*, and 100 watching *Hoot*. Eight viewers dropped *Hootenanny's* second half, with six of these going to *Gleason*, while 20 men tuned in, including three from *Gleason* and two from *Lieutenant*. The second half-hour finished with 250 for *Gleason*, *Lieutenant* holding steady with 127 and 112 watching *Hootenanny*.

With a sample size of 1,400 viewers, no more than 202, or 14%, were tuned to the show at any one time, down from 19% in mid-November. It looked like audiences were growing weary of the mixed bag *Hootenanny* had become.

2-19: United States Naval Academy, Annapolis MD #2

Recording Date: September 20, 1963.

Airdate: February 1, 1964 (*postponed from November 23, 1963*). *Repeat*: September 12, 1964.

The Chad Mitchell Trio and Glenn Yarbrough: "Hootenanny Saturday Night" (*Jack Linkletter intro*)

The Chad Mitchell Trio: "Hello, Susan Brown"

Grier Reynolds: "Those Were Other Years"

Flatt & Scruggs: "Yonder Stands Little Maggie"

Valentine Pringle: "Battle Hymn of the Republic"

Glenn Yarbrough: "Come Along Mary"

Judy Henske: "Lily Langtree" (*w/Stan Rubin & His Tigertown Five*)

The Chad Mitchell Trio: "School Song," "Ain't No More Cane on This Brazos"

Glenn Yarbrough: "Deep Blue Sea" (commercial bumper)

The Anchormen: "I'm the Man That Built the Bridges"

Charlie Manna: Stand-up comedy

Stan Rubin & His Tigertown Five: "The World is Waiting For the Sunrise"

Grier Reynolds and Glenn Yarbrough: "Where Does It Lead?"

SONGS OF THE SEA MEDLEY: "Waves on the Sea" (*Flatt & Scruggs*), "Eddystone Light" (*The Anchormen*), "Whup Jamboree" (*The Chad Mitchell Trio*)

The Chad Mitchell Trio: "Blowin' in the Wind"

FINALE: "Saro Jane" (*Everyone*)

After a two-plus month delay, the fifth of the hour-long shows aired. It's the old format, with Glenn Yarbrough and The Chad Mitchell Trio belting out the theme song, no one seated behind the performers, and Jack Linkletter introducing everybody. Possibly a few viewers thought the show had gone into reruns already, or else that the producers were suffering from schizophrenia.

The Chad Mitchell Trio are given the most to do, although not as much as in their true final appearance last December. But among their selections are two topical numbers: Tom Paxton's "What Did You Learn in School Today" (introduced by a working title, "The School Song"), which by now had appeared on the *Reflecting* album, and Dylan's "Blowin' in the Wind," a song they'd recorded and released ahead of Peter, Paul & Mary, and which might've scored the hit if their label at the time, Kapp, had put some marketing muscle behind it. It's interesting to hear the midshipmen at a military academy sing along to a musical call for war to be "forever banned."

Later in the year, Mitchell served notice he'd be leaving, and the group became simply The Mitchell Trio. After recording two more albums together, he departed in July 1965 and signed with Warner Bros. as a solo act. Mike Kobluk, Joe Frazier and their arranger Milt Okun auditioned for a replacement, choosing a singer-musician from Texas named John Denver, who'd been gigging at Randy Sparks' Ledbetter's club, among others. With Denver, the group released two more albums for Mercury. In 1967, Frazier left, was replaced with David Boise, and did one final album for Reprise. The following year, Kobluk resigned, replaced by Michael Johnson. At that point, with all original members gone, The Mitchell Trio became Denver, Boise & Johnson, and lasted another year before Denver went out on his own and, under Okun's guidance, became a superstar.

In January 1986, Mitchell, Kobluk and Frazier reunited for a surprise appearance on behalf of Washington D.C.'s World Folk Music Association (WFMA). The following year, they did a PBS special, *The Chad Mitchell Trio Reunion*, hosted by Denver, who took the stage for two songs, including the finale, "Last Night I Had the Strangest Dream" (for which they briefly became The Chad Mitchell Quartet). After that, the threesome reunited periodically for one-off concerts and performances for the WFMA until retiring for good in 2014, shortly after Frazier's passing that year.

Although they joked in these latter appearances how they were finally acceptable to folk purists because their topical material had become "songs of antiquity," the fact is The Chad Mitchell Trio were always respected by the music's old guard. Mitchell may have assumed they were disdained for making *Hootenanny* appearances, but an invitation to the 1964 Newport Folk Festival disabused anyone of that notion. Their satiric songs were often banned from radio and TV, yet they refused to compromise. Luckily for the millions watching, *Hootenanny* occasionally gave them a stage for, as one of their finest albums put it, "singing our minds."

Grier Reynolds performs her own composition, "But Those Were Other Years," and later she and Glenn Yarbrough collaborate tenderly on "Where Does it Lead?" originally written by Gwen Davis and recorded in 1960 by Miriam Makeba. By the time the show reached air, she'd divorced Jake Holmes, entrusted her future to Bill Cosby's manager Roy Silver, ditched the beehive hairdo and her ex-husband's middle name and, as Kay Reynolds, embarked on a career of writing, singing, coaching other singers, performing in the Broadway and motion picture versions of *How To Succeed In Business Without Really Trying*, and acting on the side. "I'm not a folk singer, really," she told *Wilmington News* reporter Gloria Galloway in June 1964. "I hate sopranos who sing nothing but sweet folk songs. You need 'up' numbers as well as slow, and it's hard to find 'up' soprano numbers in folk music."

Flatt & Scruggs, last seen early on during season one, make a welcome return with "Yonder Stands Little Maggie." They're followed by Valentine Pringle, another Harry Belafonte discovery whose debut album, *I Hear America Singing*, had just been released the month before taping. With a voice favorably compared to that of Paul Robeson, Pringle gives a memorable performance of "Battle Hymn of the Republic." Before his life ended tragically, he'd added songwriter, actor and playwright to his resumé. On December 13, 1999, Pringle was stabbed to death by burglars who'd broken into his home in Lesotho, South Africa.

Yarbrough sings "Come Along, Mary," a 'repeat after me' tune that had been around for over a century, although with verses likely modified for the "Hootenanny USA." tour he'd been on at the time ("Come along, Mary, to the hootenanny"). About halfway through, he announces they're going to whistle a verse, and the audience follows his lead. At one point, he does a fancy trill; when the midshipmen match him perfectly, it causes him to break up. When he's finished, Linkletter tells us, "You've seen him on our show many times with The Limeliters. This marks his debut on our show as a solo." Well, no it's not, but that isn't Linkletter's fault, because this show was taped the day before the one that aired last October.

"One of our favorite experiments on *Hootenanny* is when we blend different styles of artists who've never worked before together." With that awkward introduction, Linkletter gives way to Judy Henske accompanied by Stan Rubin & His Tigertown Five and a Dixieland-infused rendition of "Lily Langtree." Rubin and his combo have it all over the staid orchestral arrangement on Henske's debut album; the performance here sets the audience ablaze with joy. Although she'd told Linda Solomon she'd signed for four appearances this season, this was her final *Hoot*. Except for a hiatus to raise her daughter, Henske remained active almost up to her passing at age 85 in April 2022.

The first true collegiate group to appear on the show, The Anchormen were a trio of midshipmen at Annapolis: guitarists Larry Benson and Bob Lawrence and banjoist Connie Lautenbacher, and backed by Wayne Arny on bass. They sing the second Tom Paxton composition of the evening, "I'm The Man That Built the Bridges" and get to participate in the multi-artist medley later in the show.

For those who may have wondered what midshipmen of 1963 might have done upon graduation, Benson gave *TVParty.com* a brief rundown: Lawrence "went off to submarine and nuclear power school while taking flying lessons, served in the Submarine Service for five years and [became] a pilot for United." Lautenbacher "got a Master's and PhD at Harvard in applied mathematics, drove many surface ships around the oceans, ran the Navy's money for something close to 15 years" and retired at the rank of Vice Admiral. Benson "drove destroyers around the Atlantic, Caribbean, Mediterranean, skippered a Swift boat in Vietnam, directed the Navy's Leadership School, and [served as] Special Consultant to the Surgeon General for 16 years as a Naval Reservist." Arny "flew Navy fighters for many years, was a test pilot, acted as counsel to the Senate Armed Services Committee for several years, then

Assistant Director of the Office of Budget and Management" before becoming a freelance management consultant in Washington DC.

The creative and very funny Charlie Manna. *From the author's collection*

Comedian Charlie Manna appears for the third time, but this was actually his *Hootenanny* debut. He does another routine that had appeared on *Manna Overboard* about the workings of the human body, which he begins with a marvelous one-liner: "I'd like to talk this evening about a subject that's very close to your hearts: blood." Linkletter's intro tells us how Manna had studied opera, which he did for six years. Then "he went into the Army instead [and] got so many laughs from his Signal Corps buddies, that he switched from opera to comedy." The laughs are tremendous here, thanks to such lines as "It's amazing what a marvelous mechanism the human body is. If you took a man's veins, capillaries, arteries and laid them end-to-end, that man would die."

After his duet with Grier Reynolds, Yarbrough introduces the multi-artist medley with this: "I just returned recently from an extended sail trip across the Pacific ocean. And I get asked many times by friends what it's like out there on a 40-foot sailboat. And it's kind of hard to explain to landlubbers what it means to be in a gale-force wind or on waves that seem to be as high as mountains. But, Flatt & Scruggs here, and The Anchormen and The Chad Mitchell Trio have put together a group of folk songs that tell eloquently of the excitement and the danger that is faced by those who spend their lives on the rolling sea." In truth, the subsequent medley captures very little of that, and almost goes off the rails when The Anchormen add a rockabilly beat to "Eddystone Light." Yarbrough would do much more sailing, with a few more close calls, in years to come, even after periodically reuniting with The Limeliters between 1973-82. He passed away at age 86 in 2016, twenty years after Lou Gottlieb's death at 72 and ten years after Alex Hassilev retired from performing.

Everything but the show's finale exists on a substandard quality audio tape in the author's collection.

2-20: University of Florida, Gainesville #2

Recording Date: January 8, 1964.

Airdate: February 8, 1964. *Repeat*: June 20, 1964.

Video: 16mm kinescope of the repeat broadcast. Licensing: Historic Films Archive, LLC, #V-1009. Viewing: The Library of Congress, catalog # MAVIS 2899695. Excerpted on ***The Best of Hootenanny***.

"Hootenanny Saturday Night" (*Everyone*) (*Jack Linkletter intro*)

The Tarriers: "Pick A Bale O' Cotton," "Poor Lazarus"

Joan Meyers: "All the Pretty Little Horses"

Jimmie Rodgers: "Wayfarin' Stranger," "Midnight Special"

Josh White Jr.: "Delia's Gone"

Beverly White: "Maid of Constant Sorrow"

Hoyt Axton: "One More Round" & "Trombone Charlie"

Joan Meyers: "Twelve Gates to the City" (commercial bumper)

Bob Gibson: "Good News"

Jackie Vernon: Stand-up comedy

The Tarriers: "Rawhide" (Bluegrass instrumental)

Bob Gibson and Josh White Jr.: "Betty and Dupree"

The Tarriers: "Wimoweh"

FINALE: "Marching to Pretoria" (*Everyone*)

The Further Perils of Jack Linkletter: Shortly after welcoming us to this week's college, we see he's standing behind a very, very large alligator. "This is Albert the First," he tells us, "and he's the mascot of the University of Florida. It's this good fellow who gave the football team its nickname, 'the Fighting Gators.'" Throughout, the creature is completely immobile. "He's not fighting too much, is he? I threaten him; he's kind of peaceful," says the undoubtedly relieved host. A photo in the University's student paper, *The Alligator*, shows Albert tussling with a handler positioning him on the campus Plaza of Americas where the sequence was shot; it's easy to suspect a sedative was employed. Two years earlier, Albert had been retired and sent to Ross Allen's Reptile Ranch in Ocala to live out his days. According to *The Alligator*, the shoot took only "a few minutes before handlers put him back in the truck for his journey back home."

As with Salem College, sponsor influence had a hand in the choice of this locale: the Florida Citrus Commission had purchased time on the series to plug "fresh, frozen, Florida orange juice… the real thing, from Florida!" The *Tampa Tribune* reported, "On hand [for the taping], in addition to members of the commission, will be the Campbell-Ewald Advertising Agency which handles the account."

With this show, The Tarriers—Marshall Brickman, Clarence Cooper, Eric Weissburg—make their final *Hootenanny* appearance. *From the author's collection*

The Tarriers open the show and, this being the new format, they do two numbers: "Pick a Bale O' Cotton" from their newest album *Gather 'Round* and "Poor Lazurus," another superb showcase for Clarence Cooper. Marshall Brickman introduces Joan Meyers: born in Brooklyn, NY, graduate of Brooklyn College, anthropology major, licensed teacher, folksinger. Her show business career lasted less than a decade and ended mysteriously. She was part of "The American Hootenanny Festival" the previous summer, and recorded sporadically but her career never took off, even after switching from folk to pop standards. In June 1967, presumably influenced by a devotion to astrology, she changed her professional name to Taro Delphi, made a few more records, worked the nightclub circuit until 1970, then suddenly disappeared from the public eye. Her subsequent life and present whereabouts are unknown.

Jimmie Rodgers, minus The Fairmont Singers but including their bassist and a jazz guitarist, croons the traditional "Wayfaring Stranger," followed by Leadbelly's "Midnight Special." Rodgers' career continued in this vein; in November 1967, he was quoted: "I consider myself a folksinger. It's the kind of music I like best and always have." On December 1 of that year, he was pulled over on a Los Angeles freeway for erratic driving. What happened next has never been resolved: a police officer at the scene stated Rodgers fell and struck his head. The officer and two others helped him back into his car and departed; he was later discovered by a worried friend. Rodgers, although he had no memory of it, contended he was beaten by the officers and left to die. He required three surgeries before he was able to resume his career. Lawsuits were filed on both sides; in the end, the three policemen were suspended for two weeks for leaving Rodgers without first radioing for an ambulance, and the city settled with him out of court for $200,000. Rodgers continued entertaining in clubs and on television into the 2010s. He died of kidney disease in December 2021.

Josh White, Jr. is seated behind Rodgers and can be seen singing along to "Midnight Special" and cheerfully applauding at its end. Only 23, White was just beginning to seek his way in music. Being Josh White's son, "opened some doors," he admitted in 1972, "but once the doors are opened, you have to make it on your own." He leads the students in the refrain of "Delia's Gone" before introducing his older sister, Beverly, who sings "Maid of Constant Sorrow." Brother and sister had appeared on stages with their father since 1950. Beverly would retire from performing within a year of this broadcast, while Josh Jr., like his dad, continued singing and acting. As would any son of a legend, he sought his own identity as a performer ("He found his songs and I have to find mine"), but in 1984, he portrayed his father in a one-man show,

Josh: The Man and His Music. From that point until the present day, he has mixed the best of his dad's material into his repertoire.

The brawny, bluesy Oklahoman, Hoyt Axton, begins his second *Hoot* appearance with "One More Round." Penned by Art Podell and his then-writing partner Walter Schorr in 1962, the song begins with the birth of Christ and wraps God's love for humankind into a message of hope for its future. Axton follows this with a tune originally recorded by Bessie Smith in 1927, "Trombone Charlie," with a growling vocal that must have given his throat a workout. The commercial bumper gives us Joan Meyers' "Twelve Gates to the City" outdoors, surrounded by the same students that enjoyed The Coventry Singers' open-air performance in the previous U-FL show.

When we return, Bob Gibson leads the audience in "Good News," which he'd done on his first *Hootenanny* appearance. He divides the room in half for the refrain's two parts, and the camera uses a split-screen effect to show them singing each part simultaneously. Meanwhile, he sings a third part "which may confuse you. It's from another song." Later in the program, he and Josh Jr. turn in a fantastic duet on "Betty and Dupree."

In 1955, a Bronx, New York, native named Ralph Verrone had just given up music to try for a stand-up career, only to bomb in a small San Francisco club. That night, "I went to the bar, ordered a double bourbon, and while I was contemplating what new business to go into, Danny Kaye approached me and said the five words that changed my life… 'Kid, where's the men's room?'" In truth, Kaye offered some encouragement, but Varrone, who soon changed his name to Jackie Vernon, still faced some lean years. "In the beginning, I was loud and raucous, the way everybody thought a comedian should be," he said in 1978, "but I was never comfortable with that. It just wasn't *me*. So later, in the '60s, I started taking it easy." That turned the trick. His first big TV break was on Steve Allen's syndicated series for Westinghouse Broadcasting, which led to bookings with Ed Sullivan and *The Tonight Show*. He does here his by-then famous "slide show" routine, narrating a series of vacation photos that are merely implied by the clicker he uses. At the finish, he says, "I'd like to thank the producer of this show, Mister Nanny… for having me back," which may have puzzled regular viewers. This was his first *Hootenanny* to air, while his debut on the series was set to broadcast two weeks from now.

Jackie Vernon: "To look at me, you'd never believe that I used to be a dull guy." To see him perform was to believe he was never dull. *Photo courtesy of Steve Massa*

The Tarriers close out the show by teaching the students various parts on "Wimoweh" and rehearsing them briefly before playing the song. It's not a *bad* performance, but after the "Good News" sing-along, it seems unnecessarily redundant, while the song pales in comparison to the daring and dynamic "Mbube" that Miriam Makeba and The Chad Mitchell Trio had given us in season one. Sadly, *Hootenanny* would never again be so daring *or* dynamic.

2-21: Dartmouth College, Hanover NH #1

Recording Date: February 4, 1964.

Airdate: February 15, 1964. *Repeat*: May 30, 1964.

Video: 16mm kinescope of the repeat broadcast. Licensing: Historic Films Archive, LLC, #V-1014. Viewing: The Library of Congress, catalog # MAVIS 2899696. Excerpted on ***The Best of Hootenanny***.

"Hootenanny Saturday Night" (*Everyone*) (*Jack Linkletter intro*)

The Serendipity Singers: "Sing Out"

Orriel Smith: "The First Time Ever I Saw Your Face"

Mike Settle: "Hey, Li-Lee, Li-Lee"

Herbie Mann & His Sextet: "Harlem Nocturne"

The Lionel Shepherd Mime Troupe: Pantomime routines

The Phoenix Singers: "Didn't it Rain," "Lovely Choucoune"

Mike Settle: "Haul Away, Joe" (commercial bumper)

The Brandywine Singers: "Columbus Stockade Blues/Kentucky Means Paradise," "Mandy"

Jerry Shane: Stand-up comedy

Herbie Mann & His Sextet: "Down By the Riverside"

Orriel Smith and Mike Settle: "Paul and Silas"

The Serendipity Singers: "Sailing Away," "Six-Foot-Six"

FINALE: "The Music Train" (*Everyone*)

According to some newspaper columns from late 1963, *Hootenanny* was scheduled to go to Tulane University in New Orleans during the week of Mardi Gras (February 10-14). For reasons lost to time, the appearance fell through; instead of balmy Louisiana, the team wound up in snowy New Hampshire for Dartmouth College's annual Winter Carnival.

The format for this broadcast is an odd hybrid. Only the performing act is seen on stage, as of old. For the first time, the show begins with Jack Linkletter there, addressing the audience like a typical variety show host: "And now, here's *Hootenanny's* swinging folk singing group, The Serendipity Singers!" Already on stage, the nonet launches into the swiftly-paced "Sing Out;" once it's over, eight-ninths of them exit and the show returns to its then-standard pattern as Brooks Hatch introduces eighteen-year-old Orriel Smith.

Opera singer-turned-folk singer-turned-opera singer Orriel Smith. *From the author's collection*

An operatic prodigy from Sherman Oaks, California, who switched to folk after hearing Jean Ritchie perform at a summer music camp, Smith had been performing classical pieces since age six. "I love singing opera most of all, but there are limitations in that field," she told Maria Metlova of Van Nuys' *Valley News* some years later. "I feel I want to do everything well." She taught herself guitar by playing Joan Baez records at half-speed, tuning the instrument down as well, and working out the fingering. Performing at Greenwich Village hoots in 1963 led to discovery, which led to a *Tonight Show* appearance, which led to a Columbia Records audition for which she chose Ewan MacColl's "The First Time Ever I Saw Your Face," presumably performing it as she does here. The label signed her and soon released an album, *A Voice in the Wind*.

Smith performed in various small clubs at least into 1975, then gave it up to join The Ray Conniff Singers on a tour of Japan. Later she would back Dolly Parton on a U.S./Canada tour and Charo in Las Vegas, before returning to her first love, opera, in 2002 with an unusual CD project: *Cluckoratura Arias*, which became something of a guilty pleasure among those who love the genre. In May 2007, she told *Terrascope Online*, "I was rehearsing some music with my teacher, Jill Goodsell, when I noted that they don't seem to teach agility and vocal gymnastics much anymore.... I was saying to her that it was a shame and that 'staccato' to a lot of people might as well be a chicken clucking, so I started clucking away. I thought 'Why not?' They say to 'do what you love.' I love the *arias*, being silly, and making animal sounds...so why not do them all at once?"

Mike Settle introduces himself and the song "Hey, Li Lee," inviting the audience to join in. After going through the refrain, he begins with an original verse that lampoons both the college's Carnival poster, which that year depicted a downhill skier, and a famous watch advertisement:

> *Your Carnival poster cannot miss, (Hey, Li Lee, Li Lee Lo)*
>
> *It was tested by the Swiss (Hey, Li Lee, Li Lee Lo)*

In keeping with the spirit, students contribute verses, as Linkletter roves through the crowd with his hand-held mic, which results in such couplets as:

> *Fee-Fi-Fo-Fum,*
>
> *I think I smell a Harvard bum*

Settle introduces Herbie Mann & His Sextet, telling us the flautist has "a composition that merges jazz with the American folk influence." The former Herbert Solomon was born in Brooklyn in 1930, and began playing professionally at Catskill Mountain resorts at age fourteen. Originally a saxophonist, he was persuaded to try the flute for a recording session, and consequently became the instrument's leading jazz musician. He formed his own band in the late 1950s and ensured it included Afro-Cuban percussionists. In 1961, he traveled to Brazil where he forged "his intriguing blend of African and Latin rhythms into American jazz," as Settle describes it. A few critics resented his success, which he understood: "I play Brazilian music, but I'm not Brazilian. I play jazz, but I'm not African-American. I'm an Eastern European Jew." Maybe so, but his recordings and concerts were among the most popular jazz works in the nation, and such success couldn't be derided. Mann worked almost literally to his dying day, succumbing to inoperable prostate cancer at age 73 in 2003.

When we return from the commercial break, Linkletter is back on stage to introduce The Lionel Shepherd Mime Troupe. Unquestionably the oddest act to ever appear on *Hootenanny*, Shepherd uses percussion and discords from a muted trumpet, plus narration, to accompany what is basically a typical performance in the Marcel Marceau vein. And yet, a *London Evening Standard* correspondent named Jean Campbell caught his act at a tiny Manhattan venue in early 1963 and was moved to label it "a masterpiece that leaves anything I have seen in the theatre far behind. The giants like Brecht and Genet seem like the mutterings of a broken gramophone record after the impact of this new form of theatre." Shepherd's goal, in his words was "reaching towards the nobleness inherent in man's nature rather than in futility and degradation." After this appearance, however, he seems to have vanished into obscurity and should not be confused with his far more prolific contemporary Richmond Shepard.

Again from the stage Linkletter brings on The Phoenix Singers, not seen since week three of season one, although this was actually their second performance for season two thanks to ABC's scattershot scheduling. Back in November, they'd appeared at Fordham; that show would be airing next week. They were also booked for the second Dartmouth show, set to air on March 21. Here, their highly-charged spiritual "Didn't It Rain?" is nicely balanced by a Haitian ballad, "Lovely Choucoune," which, as Linkletter pointed out, had already been Americanized as "Yellow Bird."

As Mike Settle and the students hoot the sea chanty "Haul Away, Joe" during the commercial bumper, the cameras take us outside to televise the snow sculptures created by students for the Carnival. When we return, Linkletter's back on stage introducing The Brandywine Singers, who begin with an odd medley of the traditional "Columbus Stockade Blues" and Merle Travis' "Kentucky Means Paradise." What one has to do with the other is a puzzle left for musicologists to discern. More impressive is their own composition "Mandy," a tragic ballad with simple lyrics and a lilting melody. Joy Records released the tune on a single that April but it failed to place on a chart now swamped with British acts. Curiously, the flip side of "Mandy" was "Two Little Boys," a song written in 1902 about two brothers who play at soldiering as children and become the real thing as adults. It also went nowhere chart-wise, but five years later Rolf Harris would have the biggest seller of his career with it, and Joy would attempt to capitalize by licensing the Brandywines' 1964 recording to U.K. and Australian labels.

By then, Craig, Corbett and Brown had moved on with their lives. Ron and Rick Shaw remained in the music business and, in true modern folk tradition, made their biggest splash with a Coca-Cola commercial as members of The Hillside Singers, a group formed by Al Ham who was then a freelance producer. With lyrics slightly rewritten by Ham, "I'd Like To Teach The World To Sing" went to #13 on the Hot 100 in 1971, eventually earning a gold record. The ad-hoc conglomeration was never able to duplicate that success and parted ways about a year later, after which the twins became a duo, The Shaw Brothers, and performed regularly for several years, often as an opener for some of their better-known folk brethren and occasionally for functions held in their home state of New Hampshire. Ron Shaw died there in 2018; brother Rick followed in 2021.

Linkletter tells the audience Jerry Shane "is part of the new breed of satiric commentators that find their fun fooling around with the topics of the day." "New breed" or not, Shane got his start in a very "old breed" way: at a Catskills hotel. Although it takes him a minute or so to warm up, he wins over the students with his take on planned obsolescence, especially where the automobile is concerned. The crux of his routine centers on an assembly line manager speaking to the big boss on the phone: "Yeah, we got all the parts installed this morning. When do you want 'em to break down?" Described by his agent as "a little like Alan King, a little like Joey Bishop," Shane lacked anything distinctly his own and consequently was lost amongst a sea of more interesting "new breed" comedians. He earned extra money as a monologue writer when Bishop would sub for Johnny Carson; otherwise, he'd perform at various niteries and was most often seen on Merv Griffin's talk show. *Hootenanny* was far from the only place this lifelong New Yorker told automobile jokes; ironically, on January 19, 1974, he died at age 43 while driving to his Roslyn Heights home from an engagement in Lancaster, Pennsylvania, when his car hit a patch of ice and skidded into an oncoming tractor-trailer.

Herbie Mann and his combo return with a swinging take on "Down By the Riverside" while the students heartily clap along. After that, the fourth quarter-hour begins with Mike Settle and Orriel Smith seated outside the campus and dueting on "Paul and Silas." Smith's range is such that she has no difficulty carrying the melody and harmonizing with Settle, and the result is a joyful pairing, a highlight for what has otherwise been a lackluster show.

To close out, Linkletter brings on The Serendipity Singers for "Sailing Away," from their newly-released debut album, and "Six Foot Six," which would appear on their second album a few months later. The finale, "Music Train," was from The Phoenix Singers' repertoire, so it's fitting they're front and center and take the first verse.

Seeing Linkletter as a traditional emcee for three-quarters of the program feels odd, and there's no one surviving who'd know the thinking behind it. Was the genial host weary of having been marginalized? Was this the "pilot" for a format change ABC was considering for next season? Did one of the sponsors insist? Were there technical reasons behind the decision? Take your pick. Since this is the only known survivor of the Dartmouth pair, we have no clue if it continued for the second. The one existing show recorded after Dartmouth is the season's 27th episode, taped at Purdue University; in that, Linkletter's back to making the occasional quiet introduction while stationed among the audience.

2-22: Fordham University, Bronx NY #2

Recording Date: November 13, 1963.

Airdate: February 22, 1964. *Repeat*: May 23, 1964.

Video: 16mm kinescope of the repeat broadcast, housed in a private collection.

"Hootenanny Saturday Night" (*Everyone*) (*Jack Linkletter intro*)

The New Christy Minstrels: "Rovin' Gambler"

Naomi Brossart: "Turn Around"

Will Holt: "Lemon Tree"

The Phoenix Singers: "By and By/When the Morning Comes"

Rolf Harris: "Tie Me Kangaroo Down, Sport," "Wild Colonial Boy"

The New Christy Minstrels: "Go Tell it on the Mountain," "Billy's Mule," "Mighty Mississippi"

Will Holt: "Maid in Amsterdam" (commercial bumper)

The Phoenix Singers: "Little Rosie"

Jackie Vernon: Stand-up comedy

The Even Dozen Jug Band: "Log Cabin Blues"

DIFFERENT VERSIONS MEDLEY: "Waltzing Matilda" (*Rolf Harris, Will Holt, The Phoenix Singers*)

The New Christy Minstrels: "Big Rock Candy Mountain," "Muddy Road to Freedom"

FINALE: "One More River" (*Everyone*)

The planned airdate for this one was January 4. There's nothing on record explaining why it was delayed for so long, unless it was because ABC wanted The New Christy Minstrels to continue appearing monthly and they already had the first Salem show queued up for that month, with the second to follow in March. Or perhaps it had to do with the appearance of a prominent participant from the now-discontinued *First Family* record.

As mentioned earlier, Naomi Brossart portrayed the First Lady for that smash comedy LP. In a 2006 email to the author, Ms. Brossart had some clear memories of that, and how and why she came to do this show: "In 1962 I was a struggling young actress in New York. In June, I auditioned to do the voice of Jackie Kennedy on *The First Family* album. I was thrilled when I got the job, (and so was my landlord). The success of the album opened many doors, and one of those doors was the *Hootenanny* show. My agent told me she could get me an audition on the show, if I could sing. I wasn't a singer, but my eye was fixed, as it usually was in those days, on next month's rent.

"Instead of being thrilled when I got the *Hootenanny* job, I was scared to death. I had never sung a note professionally, and I was going to perform alongside some of the best folk singers in America? What could I have been thinking? What professional singers have in common is that they've worked at it long enough to know their own voices. So, when I found myself wondering what voice I was going to use, it was a little disquieting. I decided I'd be safer singing bel canto than full voice. The next thing I knew, my accompanist was playing the intro, and I was on. Out came a voice that was a cross between Jackie Kennedy's and my own. But it got me through, and taught me to be a little careful about saying 'I can do that.'"

Will Holt took a few days off from *The World of Kurt Weill in Song* to appear and reprise his most enduring composition, but before long the theater would fully absorb his professional life. During the 1970s, he wrote lyrics for the hit show *The Me Nobody Knows*, then the book for *Over Here!*, the 1974 musical that starred the surviving Andrews Sisters, Patty and Maxine. The following year, in collaboration with actress/singer Linda Hopkins, he wrote *Me and Bessie*, a show about blues singer Bessie Smith for which Hopkins played the lead and ran for over 450 performances. Later shows were not as high profile but kept Holt busy well into the 21st century. Nevertheless, upon his 2015 passing from complications of Alzheimer's disease, the obituary notices headlined him as "Writer of 'Lemon Tree.'"

Rolf Harris of Perth, Australia, wrote "Tie Me Kangaroo Down, Sport" in 1958. He recorded it two years later where it became a became a best seller in both his homeland and neighboring New Zealand. Under the guidance of producer George Martin, he re-recorded it in 1963 in England; picked up by Epic for the U.S. market, it went to #3 on the Hot 100, which is why everyone in Fordham's Campus Center ballroom knows the lyrics. His second number is the Australian interpretation of "The Wild Colonial Boy." This also goes over well, although the predominantly Catholic student body indicates at the start they're more familiar with the Irish version.

Over the years, Harris became a national treasure in Australia and the U.K., hosting several television shows in each, and honored multiple times, including Member of the Order of the British Empire (later, he was advanced to Officer and later still to Commander) and Member (later Officer) of the Order of Australia. He received honorary doctorates from the University of East London and Liverpool Hope University. In 2008, he was inducted into the Australian Recording Industry Association's Hall of Fame; three years later he was named "Best Selling Published Artist" by the Fine Art Trade Guild.

All of these were stripped away after Harris was convicted in July 2014 of twelve counts of indecent assault on four female victims, some of whom were minors and which dated as far back as 1968. Harris pleaded Not Guilty, staunchly maintained his innocence throughout, and tried to appeal his conviction in October but was rebuffed. He was sentenced to five years, nine months' imprisonment and such was his fall from popularity that accusations of leniency were directed to the Attorney General. In 2016, seven additional charges, mostly of "unwanted groping," were lodged after additional victims came forward. Harris appeared via video from Stafford Prison and again disputed all charges. He was acquitted of three, and a retrial for the remainder resulted in a hung jury. He was released on license (the British version of parole) in May 2017 after serving half his sentence; in November of that year, one of the twelve charges was overturned as a miscarriage of justice. He applied for overturning of the remaining charges, but again the Court of Appeal dismissed it. Reportedly in ill health, Harris has kept an understandably low profile in the years since.

Rolf Harris rehearses "The Wild Colonial Boy." *From the author's collection*

Within weeks after this show was broadcast, The Even Dozen Jug Band were history, but in its brief existence was something of a "who's who" in music. Among its members were The Lovin' Spoonful's John Sebastian; Blood, Sweat & Tears' Steve Katz; mandolinist David Grisman, future "Guitar Workshop" founder Stefan Grossman; future arranger Joshua Rifkin, future producer Peter K. Siegel and a twenty-one-year-old Italian brunette with pigtails named Maria Grazia Rosa Domenica D'Amato. At the time of the show's taping, the band was in the process of recording an album for Elektra; when they split up, Miss D'Amato joined a similar group under contract to Vanguard: Jim Kweskin & the Jug Band. She married one of its members, Geoff Muldaur; although the marriage ended in 1972, she remained Maria Muldaur and embarked on a solo career that led to a top ten pop single, "Midnight at the Oasis." In what is a definite anomaly for short-lived Folk Era groups, all of the ex-Even Dozen Jug Band members remain active in music up to the time of this writing.

Hootenanny's final multi-artist medley to air was a look at various ways "Waltzing Matilda" can be treated. It begins with Rolf Harris' Aussie perspective, followed by a statelier rendition from Will Holt that's actually in waltz time, and lastly The Phoenix Singers' interpretation of Harry Belafonte's arrangement.

2-23: University of Tennessee, Knoxville #2

Recording Date: January 22, 1964.

Airdate: March 7, 1964.

Video: 16mm incomplete kinescope. Licensing: Historic Films Archive, LLC, #V-1010. Viewing: The Library of Congress, catalog # MAVIS 2311883. Excerpted on ***The Best of Hootenanny***.

"Hootenanny Saturday Night" (*Everyone*) (*Jack Linkletter intro*)

The Travelers 3: "Roll Along," "Tamure"

The Carter Family: "Fair and Tender Ladies"

Hoyt Axton: "Grizzly Bear"

The Simon Sisters: "Turn, Turn, Turn (To Everything There is a Season)," "Wynken, Blynken and Nod"

Eddy Arnold: "Song of the Coo-Coo," "Poor Howard"

The Carter Family: "Worried Man Blues" (*commercial bumper*)

The Travelers 3: "Land of Odin"

Vaughn Meader: Stand-up comedy

Hoyt Axton: "Thunder 'n' Lightin'"

Sheb Wooley: "That's My Pa," "Building a Railroad"

The Serendipity Singers: "Chilly Winds," "Goin' Home"

FINALE: "Feast Here Tonight" (*Everyone*)

The second of the U-Tenn shows survives on a slightly incomplete kinescope, and is another unsatisfying hour. The Travelers 3 are ostensibly the headliners, since they get three songs and everyone else gets two (or, as in the case of The Simon Sisters, one-and-a-half), and offer up a little more variety than their last appearance. After a brisk version of "Roll Along," they do a number in Hawaiian, during which bassist Dick Shirley playfully invites the students to join in. In the second half, they cover "Land of Odin" at a slow, somber pace. But as with the UCLA program, all the selections are from their 1962 debut album. They had two newer releases on the market by this time, each with up-tempo and slow (and Hawaiian) numbers; it's odd they weren't able to utilize anything from them.

The week after this show aired, the threesome were in Hawaii, a stop along a campus circuit tour, and speaking with reporter David Butwin of *The Honolulu Advertiser*. "Folk music is peaking as a craze," asserted Shirley. "It started out just the way rock 'n' roll did—all kinds of lousy groups competing with each other for the buck, but gradually the bad ones are getting weeded out. Quality [is] replacing quantity now. Radio stations are playing 15 per cent folk music, and the people are getting more selective." By the following year, the trio would be climbing on the folk-rock bandwagon and release an up-tempo, partially electrified album on Capitol titled *New Sounds*. When Shirley left in 1966, Pete Apo and Charlie Oyama picked up electric guitars and a rhythm section and became simply The Travelers. That ended before the sixties did.

An early publicity photo of The Travelers 3. From the top: Pete Apo, Dick Shirley, Charlie Oyama. *From the author's collection*

Anita Carter's shot at folk songstress success had missed its target, and so The Carter Family returned to *Hootenanny* as a unit, and would remain so for decades. By the time of this taping, they'd become regulars on Johnny Cash's touring show, and June Carter was dealing with the pressures that come from falling in love with a married man who happens to be a big star and a drug addict. Happily, that all worked itself out and the family foursome would have a regular spot on Cash's 1969-71 ABC variety series and throughout his career. Even after mother Maybelle's 1976 retirement, others would be recruited to complete the quartet, including one or both of June's daughters from prior marriages. Maybelle died in 1978; the eldest Carter sister, Helen, passed away in 1998; the youngest, Anita, followed a year later, but not until June's 2003 death did the saga of The Carter Family truly come to an end.

Serendipity Singer John Madden recalls their introduction to Hoyt Axton. "We were on stage, our instrument cases in hand, when we see this burly fellow walking toward us from the far end. He comes up to us and the first thing he says is, 'Hey, are you guys hip to grass?'" It should, perhaps, be noted the future co-author of "The 'No, No' Song" didn't write it based on hearsay.

Introduced by June Carter, Axton does "Grizzly Bear" from his second album, as well as its title song, "Thunder 'n' Lightnin'" later on. Axton tried his hand at acting during the latter half of the decade, then returned to music in a big way in 1970 as writer of "Joy to the World," a number one hit for Three Dog Night. The following year, Axton released an album on Capitol by that title that also included his song "Never Been to Spain," which Three Dog Night subsequently recorded and took to number five. In 1972, he moved over to A&M Records and found favor on the country music charts with such songs as "When The Morning Comes," "Boney Fingers" and "Della and the Dealer." He also kept his hand in acting, appearing in films such as *Gremlins* (1984) and *We're No Angels* (1989), plus several made-for-TV movies and series episodes. He suffered a stroke in 1995, and passed away four years later from the effects of two heart attacks within two weeks.

The Simon Sisters, now full-fledged recording artists, begin their set with Pete Seeger's musical setting of a passage from chapter three of the Book of Ecclesiastes: "Turn, Turn, Turn;" they would release it on their second Kapp album, *Cuddlebug (The Happiness Blanket)* later in the year. It's a fine performance, but what follows classifies as one of the sorriest moments of the series. Linkletter (erroneously calling them "Lucy and Carly *Simone*") reminds us of their first *Hootenanny* appearance and the piece they sang, and informs us the show received more favorable mail about that song than for any other, "so we thought you'd like to hear it again." All well-and-good, but they only get to sing the first and last of what is a four-verse song because of time constraints. It hardly did them, much less the single that had just been released and would peak at number 73, any favors.

Carly and Lucy Simon from around the time of this *Hootenanny* taping.

The two sisters continued as a team until Lucy's 1967 marriage. Eight years later she released a solo album; another followed two years after that. She became a producer during the 1980s and the composer for a smash Broadway production of *The Secret Garden* in the 1990s. Concurrent with all this, of course, her younger sister established herself as a fine artist and composer in her own right, tallying many chart successes along the way. Lucy Simon passed at age 82 on October 20, 2022.

For his *Hoot* finale, Eddy Arnold sings two songs from his newest RCA release, *Folk Song Book*. The mildly topical "Song of the Coo-Coo," written by Billy Faier, was also released as a single. The album included covers of "Green, Green," "Blowin' in the Wind" and "Where Have All the Flowers Gone." Neither disc made much of a dent in the country charts, but Arnold would return there in a big way just a few months later after the sudden death of his labelmate, Jim Reeves, on July 31. One of the pioneers of the "countrypolitan" style known as the Nashville Sound, Reeves' gentle baritone was forever silenced when his private plane, caught in a sudden thunderstorm, crashed in nearby Brentwood. Producer Chet Atkins thought it only natural for Arnold's smooth vocals to carry the countrypolitan torch, which he did to great acclaim with such hits as "Make the World Go Away" and "What's He Doin' in My World." Arnold died of natural causes in 2008, one week shy of his 90th birthday.

On November 22, 1963, Vaughn Meader, booked to perform at a Democratic National Committee banquet in Milwaukee, was headed to the location in a taxi when the driver asked him, "Did you hear about Kennedy getting shot in Dallas?"

"No," said Meader. "What's the punch line?"

He soon learned there wasn't one. The banquet was cancelled, as were two-week engagements in Syracuse and Los Angeles, plus other network TV appearances, including *Hootenanny* at the University of Maryland. According to *Variety*, he used the time off to write "an entirely new nightclub turn," and to replace a Kennedy impersonation track for his first self-produced comedy album, *Have Some Nuts*. A fiercely proud man, he was determined to succeed on his own terms.

The existing kinescope has a jump splice after Meader enters and speaks briefly about folk music, citing the Singing Nuns and their forthcoming album "The New Christian Minstrels." According to Kaye Franklin Veal, who covered the dress rehearsal for *The Knoxville News-Sentinel*, Meader did some topical jokes that probably got his biggest laughs: "I guess you've noticed that Barry Goldwater has been wearing a cast on one of his legs for the past few weeks. But finally the doctors told him they just couldn't give him two right feet.... And Colonel Glenn, now that he has entered the political field, instead of going to the moon, will probably promise it." If the main routine on this show was indicative of his new act, however, Meader was sorely in need of help. He picks up a guitar, which he labels "an ethnic Stradivarius folk-alonger," and talks about his birthplace, Waterville, Maine, with a series of one-note small town jokes: "The Howard Johnson's there only has one flavor.... For excitement, we used to go downtown to the hotel and see who rented the room." Then, with accompaniment from some of the musicians seated behind him, he sings a segment of "songs of our times," beginning with this ditty to the tune of "Red River Valley":

Just remember that sooner or later,

You'll be needing a mortuary.

We will let you pay now and die later.

Call Judson six-two-four-nine-three!

For the most part, the laughs are polite, with gaps between them and the occasional applause that was likely prompted. So it would go for Mr. Meader. Always a drinker, he began imbibing between shows, and before long his humor became bitter and caustic, and engagements fell off. He blew through his money over a two-year drinking and drugging binge, divorced and remarried a handful of times, became a San Francisco flower child, got arrested in Los Angeles for indecent exposure, tried to make it as a songwriter, created a parodic singing evangelist preacher named Johnny Sunday, and moved to Florida where, as Abbott Meader, he worked sporadically as a country singer, never performing anything but his own compositions. He returned to Maine, still his own man, stubborn enough to not quit smoking even after being diagnosed with the emphysema that ultimately killed him at age 68 on October 29, 2004.

Eddy Arnold introduces Sheb Wooley, who gets to sing "That's My Pa," his number one country release from early 1962, and the more recent "Building a Railroad," which was featured in *Hootenanny Hoot*; the latter ends abruptly due to another splice in the kinescope. Wooley, like his fellow Oklahoman Hoyt Axton, parlayed musical talent into an acting career and was then costarring in the CBS series *Rawhide* as Pete Nolan. One of his earliest screen roles was as Frank Miller (*Ian MacDonald*)'s brother outlaw Ben Miller in *High Noon* (1952). His biggest hit also came early: the novelty record "The Purple People Eater," which went to number one on *Billboard's* Hot 100 in 1958. He later introduced a comedic alter ego, "Ben Colder," under which he'd record parodies of country-western hits that usually kept their original titles with "#2" appended. Wooley succumbed to leukemia in September 2003 at age 82.

The Serendipity Singers close out the main program with a nice rendition of "Chilly Winds," written by John Stewart and John Phillips, and the lively "Goin' Home," written by Bryan Sennett and Brooks Hatch, who each take a verse. The all-star finale, "Feast Here Tonight," goes for over two minutes before the credits appear, which is much longer than usual. The performers run out of verses before the "brought to you by" announcement arrives, and so just repeat the refrain. It's almost as if Lewine or somebody underestimated how much time was left. It would've been nice if a minute of that had gone to The Simon Sisters for "Wynken, Blynken and Nod."

2-24: Salem College, Salem WV #2

Recording Date: December 11, 1963.

Airdate: March 14, 1964. *Repeat*: June 27, 1964.

Video: 16mm kinescope minus commercials. Licensing: Historic Films Archive, LLC, #V-1018. Viewing: The Library of Congress, catalog # MAVIS 2275847. Excerpted on ***The Best of Hootenanny***.

"Hootenanny Saturday Night" (*Everyone*) (*Jack Linkletter intro*)

The New Christy Minstrels: "Hi Jolly"

Gale Garnett: "Wanderin'"

Steve DePass: "Town Crier" (improvisational singing; the audience calls out topics and he sings about them)

The Three Young Men from Montana: "Make Your Back Strong"

The New Christy Minstrels: "Blacksmith of Brandywine," "The Banjo," "Vayivan," "Mighty Big Ways"

Steve DePass: "Got My Mind Set on Freedom" (commercial bumper)

Flatt & Scruggs: "Hot Corn, Cold Corn," "Reuben"

Pat Harrington Jr. (in character as "Guido Panzini"): Stand-up comedy

The Three Young Men from Montana: "Bill Bailey"

The New Christy Minstrels: "Joe Magarac," "Today," "This Land is Your Land"

FINALE: "In That Great Gettin' Up Morning" (Everyone)

By the time this one reached air, The New Christy Minstrels' lineup had changed by a third. We'd be seeing the newcomers in as many weeks; meanwhile, the group brings us three more from the *Land of Giants* album, a handful of older tunes (including "Vayivan" by McGuire and Kane from their "Barry & Barry" days) and an early performance of what would become their second and final top 20 hit: "Today."

Gale Garnett was, like Joan Toliver and Grier Reynolds, of the "not-really-a-folksinger" school. "I think I've been influenced by jazz, blues and folk music and people," she would say in 1965, "but I make no claim on any kind of 'ethnicity.' I sing a song out of my own bag." Born in New Zealand and raised in the U.S. since age nine, she quit high school after her sophomore year and successfully auditioned for off-Broadway productions, which led to a part in *The World of Suzie Wong*. Then she went to Hollywood and appeared in several TV shows between 1960-62; wearying of being "typecast into the exotic, Mexican-Polynesian type roles," she traded acting for a music career of writer-performer. Some weeks after this show's rerun, RCA-Victor would release her composition "We'll Sing in the Sunshine," which peaked at number four in the Hot 100. The mildly risqué song appeared on her debut album *My Kind of Folk Songs*, which also includes the bluesy one she does here, "Wanderin'."

Vice-President Nelson Rockefeller dubbed Steve DePass "America's Singing Poet" in 1975 and the title stuck. "I'm constantly constructing words in rhyme and meter," the Jamaican-native artist told the *Atlantic City Press* in 1982. Per a 1963 press release, DePass "composes improvisational ballads from audience suggestions" as the "Town Crier." Here, students call out "leap year," "income tax," "cutting class" and "the hootenanny craze," and he's right there with a four-stanza mini-ballad for each. During the commercial bumper, he leads them in "Got My Mind Set on Freedom." DePass made his debut in 1958 on Jack Paar's *Tonight Show* and continued performing into the 2010s.

The Three Young Men—Dick Riddle, Pat Fox and Bob Ruby— came together as fraternity brothers at the University of Montana in 1956, two years ahead of The Kingston Trio's breakthrough. Whatever momentum they had was interrupted by service hitches until 1960, after which they went to New York and were soon signed by Columbia. According to a March 31, 1963 *Great Falls Tribune* article, they were booked for *Hootenanny's* University of Virginia taping, but for undisclosed reasons the appearance fell through: at the time of production, they were in the midst of an engagement at The Skyroom nightclub in Tucson, Arizona. Here, their only accompaniment is piano and Keenan's bass; with heavily stylized vocals, they're more the show's jazz act than a folk group. The trio went their separate ways not long after this appearance. Riddle, who remained the most active over the years, composed music and lyrics for the critically-acclaimed off-Broadway show *Cowboy*, and passed away from leukemia at 51 in 1988.

Flatt & Scruggs make their third and final *Hoot* appearance, opening with "Hot Corn, Cold Corn," a tune composed by their contemporary (and fellow ex-Bluegrass Boy) David "Stringbean" Aiken. After this, they perform the instrumental "Reuben." As Earl Scruggs plays, Linkletter quietly points out each fingering variant employed by the already-legendary musician. Depending on your point of view, this Banjo 101 lesson is either informative or intrusive. Lester and Earl would split in 1969 when the latter, influenced by his young sons, wanted to explore a rock-bluegrass fusion that the former wanted no part of. Scruggs formed The Earl Scruggs Review with his boys and toured internationally, while Flatt formed The Nashville Grass and remained a Grand Ole Opry fixture. Flatt passed away from heart failure in May 1979 at age 64; Scruggs outlived him by nearly 33 years, dying of natural causes at age 88 in March 2012.

In the midst of this musical grab-bag, Pat Harrington, Jr. returns as "folk authority Guido Panzini," and the less said about that, the better.

2-25: Dartmouth College, Hanover NH #2

Recording Date: February 5, 1964.

Airdate: March 21, 1964.

"Hootenanny Saturday Night" (*Everyone*) (*Jack Linkletter intro*)

The Serendipity Singers: "Don't Let the Rain Come Down," "He's Gone Away"

Johnny Cash: "When Papa Played the Dobro," "Understand Your Man"

Addiss & Crofut: Unknown

Mike Settle: Unknown

Joan Toliver: "Oh Mary, Where's Your Baby," "High Flying Bird"

The Phoenix Singers: "I'm The Man That Built the Bridges," "Oh, Waly, Waly," "Ol' Gator"

Wild Bill Davison & The Salt City Six: Unknown

Adam Keefe: Comedy impressions

For their final *Hoot* taping, The Serendipity Singers repeat "Don't Let the Rain Come Down." Since the broadcast doesn't survive in any format, Jack Linkletter can't inform us if this was prompted by viewer demand. The most likely reason, though, is the record was making its journey to the turntables of the nation's disk jockeys at the time the show was recorded. As of the airdate, it had reached #34 on the Hot 100; one week later it leapt to #19.

The Serendipity Singers, dressed for New Hampshire's frosty weather, rehearse at Dartmouth.
Photo courtesy of Eugene Tiemann

"Understand Your Man," Johnny Cash's reimagining of Dylan's "Don't Think Twice," had reached #2 on *Billboard's* Hot Country Singles chart when this show aired; two weeks later, it hit the top spot. Years later, Cash admitted the song was aimed at his first wife, the former Vivian Liberto; by then he was deeply involved with June Carter of The Carter Family. Vivian's refusal to seek a divorce fueled his rebellion, which was abetted by the copious quantity of amphetamines he was downing daily. For her part, June refused any commitment until he straightened up, which he did once Vivian threw in the towel for the sake of her own health. The rest of his story didn't unfold as happily as legend would have it—there were relapses and other misfires along the way— but Johnny Cash was deemed a legend in his own time early on, and that consensus never wavered.

After returning from a State Department tour of Viet Nam villages, Steve Addis and Bill Crofut perform Vietnamese folk songs for President Johnson in April 1965. *From the author's collection*

Steve Addiss & Bill Crofut remained together for another ten years, traveling the world for various cultural exchange goodwill tours as well as performances at home. Although Addiss initiated the break to study Japanese art—he later became Professor at the University of Richmond and author of over thirty books on East Asian art—Crofut was ready for it, telling the *Mount Vernon Argus* years later that he "fell asleep in a concert. I was playing [and] we were cranking out the same old stuff night after night." He was also weary of presenting music as a protest tool: "It didn't work for me," he said in 1993. "I've found life is a little more complex than I ever dreamt it was when I was singing 'We Shall Overcome.'" After several years of experimentation with classical and jazz, he teamed successfully with Chris Brubeck, son of jazz legend Dave Brubeck, who began his career as an Addiss & Crofut sideman. Crofut died of cancer in 1999 at age 64. Addiss passed away in May 2022.

Mike Settle's solo career would last only two more years. In 1966, he joined The New Christy Minstrels, serving as their musical director. Two years after that, he and four other latter-day Christies—Terry Williams, Thelma Camacho, Mickey Jones and Kenny Rogers—departed en masse and formed The First Edition. During his three-year tenure with the group, he contributed songs as well as vocals, including the much-covered "But You Know I Love You." In 2020, Settle was inducted into the Oklahoma Music Hall of Fame in Tulsa.

Fred Weintraub could see the hootenanny tide was ebbing, and he encouraged Joan Toliver to wean off folk music toward pop standards. In August, she represented the U.S. in the International Light Music Festival held in Poland; she won two second-place prizes but had mixed feelings about her performance, calling it "a success artistically and with the critics, but as entertainment for the Polish audience it was a flop." Weintraub kept her on at The Bitter End, and in 1965 Phillips released her second album, *The Most Unusual Joan Toliver*, but like her first for Kapp, it failed to set the world on fire. By the end of the following year, she'd abandoned the music scene and eventually settled in Elkton, Maryland, where she died in June 2017.

In early 1965, The Phoenix Singers hired a young guitarist-banjoist named Peter Thorkelson as accompanist for a six-month tour from east coast to west. Not long after it ended Thorkelson became a Monkee named Peter Tork. As for his former employers, they toured Africa in 1966 and the Far East in 1967, with US appearances scheduled in between. Both Roy Thompson and Arthur Williams left by October 1967, after which Ned Wright refashioned the group into a 10-member "Singing and Dance Ensemble" that performed in church concerts up to his 1981 passing at age 55.

Chicago cornetist Wild Bill Davison, and Syracuse's Salt City Six led by clarinetist Jack Maheu, were normally two separate acts, but had come together for a tour the previous year. Formed in 1952 at Syracuse University, the Six specialized in the same brand of Dixieland as Pete Fountain and the Dukes, but with Davison (often billed as "Davidson") adding a touch of Louis Armstrong inspiration to the mix, the result was something unique. Maheu's group continued performing into the 1980s, occasionally appearing with Davison, who died in 1989.

Adam Keefe's second and final appearance presumably showcased more of his "old movie" impressions. In the coming years, he lampooned Bela Lugosi's Dracula for a series of Isodette throat lozenge commercials that gradually typecast him out of TV appearances. By the mid-1970s, his career had devolved to small town niteries, church and school auditoriums and the occasional stock company production. Keefe passed away from complications of diabetes in November 1994 at age 63. Three months earlier, several of his contemporaries, including George Carlin, Rodney Dangerfield, Shelly Berman and Norm Crosby gathered at the Los Angeles Improv for a benefit to help defray his medical expenses.

Neither audio nor video are known to survive of this broadcast.

2-26: West Point Academy, West Point, NY #2

Recording Date: December 22, 1963.

Airdate: March 28, 1964.

"Hootenanny Saturday Night" (*Everyone*) (*Jack Linkletter intro*)

The Brothers Four: "Do Lord," "Green Leaves of Summer," "Pastures of Plenty," "Thinking Man's John Henry," "Wolverton Mountain"

The Serendipity Singers: "Cloudy Afternoon," "Waggoner's Lad," "Boots and Stetsons"

Cedric Smith: "Will Ye Go, Lassie Go?"

The Robert DeCormier Singers: "Amen," "Greensleeves," "Old King Cole"

Lydia & Brooks: "Green Rocky Road," "Hangman"

Olatunji: "Moluka," "Abana"

Orson Bean: Stand-up comedy

The Brothers Four and The Serendipity Singers again carried most of the load in this second of the currently lost West Point *Hoots*.

The Cedric Smith who here performs the Scottish-Irish tune "Will Ye Go, Lassie, Go?" is the same Cedric Smith who voiced Professor Charles Xavier in *X-Men: The Animated Series* thirty-some years later. Born in England, his family moved to Ontario when he was ten; now, at age 20, Smith was just getting started in acting (the prior year he'd played in Shakespeare's *Othello*), but had been singing folk material in Canada for about three years. When performing in coffee houses and nightclubs, he was known for satiric songs. "Smith is not a protester," a *Detroit Free Press* reviewer would write in 1966. "He simply and wittily carves out frightening cameos of the world we live in and, crouching over his guitar, sings them out."

The Robert DeCormier Singers were the type of carefully assembled, diligently rehearsed chorale that inspired Randy Sparks to form the Christies. Look for them in today's streaming services and you'll find Christmas albums galore, but at the time of this show, they were rendering traditional folk songs and spirituals into complex, multi-part arrangements. The man himself, who passed away in 2017, worked with Belafonte, Seeger and Peter, Paul & Mary. "Classically versed and Julliard trained, with a great knowledge of folklore," reads a 1976 publicity piece, "DeCormier uses exquisite musical talent to enhance the simple folk tune with expanded chorale dimensions." It must have made quite a contrast with the Serendipities. How pleasing it was to the cadets will have to wait until audio or video of the show surfaces.

Lydia Wood and Brooks Jones met in Cincinnati, Ohio. Jones, originally from Columbus, relocated to New York and its thriving theater district in 1959 where, among other things, he'd been part of 3 Folk Sing with Molly Scott and Walt Winter. Four years later, he'd become Production Director for Cincinnati's Playhouse in the Park. One evening at a private gathering, he heard Wood sing and play. He picked up a guitar as well and joined in. That led to a gig at a Baltimore nightclub, followed by five weeks at The Blue Angel and three at The Bitter End where they were heard by Weintraub who, naturally, recommended them to Dankar, who signed them for two appearances. According to *The*

Cincinnati Post, their arrangement of "Hangman" had been worked out the night they met.

In the jazz spot, Babatunde Olatunji of Nigeria brings his "Drums of Passion" along with a supporting combo. Olatunji was born in Ajido, a small village some 40 miles from Lagos. As a youngster, "I was very inquisitive," he told the *London Guardian's* Ken Hunt, "and every weekend I would go to village festivals. I was always behind those master drummers, watching them play." Desiring to study in the U.S., he won a four-year scholarship to Morehouse College in Atlanta where, according to Hunt, "his fellow students… were steeped in the stereotypes of Tarzan and other Hollywood images of Africa." Opting not to become a diplomat, as he'd originally planned, he used the music of his homeland to change Americans' perspective. He recorded five albums for Columbia beginning in 1959, co-authored *Musical Instruments of Africa: Their Nature, Use and Place in the Life of a Deeply Musical People* in 1965, founded the Olatunji Centre for African Culture in Harlem, and ran workshops on drumming as a spiritual tool at the Esalen Institute's health and therapy center located in Big Sur, California, where he passed away in April 2003.

Orson Bean is best remembered by baby boomers as a panelist on the game show *To Tell The Truth* from the 1960s into the 1990s, but he'd been house comic at New York's Blue Angel nightclub for ten years beginning in 1951. Born Dallas Frederick Burrows in 1928, the Boston-reared comic devised his stage name because "the pomposity of 'Orson' followed by the comic simplicity of 'Bean' appealed to his sense of the ludicrous," wrote Beulah Schacht for the *St. Louis Globe-Democrat* in 1952. In between gigs on *Truth* and other game shows, Bean acted on television, Broadway and in stock companies until well into old age. Still spry in his early nineties, he was crossing Venice Boulevard in February 2020 when he was clipped by a motorist that didn't see him. According to LAPD Captain Brian Wendling, "A second vehicle's driver was distracted by people trying to slow him down [and] a second collision occurred [that] caused the death of Bean."

2-27: Purdue University, Lafayette, IN #1

Recording Date: March 2, 1964.

Airdate: April 4, 1964.

Video 1: Digital file of a worn 16mm kinescope minus commercials. Viewable at The Paley Center, digitized catalog #T85-0744.

Video 2: Incomplete 16mm kinescope (includes commercials, but the entire performance of "The Cat" was removed prior to receipt), housed in a private collection.

"Hootenanny Saturday Night" (*Everyone*) (*Jack Linkletter intro*)

The New Christy Minstrels: "Way Down in Arkansas"

Liz Seneff: "Bloomin' Heather"

Stevenson Phillips: "Night Time"

The Staple Singers: "It Takes More Than a Hammer and Nails"

The New Christy Minstrels: "This Ol' Riverboat," "Shenendoah," "The Cat"

Deirdre O'Callaghan and Liz Seneff: "Whistling Gypsy" (commercial bumper)

The New Christy Minstrels: "Charleston Town"

Pat Harrington Jr.: (in character as "Guido Panzini") Stand-up comedy (includes comments on Beatlemania, Winter Olympics and other current events)

Stan Getz (jazz saxophonist): "Waltz for a Lovely Wife"

Deirdre O'Callaghan (Irish harpist and singer): "Bonnie Boy"

The New Christy Minstrels: "The Last Farewell," "Glory, Glory"

FINALE: "Walk the Road" (*Everyone*)

If The New Christy Minstrels looked different to the more-than-casual viewer, it's because three of them were brand new. Jackie Miller and Gayle Caldwell departed together in January, ostensibly to "retire," but they soon formed a pop-rock duo named, conveniently enough, Jackie & Gayle. They were replaced by Ann White and Karen Gunderson, respectively. Gene Clark had also left, eventually to become a founding Byrd; he was replaced by Paul Potash, a former singing partner with Art Podell who'd been working in another Randy Sparks group, The Back Porch Majority.

The newest New Christies had joined only three weeks before and with the others were primarily focused on learning the soundtrack songs for *Advance to the Rear*, three of which appear in this show. There's a very funny flub during "The Cat," a tune from the group's third album: Potash, assigned Dolan Ellis' verse, forgets the words halfway through and gamely ad libs new ones. When he's done, he sheepishly wanders away from the mic muttering, "I forgot the verse," while the others are heard giggling. Earlier, Barry McGuire had his own memory fail: tasked with introducing Liz Seneff, he calls her selection "one of my favorites," but blanks on its title and she has to cue him. Aside from those minor mishaps, the group is on its game; Ann White's enthusiasm is particularly enchanting.

When Judy Henske dropped out of The Whiskeyhill Singers in mid-1962, Dave Guard replaced her with Liz Seneff, as different a singer imaginable in appearance and style. Whereas the tall, brunette Henske stood, swayed and gave her songs a bluesy growl and a gospel shout, the diminutive, blonde Seneff sits on a stool, plays a plaintive guitar and gently sings "The Bloomin' Heather," which is actually "Will Ye Go, Lassie, Go," the same song Cedric Smith performed last week. Yet Seneff did share one trait with her predecessor: outspokenness. "I'm glad the Beatles are around," she told the *Pittsburgh Press* a week after this taping. "They help keep the nation's mind off hootenanny. And the less exposure there is to some of the hootenanny shows now making the rounds, the better it is for singers who are dedicated to the art of folk singing. The public has been flooded with inferior folk singing groups and this has given all folk music a bad name." Seneff tried to remain dedicated, but when the hootenannies dissipated, so did her bookings, and she subsequently made her living with radio and TV commercials. Her biggest claim to pop culture posterity would be as singer of the opening theme for *The New Candid Camera* during the mid-1970s.

Stevenson Phillips, neé Phillip Stevens of Lake Charles, Louisiana, endeavored to combine folk music and acting in a way that other singer-actors didn't approach. Unfortunately, he doesn't get to do so here, owing to the usual time constraints and Lewine's desire to get the Christies back on stage. As it stands, Phillips' song "Night Time" is just a simple slice of life from the eyes and ears of a rambler. On his newly-released *Songs and Stories of Stevenson Phillips* album, the singing stops about two-thirds through for a poignant dialogue between himself and a sad-but-resigned lover. He alters his voice where appropriate for characterization as he tries to explain why he keeps moving on and she tries to understand. He kept up this modus operandi at least into 1982, where he performed a self-created one-man show, *It's Hard to Be a Jewish Cowboy*, at the Richmond Shepard Theater in Los Angeles. "This is not a sophisticated evening of entertainment, but it is a captivating one," wrote the *LA Weekly*. "Phillips has no stage presence to speak of, but his informal presentation and rambling, good-natured style of speaking are thoroughly ingratiating and never boring."

The dynamic Staple Singers: 'Pops,' Cleotha, Pervis and Mavis Staples.

The Staple Singers were primarily a gospel group, although their selection, "It Takes More Than a Hammer and Nails," mainly dwells on the credo of "Love Thy Neighbor" with only an oblique reference to God ("a whole lot of guidance from above"). The tune rocks, with Roebuck 'Pops' Staples playing a Fender Jaguar and daughter Mavis taking lead and belting out the refrain, proving early on she could stand tall among the most soulful vocalists in history. The group, first formed in 1948, remained together, moving easily between gospel, soul and rhythm & blues, until Pops' death in December 2000. Mavis launched a solo career shortly afterward; with her siblings having also passed, as of this writing she remains active in the music world.

Although this show preceded it in taping order, Dublin's Deirdre O'Callaghan made her American TV debut on Ed Sullivan's annual salute to St. Patrick's Day on March 15. Here, accompanying herself on an Irish harp, she trills the wistful "Bonny Boy." She'd begun her professional career eight years earlier, at age 16, after six years of musical education. Along with local appearances she found work in England, where she also did her earliest recordings. Bucking the stereotype, she delighted in the U.K. "So many Irish people come to listen that it's like appearing at home," she said in 1959. "As for Liverpool, it's even more Irish than Ireland." O'Callaghan has continued performing into the 21st century. "I'm lucky," she reflected in 1976. "Things always go well for me. I guess playing the harp is different. People like something different."

Speaking of Liverpool, Pat Harrington's Guido Panzini uses part of his spot to comment on a certain foursome from that city who'd recently visited the U.S. for three *Ed Sullivan Show* appearances. "That's a wild group, The Beatles. Most singers hire a manager. They have a gardener. It's a wild *looking* group; when they put their heads together, they look like a welcome mat." The rest of Harrington's material is just as topical: he touches on Fidel Castro, General de Gaulle's treaty with Red China, and the Winter Olympics ("where America showed the world that when the chips are down, we can lose"), and none of the jokes have held up. His best line and biggest laugh comes at the start of the routine: "Well, kids, I understand you've been snowed in all winter… by the faculty." The comedy is all downhill from there. Harrington would spend another eleven years of floundering in television and elsewhere before striking gold as landlord Dwayne Schneider in the sitcom *One Day At a Time*; the role would win him both an Emmy and a Golden Globe award.

"Waltz For a Lovely Wife" is saxophonist Stan Getz's contribution. A pioneer in the "cool jazz" sound, Getz got his first break in 1948 at age 21 when he recorded "Early Autumn" with Woody Herman's band. His 1962 album with Charlie Byrd, *Jazz Samba* and its Grammy-winning track "Desafinado," launched the bossa nova craze in America. His personal life, though, was a mess; abuse of alcohol and heroin clouded his mind and frequently turned him into a raging abuser of his own "Lovely Wife." He would record "Waltz…" two days after this taping but it and the rest of the session's tracks would remain unreleased for thirty years, thanks to the attention surrounding his soon-to-be biggest hit: "The Girl from Ipanema." Getz passed away from liver cancer in 1991 at age 64.

"Last night was one of the best audiences we've had," the Christies' bassist Clarence Treat told student reporter Donna Steidinger of the *Purdue Exponent* at the following day's rehearsal. "It seemed as if they genuinely enjoyed it. Some other campuses completely tie-up on the *Hootenanny*, just clap when they are told to, laugh just because they think they should." McGuire cynically concurred on Treat's latter point: "Kids just come to [this] show for the glamor and wonder of being on TV. They don't come to hear the actual stories that the songs tell. I appreciate college audiences, but not under these circumstances." McGuire also informed the reporter he would be leaving the group come September.

The day this segment aired, ABC announced its Fall schedule, and *Hootenanny* was listed for 7:30 p.m. Saturday, which several critics, including Rick DuBrow, had termed "surprising," given its nearly season-long berth in the bottom 50 of the ratings. That miserly $60,000 weekly budget, though, was still more influential to the third-place network than any Nielsen and Trendex numbers.

But, as McGuire, Liz Seneff and "Guido Panzini" knew, a much bigger fad than folk was brewing in the music industry.

2-28: College of William and Mary, Williamsburg VA #1

Recording Date: February 18, 1964.

Airdate: April 11, 1964.

"Hootenanny Saturday Night" (*Everyone*) (*Jack Linkletter intro*)

The Brothers Four: "Greenfields," "The Ox-Driver's Song," "Beautiful Brown Eyes," "Beans Taste Fine," "Long Ago, Far Away"

Bob Gibson: "Sweet Betsy From Pike," "Fare Thee Well"

Enid Mosier: "Keep Your Hands on That Plow," "Banana Tree"

The Romeros (Flamenco guitarists): "Fandangos de Huelva"

The Ivy League Trio: "Bells," "Women From Liberia"

Elaine Malbin: "Black is the Color of My True Love's Hair"

Stan Rubin & His Tigertown Five: "I Would Do Most Anything For You"

Charlie Manna: Stand-up comedy

FINALE: "Come Go With Me To That Land (Where I'm Bound)" (*Everyone*)

William and Mary holds a unique place in *Hootenanny* history: it's the only institution where students organized a protest in *support* of a taping.

Back in late October when ABC extended the series to a full 26-week season, Dankar initiated a search for six more photogenic campuses, followed by inquiries. The Williamsburg school, founded in 1693 by royal charter of King William III and Queen Mary II, was on the list. Dankar's booking agent, Sylvan Markman, called on November 6: Would William and Mary like to host *Hootenanny* tapings on January 21 and 22? Dr. Davis Y. Paschall, president of W&M, consulted his fellow administrators and the faculty and informed Markman, sorry, those are mid-year examination days. Dr. Paschall assured Dankar the college would gladly cooperate with a different set of dates. Markman noted this and moved on down the list; eventually, the University of Tennessee was selected.

Word got out. An editorial in the student paper *The Flat Hat* said in part, "we feel the college passed up this opportunity for reasons which are not strong enough to merit William and Mary's losing the chance for such an appearance." Dr. Paschall maintained "this activity would affect adversely the study opportunities which are so desired during such an important period." By contrast, according to *The Newport News Daily Press*, "[the] students expressed the belief the show would provide a welcome relief from the tension of studying for mid-year exams."

An official demonstration was held. In attendance was Mark A. Bush, a junior at the college, who recalls, "The main instigator was a fellow named John Bingham 'Bing' Munroe. He was a happy-go-lucky type who played guitar and banjo." A member of a campus folk trio, The Postroad Singers, Munroe provided accompaniment, "and he also spoke," says Bush. "Bing was standing at the Wren Building end of the Sunken Garden," a piece of landscape designated for "relaxation and recreation," according to campus literature.

Seen from behind, John 'Bing' Munroe leads a demonstration in support of *Hootenanny* at the College of William and Mary.

"He said, 'I just want you to imagine something. On this side, we have the administration. And down there on that side, we have the lions. Let's hear it for the lions!'"

"Approximately 700 students gathered around the top of the entrance to the Sunken Garden to protest the administration's action regarding the ABC TV 'Hootenanny,'" reported *The Flat Hat*. "A portable loudspeaker enabled the fast-growing crowd of students—sprinkled here and there with faculty members—to hear the songs of social protest." The ad-hoc concert began with a take-off on "Mama Don't 'Low" ("Mama don't 'low no hoot-*Hootenanny* 'round here"). A few students spoke between songs expressing their disagreement with the decision. "The rally lasted 20 minutes, and ended with the orderly crowd singing 'We Shall Overcome.'"

The demonstration was held at noon on Friday, November 22. It had been "a gala affair. Students clapped and sang and laughed. Then they went to lunch or back to classes. It was a pretty day." Less than seventy minutes later, everything changed.

"I got back to the dorm," says Bush, "and someone told me 'the President's been shot.' I thought they meant Dr. Paschall. I said, 'When did this happen?' He said, 'A few minutes ago.' I thought, 'No, no… Dr. Paschall's in New York for something this week.' I said, 'Tell me which president was shot.' He said, 'Kennedy, of course!' Well, that pretty much drove everything out of everybody's mind."

Ironically, the national tragedy of that afternoon made *Hootenanny* possible for William and Mary. ABC quickly realized there were shows containing Kennedy references that couldn't be repeated and made the decision to order four more, taking the program through April. Suddenly Dankar needed two more colleges… and Markman got back on the phone with Dr. Paschall.

The Brothers Four headlined; they, Bob Gibson and The Ivy League Trio present the folk music for this segment. It's certainly a welcome return for Gibson, not seen since February 8.

The Ivy League Trio, another all-male threesome in the Kingston Trio vein, originally consisted of college graduates Bob Hider, Norris

O'Neill and Beverly Galloway. Like the one-shot Wanderers Three, they arrived late to the party, recorded for the budget line of a major label (in this case, Decca subsidiary Coral Records) and failed to set the charts on fire. Galloway departed and was replaced with Ronn Langford, a classmate of Hider's at Princeton. Having switched to the hungry Reprise label in '63 they retooled to a more MFQ-esque sound and hoped to make waves with a concept album: *Folk Ballads from the World of Edgar Allan Poe*, from which comes the interpretation of "The Bells"[3] performed here. They did a "Hootenanny USA" tour the previous fall and had guested on some early *Let's Sing Out* programs in Canada. "Maybe in some ways, it's a little better than the American version," Hider opined for *The Flat Hat*. "It's a real 'Hoot' and not necessarily a form of show with comedians and all. But don't get me wrong. Our 'Hootenanny' here has done more for folk music than almost any other medium." Sadly, it wouldn't do anything for Hider's group, which never recorded another album and quickly faded.

Enid Mosier's second visit includes the song she made famous in *House of Flowers*, the full title of which is "Two Ladies in De Shade of De Banana Tree." It appears on her debut album, *Hi Fi Calypso, Etc.*, released in 1956. By the end of the '60s, she'd changed her name to Vivian Bonnell and turned to acting in films and television, as did her husband Alfonso, under his real name, Austin Stoker. One of the movies in which she appeared was *Leadbelly* (1976), a biopic of Huddie Ledbetter that starred Roger E. Mosley. Mosier passed away in 2003 of complications from diabetes.

Like Orriel Smith, Elaine Malbin began her career singing opera, having done so professionally since 1945 at age fifteen; unlike Smith, she never gave a thought to switching to folk music. During the 1950s, she appeared with the New York City Opera company in several productions and starred in NBC's *Opera Television Theater* series. By the following decade, she'd added musical theater to her resumé with stock company productions of *Kismet* and *Carnival*, but never forsook roles in *Madame Butterfly* and *Carmen*. No doubt the Broadway-based Lewine sought her

---

[3] Singer-songwriter Phil Ochs would compose his own version of Poe's classic poem that same year, one that would have far greater staying power.

services for his show and was delighted when she accepted, but she would likely have been happier with an *aria* on *The Hollywood Palace.*

Celedonio Romero and his three sons, Celin, Pepe and Angel, were classical and Flamenco guitarists who'd performed at New York's Philharmonic Hall less than two weeks before taping. The Spanish quartet's *Hootenanny* appearance was diplomatically termed a "unique booking" by *Variety*. One wonders how the William & Mary students felt, after having lobbied so hard for their school's selection, to have wound up with artists whose folk music credentials were, at best, suspect.

With three appearances, Stan Rubin and His Tigertown Five hold the *Hootenanny* record for Dixieland combos. Rubin is second from left. *From the author's collection*

At least Stan Rubin & His Tigertown Five had appeared on the show twice before. The Dixieland combo would find the pickings considerably slim as rock 'n' roll overtook the music and college concert industries.

Rubin abandoned performing and opened a booking agency in the mid-sixties, but by 1973 had wearied of the businessman's grind. Shortly thereafter, he launched The Stan Rubin Orchestra, specializing in the big band sound of the 1940s. Removal of a brain tumor in 1984 robbed him of the muscular control needed to play clarinet; from then on, he'd step in front of the band, which continues to the present day, and conduct.

Cancer would claim Charlie Manna at age 51 on November 9, 1971. Up to that moment, he was still working and still funny. *The Buffalo News'* Jeff Simon caught him opening for singer Jerry Vale at Melody Fair three months before his passing and couldn't resist reprinting some favorite one-liners: a loser is "a guy who sends away for his family tree and they send him back a bunch of bananas." Or the jungle movie cliché "I don't like the sound of those drums" being followed by "He's not our regular drummer." Or the surrealistic observation, "As Arthur Murray once said, 'If you must dance with a waltzing bear, let him lead.'" Hopefully when Manna walked into Heaven, St. Peter handed him a box of crayons.

2-29: Purdue University, Lafayette IN #2

Recording Date: March 3, 1964.

Airdate: April 18, 1964. *Repeat*: July 18, 1964.

"Hootenanny Saturday Night" (*Everyone*) (*Jack Linkletter intro*)

The New Christy Minstrels: "Springfield Fair," "The Dying Convict," "Elijah Rock," "Mary Ann," "Fire Down Below," "Ride, Ride, Ride," "Don't Cry, Suzanne"

Bob Carey: "I'm On My Way," "Alberta (Let Your Hair Hang Down)"

Lydia & Brooks: "Almost Gone," "Seek"

Homer & Jethro: "How Much is That Hound Dog in the Window?" "Don't Let the Stars Get in Your Eyes," "Buffalo Gal"

The Levee Singers: Unknown

FINALE: "Joshua Fit the Battle of Jericho" (Everyone)

The Minstrels meet The Beatles in this snapshot from January 1965. Top row from left: Barry McGuire, George Harrison, John Lennon, Paul McCartney, Ringo Starr, Larry Ramos, Art Podell. In the center are Nick Woods, Karen Gunderson and Barry Kane.

The New Christy Minstrels had been formed by Randy Sparks for one purpose: to record Randy Sparks originals and Randy Sparks arrangements of traditional songs. Becoming an actual touring unit was foisted upon him by their record label, and he opted to delegate the nuts-

and-bolts road management duties to a pair of professionals: George Greif and Sid Garris. He'd given up performing with the troupe not long after their *Andy Williams Show* contract ended, but in the recording studio, Sparks was still calling the shots. By the time of the group's final *Hootenanny*, its long-time members were wearying of this creative straightjacket and Sparks was wearying of their discontent. Within a few months, he'd sell the Minstrels to Greif and Garris for $2,500,000.

The Christies were committed to a five-week half-hour summer series for NBC in August; Barry McGuire had planned to depart immediately after but was persuaded to stay through their first European tour the following January. Paul Potash left at the same time as McGuire, Barry Kane left in April and Clarence Treat in May. Velvet-voiced Nick Woods departed in September. Larry Ramos left in January 1966 to become one of The Association; Mike Settle replaced him. The last of the 1961 originals, Art Podell, departed in February, along with Karen Gunderson. Finally, Ann White left in July; her replacement was Kim Carnes. Around that same time, Kenny Rogers replaced one of the replacements. By then, they'd long been a pop group, having last charted in the Hot 100 the prior year with "Chim Chim Cher-ee" from *Mary Poppins* (1964).

Well over 200 musicians, both aspiring and established, became "New Christy Minstrels" during Greif and Garris's ownership period, which ended in 1991. Eventually, Sparks registered the name as a trademark. In 1994, several members of the 1961-64 editions, including McGuire, Podell, Ramos, Miller, Caldwell, Treat and Ellis, regrouped and toured as "A Gathering of Minstrels;" several other reunions followed into the 21st Century. Likewise, Sparks has toured with his own hand-picked lineup under the original name.

Biographical information on Bob Carey is almost non-existent for the years following his departure from The Tarriers. What remains is testimony from secondary sources. It's been written he was battling alcohol and/or substance abuse since his latter days with the group; that Eric Weissburg brought in his former U of Wisconsin classmate Marshall Brickman as a precaution lest Carey fail to appear; that Carey's career as a working musician ended in 1967 when he was hired to manage the

Norman-Leonard Music Company, a New York City song publishing house; that he was found dead in 1976 on a Central Park bench.

The Levee Singers were thus named because they originated at a Dallas bistro called The Levee, owned by the group's leader, Ed Bernet, a 30-year-old ex-pro footballer for the Pittsburgh Steelers. Other members included fellow Texans Marvin Montgomery, described in publicity as "the old man of the group—he voted in two elections, Lincoln and McKinley;" Bob Christopher, an ex-geologist; and most famously, Ronnie Dawson, who'd tasted rockabilly success at the Big D Jamboree in the late 1950's and would return to it after the group parted ways in the late 1970s. The primary instrumentation was similar to that of Freddie Powers' Powerhouse Four: Bernet, Montgomery and Dawson played banjo (although Dawson also played 6- and 12-string guitar for quieter pieces), and Christopher handled bass saxophone.

Despite being signed to International Talent Association, the same firm that handled Peter, Paul & Mary and The Chad Mitchell Trio, Lydia & Brooks didn't last long as a duo. In mid-year, Lydia married Joseph Spaulding, a black aspiring musician; together they formed The Spaulding Wood Affair, which quickly met with resistance on the club circuit owing to their status as an integrated couple. It took until 1968 to land a record deal, which didn't amount to much in the way of radioplay, but helped open doors for other integrated groups. Eventually Lydia left the music business, returned to Cincinnati and focused on raising the couple's four children. Citing "gross neglect of duty," she divorced Spaulding in 1985. A few years later, she and the children opened a tie-dye business, Wizard's Wardrobe, housed for many years in the Linwood district. Brooks Jones returned to Playhouse in the Park, remaining its Production Director until 1971, after which he traveled overseas, did some producing for public television, and eventually relocated to Westport, Connecticut, where he passed away in 2008.

As at University of Tennessee, when Homer & Jethro are among your guests, you don't need a stand-up comic. Asked by the *Purdue Exponent* how their comedy measured up, Jethro Burns replied, "We've found that the corny jokes and comedians last, while the so-called intellectual humorists like Mort Sahl come and go." It was certainly true in their case. Despite their bickering stage shtick, the boyhood chums remained close friends and active partners up to Homer Haynes' fatal heart attack at age 51 while on the way to a performance in August 1971. Their last major TV appearances had been as semi-regulars on the final season of ABC's *The Johnny Cash Show*. Four years later, Burns tried a new partner: Ken Edison, a 28-year-old junior high school teacher from Chicago, but "it just wasn't Homer," his son John Burns asserted years later. His father remained active as a soloist as well as instructor for a younger generation of mandolinists until diagnosed with cancer in early 1988. Jethro passed away in February 1989 at age 69.

This was the final *Hootenanny* to be taped. Unfortunately, it isn't known to survive in any format.

2-30: College of William and Mary, Williamsburg VA #2

Recording Date: February 19, 1964.

Airdate: April 25, 1964. *Repeat*: August 15, 1964.

"Hootenanny Saturday Night" (*Everyone*) (*Jack Linkletter intro*)

The Brothers Four: "Darlin' Sportin' Jenny," "Seven Daffodils," "Symphonic Variations," "Twenty-Five Minutes to Go"

Trini Lopez: "Kansas City," "Jailer, Bring Me Water," "If You Want To Be Happy"

Bob Gibson: "Bimini," "Andalusian Dance"

Marilyn Child (actress-singer): "Tell Old Bill"

Bob Gibson and Marilyn Child: "Sinner Man"

The Gateway Trio: "Foolish Questions," "A-Rovin'," "When the Stars Begin to Fall"

Jackie Vernon: Stand-up comedy

FINALE: "Heaven is So High You Can't Get Over It" (*Everyone*)

Trini Lopez's drummer, Mickey Jones, brought along his home movie camera, resulting in the only known color footage of a *Hootenanny* taping. Thankfully, it's been preserved by Historic Films and can be viewed on their website, *historicfilms.com* (catalog #MJ-2; scenes shot at the rehearsal and performance begin at roughly the 12-minute mark and continue for about three-and-a-half minutes).

Lopez's version of "Kansas City" had reached #23 on Billboard's Hot 100 the previous year. His newest single, "Jailer, Bring Me Water," would only reach #97. Nevertheless, Lopez was now a major draw and before the year was out, he'd have his own line of Gibson guitars, which the company would manufacture until 1971. For the next two decades, the original Tex-Mex star would alternate music with the occasional acting gig such as in *The Dirty Dozen* (1967) and the police series *Adam-12*. Having spent those years investing mainly in real estate, he settled down in Palm Springs, where he co-hosted the annual Palm Springs Celebrity Golf Tournament. In 1996, he wound up on the front pages when a former girlfriend accused him of a severe beating. Charged with assault, he maintained his innocence; the case went to trial in July and he was acquitted. After that, he rarely performed, mostly showcasing his talents in an occasional recording session. Lopez died at age 83 in August 2020, one of the first celebrity casualties of the COVID-19 pandemic.

An ex-school teacher, Marilyn Child began her professional career at Chicago's Gate of Horn in July 1956, opening for Bob Gibson. She'd been soloing there a year later when she teamed with fellow folksinger Glenn Yarbrough for a set. *Variety's* 'Leva' was impressed: "Their voices balance in range and volume…. This pair should shape as a sock act in most surroundings if they stick together as a duo." They gave it a run, even recording an album for Elektra, but then Yarbrough became a Limeliter. Child returned to the clubs, opening for Lenny Bruce and appearing with Will Holt and Martha Schlamme, eventually making her way to the musical stage, in stock companies and on Broadway (where she debuted in the Phil Silvers starrer, *Do Re Mi* in December 1960). This line of work would keep her occupied into the 1980s. Here, she took a step back to her career's beginning with a solo number as well as dueting with Gibson on Holt's "Sinner Man."

For his part, Gibson led the students in "(When I Go Down to) Bimini," the same sing-along that Theo Bikel had performed at SMU, and took on an instrumental, "Andalusian Dance." By then, the erratic but deeply respected troubadour "was getting nuts… really self-destructive," he would write in his autobiography. Gibson continued along a troubled path until 1978 when he found Alcoholics Anonymous and embraced sobriety. From that point on, his career maintained a steady, enjoyable pace, with occasional highlights such as touring with Tom Paxton and Anne Hills as Best of Friends in the mid '80s. In 1994, he was diagnosed with Progressive Supranuclear Palsy, a form of Parkinson's Disease. Gibson retired to Portland, Oregon, and passed away there in September 1996. Perhaps the most salient tribute came from Allan Shaw, president Folk Era Records, who unintentionally summarized precisely why Gibson was such a fixture on *Hootenanny*: "Bob and Pete Seeger were the only two who could take the stage by themselves with only a five-string banjo or 12-string guitar and carry the whole show."

The Gateway Trio, whose beginnings stretched back to 1956, finally make it to *Hootenanny*. From left: Jerry Walter, Betty Mann, Milt Chapman.

The Gateway Trio was the final iteration of the group that began as The Gateway Singers. When that foursome called it quits in 1961, founding member Jerry Walter partnered with Betty Mann and toured for eight months as a duo. Deciding to try for a bigger sound, they engaged Milt Chapman, who'd been with a San Francisco group that specialized in jazz, The Axidentals. With Chapman playing bass, Mann on guitar and Walter on banjo, the threesome went on to record two albums for

Capitol and appear in *Hootenanny Hoot*. For this show, they performed "Foolish Questions" from that film, thankfully sans trampoline. They also sang "A-Rovin'" from their debut Capitol LP, and interpreted a Weavers song, "When The Stars Begin to Fall." The group recorded a third album for the label but its release was cancelled in early 1965, a casualty of the British Invasion. Soon after, The Gateway Trio split up.

Jackie Vernon's pop culture legacy was cemented in 1969 when he voiced the title character in a Rankin-Bass animated Christmas special, *Frosty the Snowman*. By the 1980s, though, his star had cooled considerably, TV appearances having dwindled down to occasional shots on Merv Griffin's talk show. Speaking to syndicated columnist Louis Brandon in 1981, he said, "It's getting to where you work three months out of a year doing clubs, and the rest of the time you sit by the phone waiting for your manager to call. It's not a pretty business.... People like zany stuff nowadays." Six years later, he died of a heart attack at age 63.

"We never do any 'pop' music," the Brothers Four as a unit told *The Flat Hat*. Maybe not then, but they'd be releasing an album of Lennon-McCartney compositions within two years, and 1969's *Let's Get Together* included covers of "Wichita Lineman," "Revolution" and a Bee Gees medley. It was their last for Columbia, produced after Mike Kirkland departed and featuring his replacement, Mark Pearson, who left two years' later. Except for a brief period in the early seventies, the three remaining original members—Bob Flick, John Paine and Dick Foley—remained intact until 1991, first with Pearson's replacement, Bob Haworth, through 1985 when Pearson replaced his replacement. In 1991, Foley departed and was replaced by Terry Lauber. In 2004, Lauber and Paine departed and were replaced by Mike McCoy and John Hylton, respectively, leaving Flick the only founding member remaining. Four years later, Hylton left and was replaced by Karl Olsen, and this lineup has remained together since, making the occasional domestic tour as well as appearances in Thailand and Japan, where the group's popularity has never faded.

"We Did It!" said a headline in *The Flat Hat* the week after the taping. "It was a remarkable showing of enthusiasm for sometimes sedate and apathetic William and Mary," the subsequent editorial stated. "In the course of two short nights before audiences which topped 2,000 each evening (an unprecedented 4/5 of the student body), members showed how enthusiastic they could really become if given the chance." In a separate article, the paper affirmed "the productions were called by the [show's] crew 'two of the best in the series.'" Unfortunately, neither is known to exist in any format.

* * * * *

The following week, *Hootenanny* went into reruns with Lewine, Linkletter and other Dankar staffers secure in the knowledge they'd be back at it when the 1964-65 school year began. No doubt the producer already had Sylvan Markman sounding out various universities for fall taping dates.

ABC, though, was having difficulty lining up advertisers for many of its shows, and according to *Variety*, *Hootenanny's* third season was among the "virtually unsold." The problem, wrote reporter George Rosen, was the 1964 World's Fair: several blue-chip sponsors "found that [their] Flushing Meadows investment would vastly exceed previous estimates," and thus were cutting back their broadcast dollars. NBC and CBS were feeling the same pinch, but not to the extent of their third-place competitor.

To attract new sponsors, ABC needed new product. They put one of their in-house companies, Selmur Productions, on retooling a recent pilot submission into something more eye-catching. The pilot, *Young America Swings the World*, was co-created by producer Jack Good and Los Angeles deejay Jimmy O'Neill. The revamped result clearly held tremendous appeal to the 13-to-16-year-old age bracket too young to appreciate *Hootenanny* and currently pouring their allowance and odd-job money into Beatles records. Taking a lesson from the series it was about to usurp, Selmur titled the show as an event: *Shindig!* The network, touting the obvious youth appeal, promptly sold time to Lehn & Fink Products (on behalf of its Stri-Dex medicated acne pads) and the American Dairy Association (on behalf of *its* flagship product, milk).

ABC liked the idea of having *Shindig!* follow *The Patty Duke Show* on Wednesday nights, which meant moving its sci-fi series *The Outer Limits* to another timeslot. The AP's Cynthia Lowry broke the news on June 9 under the title "Monsters To Replace Folk Singers on TV."

> *In a sudden change of plans, ABC announced yesterday it would drop 'Hootenanny,' a Saturday evening folk song program, and replace it with 'The Outer Limits'…. The move is undoubtedly popular with the 'Outer Limits' people, because it had been pitted next season against both 'The Beverly Hillbillies' and 'The Dick Van Dyke Show,' two of TV's most popular shows.*

In a perceptive piece for her "TV Time" column, *Los Angeles Citizen-News* writer Arlene Garber endorsed the change: "'Shindig,' which I saw at an advance screening, isn't too far afield from the beat usually emanating from 'Hootenanny.' Matter of fact, 'Shindig' is much livelier, daring in its youthful dance numbers and filled with a far more progressive musical outlook than 'Hootenanny' ever had. After only one(*sic*) season on the air, 'Hootenanny' was getting very pedestrian… even reaching the point where it appealed to some of Mitch Miller's fans, but you can be sure that 'Shindig' will not be for the senior citizens. It might even be the 'sleeper' hit of next season."

And so, Dankar closed down and everyone moved on. Fred Weintraub had already entered artist management and in 1967 would produce and host his own music series, *From The Bitter End*, that aired locally on WOR-TV. Two years later, he joined Warner Brothers' motion picture division as a production executive ("After 'Easy Rider' did so well, they wanted to hire someone with a pony tail down to his behind," he'd tell *Variety*), where he funded the filming of Woodstock and scored a major success with *Enter the Dragon* (1972). Marital arts was a favorite theme; as an independent producer, he'd oversee Jackie Chan's *The Big Brawl* (1980). At the 2012 Creator's Project, Weintraub predicted, "In five years there'll be 10 million people paying $2 to see a new movie on its first night on the internet." He died in 2017 at age 88.

Garth Dietrick returned to WNBC in New York; during the 1970s he directed some daytime programs, with a few special tasks like the network's coverage of *Macy's Thanksgiving Day Parade* thrown in, before retiring to Florida. Presumably all the other staffers found new jobs. Norman Keenan decided he'd had enough of folk music and joined Count Basie's orchestra, which lasted until 1974. He passed away in 1980.

After several years of hosting the Miss Universe pageant, Jack Linkletter took one more fling at series television in July 1978 with an NBC mid-day current events show titled *America Alive*. Unlike *Hootenanny*, this one didn't make it past its first six months. Undaunted, he pretty much vanished from television and made overseeing Linkletter Enterprises his primary vocation; at this he was excellent. Eventually, he took on a sideline as freelance consultant, targeting CEO's wishing to expand their businesses. "I want to grow you faster than your job," he'd tell them. "Highly creative growth companies obsolete themselves before the competition does…. What you are becoming has to be the priority." Linkletter remained president of his father's company until his untimely death from lymphoma in December 2007 at age 70.

ABC tried to make it up to Richard Lewine by offering him the producer's spot for its initial entry in the late-night, compete-with-Johnny-Carson sweepstakes: *The New Les Crane Show*, which began in August. Crane was an opinionated, outspoken former radio talk show host who, it sometimes seemed, liked to provoke his guests (or audience members) simply for the fun of it. He'd moved into television in 1962; the previous season, *The Les Crane Show* appeared solely on New York City's WABC, airing after 1:00 am before shifting into a mid-afternoon slot. Crane's style was the antithesis of Lewine's and the producer lasted less than a week before handing in his notice. The following year, he'd win an Emmy for producing Barbra Streisand's first TV special, *My Name is Barbra*. He co-authored such reference books as *Encyclopedia of Theater Music* and *Songs of the American Theater*, and finished out his prolific career as managing director of the Rodgers and Hammerstein Organization, taking over the position held by Richard Rodgers himself after the latter's passing.

Lewine died at age 94 in May 2005. His personal papers, several cartons' worth, were donated to the Performing Arts Library at Lincoln Center. The contents of his *Hootenanny* file consist of the hand-written sheet music for "Hootenanny Saturday Night" and a few newspaper articles.

Clearly, producing *Hootenanny* was not Richard Lewine's idea of a legacy.

EPILOGUE

ABC-TV's folksinging "Hootenanny" series, which has toured the college campus circuit, has been scratched from the network's lineup for the new fall season. Two late entries, one a situation comedy with Tony Franciosa, the other a musical show, and each 30 minutes in length, will be filled into the ABC-TV schedule replacing "Hootenanny," which is an often-vivacious program and deserves a better fate.

Rick DuBrow, UPI

There won't be any tears shed in this corner over "Hootenanny's" demise. We never did like the artificial pablum that Jack Linkletter, Fred Weintraub and Company served up to us week after interminable week. And if the pholk music wasn't insipid enough, the producers added insult to mayhem with their political blacklisting.

Irwin Silber, *Sing Out!*

Despite posterity's claim to the contrary, the British Invasion didn't kill off folk music. The weekend of July 24-26, with The Beatles, The Dave Clark Five, Dusty Springfield, Peter & Gordon, Gerry & The Pacemakers, Cilla Black, Billy J. Kramer with The Dakotas and The Searchers all in *Billboard's* Top 40, the 1964 Newport Folk Festival drew a record-shattering crowd of 70,000. The collegiates that swarmed to Rhode Island considered The Beatles and their ilk to be meaningful only to younger siblings, while they resolutely remained Bob Dylan's disciples. The following year, attendance reached 75,000, and when Dylan left the stage after "going electric" with The Paul Butterfield Blues Band for three numbers, according to *The Newport Mercury*, "there were numerous shouts for him to come back alone and to 'throw away that electric guitar.'" He did, for an acoustic "It's All Over Now, Baby Blue" and "Mr. Tambourine Man," a song that had just been released by an electrified group of folkies called The Byrds.

Albums by Joan Baez and Peter, Paul & Mary continued to sell reliably. In 1967, the "Summer of Love," Judy Collins recorded a top ten hit: Joni Mitchell's "Both Sides Now." In 1969, the year of *Woodstock* (where Baez performed), Collins charted with "Someday Soon" and Peter, Paul & Mary went to number one with John Denver's "Leaving on a Jet Plane." Denver himself would become a musical force the following decade, as would Mitchell, Carly Simon, Gordon Lightfoot and David Crosby.

Nor did *Hootenanny's* departure spell the end of folksingers on network television. *Hullaballoo*, NBC's living-color *Shindig!* clone, presented Collins, The Mitchell Trio, Bud and Travis, The Travelers 3, Trini Lopez, The Serendipity Singers and other *Hoot* graduates as guests. The Smothers Brothers' CBS variety hour arrived in 1967 and finally broke the network blacklist against Pete Seeger. Johnny Cash got his own show on ABC beginning in 1969, and brought on not only Seeger, but Dylan, Collins, Lightfoot, Odetta, Ian & Sylvia, Nancy Ames, Joni Mitchell, Ramblin' Jack Elliot, Eric Andersen and The Dillards.

As a marketable craze, though, the Folk Era had passed its shelf life. Back in mid-March '64, *Valley News* entertainment editor John Hoggatt warned, "In the opinion of observers of the music industry, the hootenanny fad is dying and the time is long past that three fraternity brothers could take their guitars, a sheaf of Woody Guthrie ballads and become instant folk singers…. The tours of colleges and smaller cities are not playing to sell-out audiences. Many clubs are moving back into jazz."

And scores of groups disappeared. The fates of The Limeliters, The Journeymen and The Big 3 have been previously documented. Marshall

Brickman quit the The Tarriers in 1965, turning to comedy writing; first for Johnny Carson and ultimately to script Woody Allen's most memorable films. Eric Weissburg and Clarence Cooper kept the act going with Al Dana, formerly with (Garrett) Brown & Dana, but inevitably the gigs dried up. Weissburg rose from the ashes to perform (with Steve Mandell) "Dueling Banjos" for the soundtrack of *Deliverance* (1973), winning a Grammy (for Best Country Instrumental) in the process.

Surprisingly, given their contentious personal relationship, Bud and Travis held on for a couple more years. Reportedly their partnership ended at The Gate of Horn in 1965 when, according to Travis Edmonson, Bud Dashiell "pushed me into the wall, and my head was broken open," an event witnessed by guitarist Frank Hamilton. Their final appearances as a duo, though, appear to be at San Francisco's El Matador for four weeks beginning in late January 1966. Philip F. Elwood, reviewer for the *San Francisco Examiner*, caught them at this third-rate venue (with "ratchety bar equipment"), performing for an indifferent and talkative audience ("how can four 60 year-olds spend five minutes deciding whose drink is which?") and, although impressed by "gorgeous renditions of 'A Cloudy Sunday(*sic*) Afternoon' and 'It Was a Very Good Year,'" he also noted, "Some of the old Bud and Travis ability to communicate seems to have diminished." Regardless of what happened when, the two parted ways for good before spring.

Second-echelon groups like The Wanderers Three, The Gaslight Singers, The Ivy League Trio, The Coventry Singers, The Three Young Men from Montana and The Brandywine Singers faded from view not long after the final *Hootenanny* rerun had aired. As we've seen, some of their members remained in music in one capacity or another, while most went into the fields for which they were studying before the craze sidetracked them.

Some, like The Glencoves' Brian Bolger, set music aside when their nation called. "I was at Georgetown University when [the Jesuit priests] Philip and Daniel Berrigan were burning draft cards. Here I am singing 'Blowin' in the Wind' and 'Where Have all the Flowers Gone,' and a year later I was throwing bombs at the Viet Cong. But it was never in my mind that I wouldn't go." Bolger served in the Navy on a destroyer as Chief Engineer until 1971, married and raised seven children, two of whom became priests themselves.

Although consisting only of 43 shows that would never be syndicated, *Hootenanny* certainly left many a legacy. For one thing, according to accompanist Paul Prestopino, "the 'clap-along syndrome' was actually started by one of the show's producers. Folk audiences hadn't done that before…. I distinctly remember that producer starting the audience clapping on every up-tempo song. It was really annoying." Prestopino's recollection is borne out by comparing "In Concert" recordings made before and after 1963.

For another, *Hootenanny* inspired Canada's *Let's Sing Out*, hosted by Oscar Brand and taped at various Canadian colleges. That series debuted in October 1963 and because its producer, Sydney Banks, wasn't hampered by meddling executives or performers refusing to appear, it remained a half-hour show and aired for four seasons, with reruns continuing for another two. "If there's a stamp on the show, it's pure integrity," Banks told *The Vancouver Province* in April 1964. "We're doing a true hoot: folk performers and artists getting together and swapping songs and involving the student audience in the spirit of it. *Hootenanny* is more of a variety show, but I'm not knocking it. That's their concept." Or at least, it *became* their concept.

That an event could serve as a title paved the way for *Shindig!*, *Hullaballoo* and *Shivaree*. These and many similar shows became possible in part because *Hootenanny* proved young people make an attractive—and lucrative—audience. Certainly the intimacy of its staging and audience seating carried into countless music programs over the years, all the way to *MTV Unplugged*.

Hootenanny's enduring legacy is its reputation for presenting nothing but "pablum" or "pholk music," as Irwin Silber put it. As readers hopefully now realize, that's an over-generalization. Significant songs and performers were included as often as possible, for as long as they agreed to appear, but the upshot is, slick, peppy groups were popular and thus desirable for keeping viewers tuned in through the commercials. The preponderance of male trios and quartets were partially a reflection of the marketplace in those Kingston Trio days, but the loss of prominent women's voices like Judy Collins, Carolyn Hester, Miriam Makeba and Bonnie Dobson left a void the series could never effectively fill. It's depressing to conjecture, had a third season happened, how many more opera singers Lewine would've booked to plug the gap.

The show's most durable pop culture impact was in launching The Serendipity Singers. Because they came after The New Christy Minstrels, there's a perception they were merely a carbon copy, yet its members had more freedom in selecting, writing, and arranging material, and in at least one way were more successful. In the heat of the British Invasion, "Don't Let The Rain Come Down" reached #6 on the Hot 100, whereas the Minstrels' biggest hit, "Green, Green," peaked at #14, and their latest release, the romantic ballad "Today," went to #17. Unfortunately, The Serendipities' second single, Len Chandler's "Beans in My Ears," would stall at #30. Doctors griped their young patients were indeed putting beans in their ears, radio stations pulled it from rotation and at least two cities, Boston and Pittsburgh, banned the song outright. "Obviously it was a statement about adults not listening to children," said Bryan Sennett. "Some television shows asked us to do something different. Understandably so—it was dangerous."

As with the Christies, the group's founding members gradually departed and were replaced. Lynne Weintraub left in November 1964 when she married television producer Bob Kline; her replacement was Patti Davis (neé Juarez). According to John Madden, none of the newcomers became part of the corporation. By 1970, all of the originals were gone; Mike Brovsky went into management and bought out the others' interest in T.D. Shawbym. Eventually the group name was controlled by Theatrical Corporation of America; its manager, David Stanton, assembled two separate "Serendipity Singers" lineups and sent one out on the college circuit and the other on a USO tour of Europe. TV specials and direct-to-video programs were the group's bread-and-butter during the 1980s and '90s. In 1999, the original members reunited for a concert in Branson, Missouri; four years later, they regrouped to appear in a PBS special. They were inducted into the Colorado Music Hall of Fame in 2013 and reunited once more to perform at the ceremony.

* * * * *

As 1964 progressed, the craze's mass marketing dissipated. With the TV series kaput, *ABC-TV Hootenanny* magazine folded after its third issue; cover-dated July, it hit the street just before the cancellation was announced. The earlier, Bob Shelton-edited *Hootenanny* would only make it to four, the final one cover-dated November. This issue, with the striped-shirted Kingston Trio on its cover touting a Shelton-penned evaluation titled "The Kingston Trio vs. Beatlemania," sets a tone that might best be described as schizophrenic.

Although promising readers he "is not changing his preferences for real folk music," Shelton gamely gives the Kingstons, particularly their first hit, "Tom Dooley," a degree of respect not shown in prior issues: "Many ethnically oriented folk fans have forgotten that… 'Tom Dooley' was a bonafide Appalachian folk song done in a fashion that was one of the trio's least contentious performances [and that it] was to trigger the whole folk and 'hootenanny' revival…." He also, cagily, targets Beatlemania and not the group itself: "[The] shrieking of hysterical girls… fans lined up for hours for a glimpse of a quartet of four shaggy Teddy Boys… jelly beans tossed on stage…" and a "manufactured, assembly-line, hoked-up craze that 17 press agents, untold dozens of disk jockeys and a corps of promoters were able to effect on the American listening public." Shelton admits that "knowledgeable folk fans have found something of merit in the music… a certain funky, bluesy quality that rings sympathetically in their ears," while also insisting, "It would be difficult to discuss the music of The Beatles seriously" because "such mass madness" overpowers it. Conversely, "No one, to our knowledge, has ever thrown jelly beans at The Kingston Trio to show admiration."

Dave Van Ronk, in a piece titled "Beyond Folk Music," insists "the work of The Kingston Trio, The Brothers Four, Peter, Paul and Mary, etc., however pleasant and catchy it might be, will have no lasting significance. Their music will be listened to in 20 years in the same way that one might listen to an old recording of 'Yes, Sir, That's My Baby.'" Elsewhere, Peter Yarrow hails Van Ronk as one among select artists who "will embrace not only a music but also a total cultural attitude other than his own… that can be believable." And while acknowledging the craze was waning, Yarrow asserts "the phenomenon of folk music as a fad never really did feel right…. Folk music is not **like** caring about other people, it **is** those things. It is because this is the 'stuff' of which folk music is made that even thinking of it as a fad demeans it."

Amidst profiles of Joan Baez (penned by her soon-to-be brother-in-law Richard Fariña) and Homer & Jethro (penned by themselves), the rest of the magazine covered the usual gamut of record, club and concert reviews, and a bundle of song sheets, from the traditional ("Deep Blue Sea") to the modern (Gil Turner's "Carry It On"). Surprisingly, there's no write-up of the summer's Newport festival, which strongly implies the issue was assembled prior to that event. If they were saving such a piece for issue five, it was a lost cause. The compact, economically-produced *Sing Out!* would alone carry the music's literary torch for the foreseeable future. Shelton continued reviewing music for *The New York Times* and penning liner notes, and reportedly spent twenty years writing a biography of Bob Dylan, which saw publication in 1986 under the title *No Direction Home.* Within its pages, he briefly discussed *Hootenanny* and, with the perspective of time, admitted "some good performances did sneak through; some obscure musicians won recognition. The TV series probably led millions of its viewers toward quality song." In 1969, he settled in Brighton, England, and worked for the *Brighton Evening Argus* as its Arts editor. Given his withering indictment of Beatlemania at its start, it's ironic that, after his December 1995 passing, Shelton's personal papers were donated to the University of Liverpool's Institute of Popular Music.

Some may be surprised to learn *Hootenanny Hoot* wasn't the only Folk Era movie, although the second wasn't widely distributed until 2006. As 1964 began, Frederic Berney, a recent graduate of Miami University, had been recording a radio show from the city's Hootenanny Coffee House, owned by brothers Carl and Roger Yale. His father, Harold Berney, an insurance salesman by day, had invested $30,000 in the production of *Sextet* (1964), a 67-minute excuse for six unclad women to fawn over Miami nightclub comic Pauly Dash. This dubious cinematic flirtation escalated into co-owning Motion Picture Films Inc., producers of commercials that played at local drive-in theaters, as well as musical shorts for Cinebox jukeboxes. With partner Harvey Berman, the senior Berney was seeking feature properties; simultaneously, his son was conceiving one.

During the weeks of recording his radio show, Fred Berney "got to talking with the brothers, and they were telling me all the trials and tribulations of owning a coffee house. My father had just done *Sextet*, so the idea of doing a movie was in my head. And I told them, 'This sounds like a neat story. Why don't one of you write this on paper and we'll see if we can produce a movie?'" Carl Yale wrote the scenario and a dozen songs; Berney hired Jerry Winters to direct.

Next, the novice producer went to New York to sign some names, a process hampered by his budget, which was then set at $60,000. "I met with a vice-president of Epic Records," he remembers. "When I walked into their office, I saw these big posters for The GoldeBriars and The Freewheelers." The former had just completed their *Hootenanny* appearance, and the label was about to issue "Walk, Walk," the latter's debut single. "He says, 'I'll give you these groups,' because he wanted to get them into a movie and promote that. And he said, 'We'll release your soundtrack album.'" Easily the most important performer engaged was Oscar Brand, on hiatus from *Let's Sing Out*. The only one permitted to sing something other than Carl Yale's compositions, Brand chose a traditional Irish tune, "Cod Liver Oil," and his own "My Old Man." Also in the cast was the folk-comedy team of Jim, Jake and Joan that featured

Jake Holmes, formerly of Allen and Grier, and Joan Rivers. As for the leading roles, finding name actors that would accept $750 per week plus expenses proved impossible, so Berney settled for those he was offered: Curtis Taylor, a 30-year-old former NBC pageboy and TV commercial actor, and Karen Thorsell, also a TV ad veteran whose most recent endeavor, the Broadway comedy *Have I Got a Girl for You*, closed after one critically-lambasted performance.

Karen Thorsell and Curtis Taylor make their movie debut in *Once Upon a Coffee House* (1964). At right is a member of The New Coachmen, a group that headlined at Miami's Hootenanny Coffee House. *Photo courtesy of Fred Berney*

Back in Miami, eight locals were cast in supporting roles, including singer Vince Martin, who'd scored a chart hit in 1957 with "Cindy O, Cindy" (for which he was backed by The Tarriers) and Eve Tellegen, who as Eve Casanova had been active in theater, film and radio since the 1920s. Shooting had originally been slated to begin April 20. That got pushed all the way to June 8 due to time spent casting the leads and selecting a new director. "Jerry Winters had a track record," says Berney, "but he would make art movies. And I saw this as a down-to-earth movie that hits the general public, not art houses." The script, titled *Once Upon a Coffee House*, had a simple story: rich 'square' boy (*Taylor*) flies to

Miami every weekend to woo pretty girl folksinger (*Thorsell*), who isn't interested in him. The coffee house's smarmy owner (*Jerry Newby*) talks boy into buying his money-losing business, thus becoming girl's employer. All the usual 'inept-boy-eventually-wins-clever-girl' complications ensue in between a lot of singing. "When the script was written and [Winters] looked at it," says Berney, "he didn't understand the joke about the boy going horseback riding [for the first time] and later has to eat his dinner standing by the fireplace mantle. When I realized he didn't understand that basic joke, I thought, 'I've got the wrong man as director.'"

Winters was released and Shepard Traube was engaged. "Shep," as everyone knew him, at least had mainstream cinema directorial experience, although it was mostly limited to big band short subjects of the late 1940s. Once hired, says Berney, "he'd take his hundred-dollar-a-day per diem on the weekends and fly to the Bahamas and gamble. He wasn't working on the picture. Most directors would take the weekends to plot out the following week's shooting." The inevitable result: delays that sent costs skyrocketing. "In order to try coming in under budget, Shep tore fifteen-to-twenty pages out of the script, which is why the movie runs only 82 minutes." Along with the pages went Berney Productions' hope that their finished product could run on its own and not as half of a double feature.

As shooting finally wound down, the company was hit with two lawsuits: one from Winters over his dismissal, who sought $5,000 in actual damages and a quarter-million in punitive damages, and another from a vocalist named Aileen Frances, seeking $750,000, claiming she'd been promised Thorsell's role, then was downgraded to the second lead and eventually shut out altogether. "I met her brother, who was an attorney, the year before and he told us about her," Berney recalls. "She'd just recorded a song ["You Better Leave Him Alone" for Roulette Records] and was starting to get some publicity. Shep didn't want to use her, but I did, so I mailed her a contract. Shep would not shoot a scene with her, and basically her brother sued us." Both lawsuits were settled out of court.

Berney returned to New York to assist with editing and oversee the sweetening of the music and effects. While there, "I went back to Epic and [a poster of] The Dave Clark Five had replaced The Freewheelers… and I thought 'Uh-oh. They're not [promoting] these groups anymore.'" The promise of a soundtrack release by Columbia's subsidiary label quickly vanished. There was also zero excitement generated by distributors when a finished print was screened. The only theatrical distribution *Once Upon a Coffee House* would see came in late April 1965, when it played in Miami as a supporting feature at one hardtop and three drive-ins owned by the city's Wometco Theater chain… and *that* was because the daughter of Sonny Shepherd, Wometco's vice-president, had been an extra.

Newspaper advertisement for *Once Upon a Coffee House's* sole theatrical run in April 1965.

In the interim, Joan Rivers had gone solo and became a star but not enough to aid the box office, and folk groups who weren't Peter, Paul & Mary were fading from view. Reviewers for both the *Miami Herald* and *Miami News* panned the picture. Once the run ended in early May, that was that… for forty-one years.

The finished film has a sort of quirky charm that makes it more likeable than the purely exploitative *Hootenanny Hoot*. While there's little chemistry between them, Curtis and Thorsell do the best they can with the contrivances they're given. As for the music, a couple of Yale's originals, particularly the spiritual on which The GoldeBriars and The Freewheelers duet, are quite good; the rest at least don't embarrass anyone. Oscar Brand is excellent; the GoldeBriars' "Honey Bunny" is cute; The Freewheelers make a fine ersatz Brothers Four; Jim, Jake and Joan are easily the funniest ones in the film; and Thorsell, despite the distraction that her six-string acoustic is overdubbed by an electric guitar, holds her own vocally. On the downside are the claustrophobic sets, an abundance of interior shots, and Traube's lackadaisical pacing and heavy-handed approach to comedy. Worst of all is Jerry Newby as the sleazeball coffee house owner. A local actor whose experience up to then was limited to "musicals around town" according to *Miami News* columnist Herb Kelly, Newby's every gesture is aimed at the last row of the local playhouse. Traube should've reminded him that in motion pictures, less is more.

In truth, there was a lot Traube should've done, but didn't. "After about five days of shooting, we were running behind," Berney recalls, "and people were saying, 'Fred, *you* could direct this.' Everybody on the crew said, 'We'll help you do this. We'll work with you.' It was my father's money and I was afraid. I'd never directed anything except a couple of commercials, telling people to stand next to a refrigerator." With the perspective of time, Berney admits "it would've been interesting. And it couldn't have been any worse, and might've been better."

Over the ensuing years, Berney would try to get somebody to distribute *Once Upon a Coffee House*, and his efforts finally paid off in 2006, when Steve Kaplan of Alpha Video, a budget-line DVD manufacturer, agreed to a release under their "New Cinema" division. However, they wanted to change the title to something more commercial, and better able to communicate the youth appeal for folk music that Berney Productions had sought from the beginning. Alpha's choice: *Hootenanny-a-Go-Go*.

* * * * *

The original Weavers are filmed by Jim Brown for his moving documentary *Wasn't That a Time* (1982) From left-to-right: Pete Seeger, Lee Hays, Ronnie Gilbert, Fred Hellerman. *From the author's collection*

In 1980, a young filmmaker named Jim Brown was asked to produce and direct a documentary about a long-time friend and neighbor, Lee Hays, and the group with which he used to perform. Hays wrote and narrated The Weavers' story, designed to conclude with the original foursome reminiscing and performing together for the first time since 1963 at a picnic in Hays' backyard. The high spirits that enveloped this informal concert, with family and neighbors gathered around and clearly enjoying themselves, prompted Pete Seeger to suggest they give Carnegie Hall one more fling. Although the others were skeptical, especially the ailing double-amputee Hays, it didn't take a great deal of persuasion to convince them; as Ronnie Gilbert wistfully put it, "Ahh, to do it for one more moment...." Seeger's manager Howard Leventhal set up a two-night appearance in November. The resulting documentary, titled *Wasn't*

That a Time! after one of Hays' more controversial songs, was released in mid-1982 and won plaudits from critics nationwide, but it was the concert itself that opened a floodgate.

In 1981, the Kingston Trio's original members were persuaded to reunite for a show that would be recorded for television's Public Broadcasting System (PBS). Any hope this would be another warm and fuzzy reunion of old friends and colleagues was quickly dashed. Although Dave Guard had mellowed in the intervening years, his 1961 departure was contentious, and Bob Shane in particular had little desire to work with him again. Nick Reynolds had remained friends with John Stewart, who'd logged more years than Guard, and felt Stewart should also participate in any reunion. Stewart wanted the opportunity to perform his new release, "Gold," and invited Fleetwood Mac's Lindsay Buckingham to play bass during his set with Bob and Nick. Shane owned the Kingston Trio name, had been touring under it with two others since 1972, and wanted the current "others"—Roger Gambill and George Grove—on the program. (Shane actually told the *Palm Beach Post*, after rehearsing with Reynolds and Guard, "it made me realize the group I have now is better.") Everyone acquiesced to everything; Tom Smothers was engaged to host; Mary Travers did a guest vocal with the trio on "Where Have All the Flowers Gone." The resulting show was titled *The Kingston Trio and Friends: Reunion*, and took place at Six Flags Magic Mountain's Showcase Theater on November 7 for airing over the PBS network the following March.

During the '70s, folk music became the purview of PBS, with both veterans and a newer breed of practitioners making appearances on *Soundstage* and *Austin City Limits*. With the success of the Kingston Trio program, the network discovered the original folkies were a good pledge week drawing card and would trot out various specials over the next twenty-some years, starring Peter, Paul & Mary, Joan Baez, The Chad Mitchell Trio, Judy Collins, Pete Seeger and Arlo Guthrie, Ian & Sylvia, and more, culminating in 2003's *This Land is Our Land: The Pop-Folk Years*, a program filled with *Hootenanny* alumni: Collins, Tommy Makem, Erik Darling, Scott McKenzie, Trini Lopez, The Shaw Brothers, Jerry Yester, Eric Weissburg and all nine original Serendipity Singers (as "A Serendipitous Reunion").

Two prominent *Hootenanny* holdouts are flanked by two of its participants in this promotional photo for a 1981 *Soundstage* special on PBS. From left-to-right: Bob Gibson, Odetta, Tom Paxton and Josh White, Jr. *From the author's collection*

* * * * *

Forty years after the hootenanny craze peaked, Christopher Guest paid it a loving satiric tribute with his film, *A Mighty Wind* (2003). The movie, designed as a pseudo-documentary, starred Guest, Michael McKean and Harry Shearer—who'd portrayed the titular heavy metal rock group in *This is Spinal Tap* (1986)—as The Folksmen, a clone of nearly every picking and strumming all-male threesome that arrived in the wake of The Kingston Trio. Its story centers around the passing of Irving Steinbloom, a mythical empresario who managed not only The Folksmen, but also The Main Street Singers (seven males and two females assembled from various soloists, duets and trios... sound familiar?) and "the sweethearts of folk music," Mitch & Mickey (*Eugene*

Levy and Catherine O'Hara). Steinbloom's eldest son, Jonathan (*Bob Balaban*), wants to pay tribute to his dad by bringing these long-forgotten acts together for a memorial concert. The Folksmen are all in, but Mitch & Mickey divorced bitterly years before, while the ensemble has since become The New Main Street Singers featuring one original member

(*Paul Dooley*) and the daughter (*Parker Posey*) of another, now managed by Mike LaFontaine (*Fred Willard*), a failed sitcom actor whose idea of a major deal is booking his "neuftet" on cruise ships and at amusement parks where the stage is placed next to the roller coaster. And since the nervous, finicky Jonathan thoroughly lacks his father's managerial savvy, the challenges are enormous… and very funny throughout.

Guest's modus operandi was to script (usually with a collaborator; in this case, Levy) the character biographies and individual situations, then let his actors improvise the dialogue. "We give [them] enough information," Levy told AP's Anthony Breznican. "They know what they have to come out with, we just don't tell them how to say it." Most worked steadily with the director and appeared in at least one of his two previous films, *Waiting for Guffman* (1996) and *Best in Show* (2000). Guest understood he had improvisational gold, telling Chris Garcia of the *Austin American-Statesman*, "These actors are the best at this you can get… you trust what they're going to do. There's no burden individually, because you know if you're not stepping up in an instance, someone will be there to pick up." The players understood it, too. "It looks from the outside like we're working with no net," said Shearer. "Actually, everybody is everybody else's net."

A Mighty Wind is charming and by no means a derisive slam at the Folk Era, something a few critics, based on their reviews, would have preferred. "The songs don't sound very different from the 40-year-old hootenanny tunes they're supposedly skewering," wrote the *Tampa Bay Times'* Steve Persall, adding, "Guest and Levy don't have the courage of their convictions to show this dead-ended optimism for the silly fad it was."

Guest would respond Persall and like-minded reviewers were missing the point. "It's not an attack on the music," he assured Garcia. "It's not about mocking… it's observing these people. We create these characters and it's about them going through this very specific story." Still, when crafting the film's songs and arrangements, they kept the genre's most commercial aspects at the forefront. One of their resources was 1963's *Jack Linkletter Presents a Folk Festival* LP which, as noted earlier, introduced The Yachtsmen ("What could be folksier than yachting?" McKean asked dryly). The album's opening track, "Drivin' Wheels," inspired McKean and Shearer to pen "Never Did No Wanderin'," a tune about a would-be rambler who just never got around to it. But another source, clearly, is the moving *Wasn't That a Time!* The Folksmen's initial reunion takes place at a backyard picnic, and during the concert Mitch & Mickey's duet becomes a symbol for everything they, the others and their audience ever hoped for or believed when the music was new.

Sweet as it all is, the movie does include one telling moment. During a pre-concert cocktail party, McKean's character, Jerry Palter, is conversing with an elderly African-American gentleman (*Bill Cobbs*). Palter gripes to his stoic seatmate that only slick, ultra-commercial, snow-white groups like The New Main Street Singers can "make money playing folk music." By now we're aware Palter and his two bandmates consider themselves authentic folk purists, despite the fact that their biggest hit was a novelty song. Cobbs' character, who we presume to be a performer in the Josh White mold, merely turns away while Palter continues to bad mouth the Main Streeters with his holier-than-thou mindset. The vignette passes quickly and, like everything else in the film, is not overplayed; modern audiences tend to let it slip by unnoticed. But for those who truly remember, the jibe is unmistakable: Cobbs' character, whoever he's meant to be, knows The Folksmen and The New Main Street Singers are two sides of the same counterfeit coin.

The film, which had a modest production budget of $6 million, opened on April 16, 2003. In limited release to 133 theaters, it grossed a surprising $2.1 million on opening weekend, coming in at ninth place for the weekend's top ten box office. In the end, *A Mighty Wind* played on 770 screens over three months to a respectable worldwide gross of $18.5 million. One of its songs, Mitch & Mickey's "Kiss at the End of the Rainbow" (written by McKean and his wife, Annette O'Toole) would be nominated for an Academy Award.

* * * * *

As *A Mighty Wind* did its wanderin' from concept to theaters to home video and cable channel release, some behind-the-scenes work was under way to recover what remained of *Hootenanny*.

In 1998, Richard Foos and Harold Bronson of Rhino Entertainment sold out to Warner Brothers, and once all contractual obligations within that deal were met, they were free to launch a new company: Shout Factory. Robert S. Bader, a former editor at CBS who'd done some freelance work for Foos and Bronson, was asked to join the team as a producer. Says Bader, "We made a list of things we wanted to work on. We wanted to do *Shindig!* but it was really impossible, because the ownership was in question; the Disney company was saying they owned *Shindig!* I said, 'What about *Hootenanny*? The precursor of *Shindig!*' We were looking for pop culture stuff, of music, of… things you grew up on, but never outgrew. So, I started researching where I could find episodes of *Hootenanny*. All the videotapes were erased." What remained, of course, were kinescopes, and "we got 'em from a lot of different sources. I had fifteen episodes to work from to make this collection, and everything was a kinescope, in different [degrees of] quality [including] kinescopes that were made from kinescopes."

Bader had originally thought there'd be a box set with complete programs, but "our development team thought the episodes were boring as s***. So, I thought we could make three 90-minute 'television shows' and sell them to PBS for a two-hour pledge slot, because we were really good at that; we'd done a whole bunch of them." Given the network's proclivity toward using folk performers for their perennial fundraising drives, it was a logical conclusion, but the fuzzy, uneven black & white footage proved too big a hurdle for PBS execs. They weren't even interested in using them as pledge premiums.

Instead, Shout focused on retail. Clearing music rights wasn't that big an expense, says Bader. "There were something like twenty public domain songs on each of the three discs, which is what made this thing palatable and gave me the budget to do some nice packaging." In editing the shows, Bader took out the parts the company considered dull, and the three volumes gave them flexibility. "In those days," Bader recalls, "it cost less to make 40,000 discs than it did to make 20,000. The packaging was more expensive than the replicating. So, they'd manufacture a ton of discs as if they were going to make 30,000 sets and then they'd do the packaging for 7,500 of them. They'd put them out in retail, and if they don't get reorders, they'd do some cheap slimline packaging and put out volumes one, two and three as stand-alone discs for budget stores."

The Best of Hootenanny almost does the best it could with the material available to it. There are classic performances here by those who did the show most often; by legends; by the fondly remembered; by the completely forgotten. Bader strove to keep each of his three "programs" balanced between groups, duos and soloists, and no more than two comedians per disc. There's a little gospel, a little country, a little jazz. The feel of the show remains, including some of Jack Linkletter's on-campus introductions as we move from one location to another. The superfluous has been discarded: there are no clog dancers, no opera singers, no mime troupes.

On the other hand, topical songs are represented solely by The Chad Mitchell Trio's "The John Birch Society" and Trini Lopez singing "If I Had a Hammer." Performances available but not used include Martha Schlamme's powerful interpretation of "Johnny, I Hardly Knew Ye;" Bud and Travis' rendition of Tom Lehrer's "Fiesta in Guadalajara;" the blues medley at University of Pittsburgh with Leon Bibb, The Rooftop Singers and Judy Henske (who isn't in the set at all); The Journeymen's lovely "Someone to Talk My Troubles To;" "Rum by Gum," another satiric Chad Mitchell Trio number. By far, the saddest omission is "Mbube" with the Trio and Miriam Makeba, a landmark moment of racial equality in early '60s network TV. Instead, we get The Tarriers' unremarkable sing-along "Wimoweh," inexplicably chosen over two much stronger performances: "Take This Hammer" and "Poor Lazarus."

The booklet included with the set, penned by musicologist Todd Everett, is succinct and informative, although it includes two glaring errors: misidentifying Trini Lopez's bassist Dick Brant as Glen Campbell, and mistaking Norman Keenan for Bill Lee. Chalk the former up to a slight facial resemblance and the latter to what was likely a guess fueled by Lee's presence on the most memorable Folk Era LPs.

Shout Factory's *The Best of Hootenanny* 3-DVD collection, released in 2007, uses The New Christy Minstrels' 1964 lineup as its lure.

The DVD set reached shelves on January 16, 2007. Newspaper critics that received advance copies were predictably unimpressed. *The Washington Post's* Richard Harrington simply parroted what he'd learned from Wikipedia about the show's banning of Pete Seeger and censoring of Judy Collins, then added pithy observations such as Jack Linkletter "sometimes talking over performances as if he were taping 'Wild Kingdom.' 'Mild Kingdom' was more like it." He also confesses, "It's not always easy to differentiate from among the Travelers Three, the Chad Mitchell Trio and the Journeymen," which speaks volumes about his lack of interest in the genre.

Likewise, Bruce Daniels of the *Sacramento Bee* spent about half his piece detailing the controversies before admitting "some fine groups and singers did appear on 'Hootenanny,' and there are enough other unusual performances to spark interest.... Judy Collins does an outstanding rendition of 'Anathea,' and the young Canadian duo of Ian & Sylvia demonstrate their unique harmonic sense.... Two international acts— South Africa's Mirima Makeba and Ireland's Clancy Brothers & Tommy Makem—are also excellent." But Daniels declares "the first-rate performers on 'Hootenanny' were outnumbered by lesser lights," which in his view include The New Christy Minstrels, The Serendipity Singers, The Simon Sisters, The Rooftop Singers and The Travelers 3. "Overall, one is left underwhelmed," he concluded. "A lot of powerful, engaging and provocative folk music could be heard at the time of the TV show, performed by the likes of Dylan, Baez, Seeger, Phil Ochs, Dave Van Ronk, Tom Paxton and others, but you couldn't find them on 'Hootenanny.'"

In the *Iowa City Press-Citizen*, Jim Musser's Music Beat column advised "the somewhat blurred/grainy kinescope sources won't show off your 'hi-def' plasma screen or your 'theater-surround' system" and decided "the great moments here... are far outnumbered by bizarre, rhythm-and-charisma-challenged dilettantes and frightfully earnest mediocrities—many of whom were actually 'stars' at the time." Still, Musser recommended the set as "neither definitive nor disposable... worth seeing as an intriguing slice of pop-culture history. The eager, enthusiastic campus crowds and volatile times provided ample kindling for a fire, but—at least on 'Hootenanny'—the matches too often were damp."

In what qualifies as the irony of ironies, the set's most favorable review appeared in the website maintained by *Sing Out!* magazine. Ron Olesko, long-time programmer for WFDU-FM and president of the Hurdy-Gurdy Folk Music Club in Fair Lawn, New Jersey, penned a piece that flat out rejects co-founder Silber's perspective: "I found the discs fascinating and highly entertaining—a worthy addition to the library of anyone with an interest in the history and music of the folk revival."

After thoroughly detailing the Seeger controversy, Olesko writes, "History has a way of becoming clouded with opinion as time marches on. A lot of negative opinion has been written over the years and the show is often dismissed as 'second tier' quality performers with little connection to 'real' folk music. The DVD boxed set tells a different story. Yes, there are performers that will make you cringe…. There are a number of 'collegiate' groups [whose] cleaned up styles and set patter flew in the face of the music…. Yet some of these groups are notable for the joy they seem to be truly sharing. [The Rooftop Singers'] interplay on "I've Been Working On the Railroad" turned a corny childhood ditty into an exciting musical expression of joy…. Watching the Simon Sisters was a moving experience [as] they deliver a passionate version of 'Turn, Turn, Turn.' The song brings up another point. While Pete Seeger may not have been present, his music and spirit [were]." The review also reminds readers the show took place "during the days when the Civil Rights movement was picking up momentum. Seeing an integrated group like the Tarriers must have ruffled a few feathers in parts of the country, but 'Hootenanny' appeared ready to offer the stage to artists who might not have had an opportunity to perform on television before."

Where Nat Hentoff saw artifice, Olesko saw honesty. "This was the first time I saw either Clara Ward or Marion Williams. To say that their audio recordings do not do them justice is an understatement…. Whatever staging was done for [their] songs was not done for enhancement or effect, it was a natural extension of the music." The review concludes with, "If you truly keep an open mind and watch this without any preconceived notions, I believe you will appreciate and be entertained by most of the performances…. Thanks to the technology of DVD's we can re-educate ourselves and make up our own minds on the historic legacy of *Hootenanny*."

Sadly, *The Best of Hootenanny* is now out-of-print, but copies can occasionally be found on eBay and Amazon Marketplace.

* * * * *

Olesko's review was a step toward setting the record straight for *Hootenanny*. This book is dedicated to the same purpose. There's no escaping the fact that barring Pete Seeger was both cowardly and shortsighted, hurting the series through his lack of participation and that of other performers, but the majority of those who did appear expertly represented their art. Thankfully, some of its best, brightest moments survive. Some of the era's most popular artists can be seen in their prime. Sometimes the sight and sound of a youthful audience singing along compels viewers to join in, just as it did back then. Sometimes the camera cuts to a student listening raptly, eyes riveted to the stage, and you marvel at the power of this music to touch the heart.

And sometimes we're reminded of how far we've come as a nation since 1963, and how far we still have to go.

Even prior to the rise of Guthrie and Seeger, folk music was employed for political purposes. During the *Hootenanny* period, its primary mission was aiding the integration movement, and to the extent songs like "We Shall Overcome," "If I Had a Hammer," "Blowin' in the Wind" and "What's That I Hear" helped pass the Civil Rights Act of 1964, it succeeded. With songs like "Last Night I Had the Strangest Dream," "Where Have All the Flowers Gone," "Come Away, Melinda" and "I Ain't Marching Anymore," folk musicians also hoped to end war in our lifetimes. No need to elaborate on how *that* turned out.

Molly Scott insists the Folk Era "was enormously important for how it provided a platform for the necessary expression of political discontent, and how it served culturally that way." Still, there's much more to the music than political commentary. The Weavers might've given us "If I Had a Hammer," but they also gave us "Kisses Sweeter Than Wine." The Bob Dylan who penned "Blowin' in the Wind" and "Masters of War" also wrote "Tomorrow is a Long Time" and "It Ain't Me, Babe." Work songs, drinking songs, children's songs, songs of loves won and lost, songs of hope and despair, songs of faith and redemption: they're still being written and performed by those who've lived them or believe in their messages and just want to sing… and invite you to sing along.

Organizations such as the World Folk Music Association and The Hurdy-Gurdy Folk Music Club host concerts that spotlight musicians and singer-songwriters who carry the torch into the present. Some of the era's classic commercial groups also continue: The Kingston Trio, The Limeliters and The Brothers Four tour every now and again, sometimes together, even if between them there's only one original member—the latter's Bob Flick—standing on stage. The newcomers respect their predecessors and the brand names still resonate with audiences because the music remains memorable.

"Melody is how we're wired musically," affirms Dr. Scott, who speaks as both folksinger and therapist. "And the source, melodically, for any culture's expression is what we call folk music. The thing about folk music's endurance, the gestalt of it, is that it's music that comes out of people's lives, out of people's work. And it changes, because the culture changes. So, there's a permission in folk music to change words and change stories, to let it evolve and grow. From the very beginning, with Woody Guthrie, and Cisco Houston, and Pete Seeger, [folk music] has to do with people, and sharing, and singing together."

At its very best, *Hootenanny* brought all of that before the eyes and ears of millions.

THE NATION'S TOP FOLKSINGING STARS!
WTEV 6
abc
HOOTENANNY!
SATURDAY - 8:30 PM
DIRECT FROM
BROWN UNIVERSITY
NATIONALLY TELEVISED! abc
JACK LINKLETTER
Master of Ceremonies
THEODORE BIKEL
TOMMY MAKEM
THE CLANCY BROTHERS
BROWN
JUDY COLLINS
6 WTEV

ACKNOWLEDGEMENTS

Hootenanny is among my earliest television memories. Although I mainly watched cartoons, *Captain Kangaroo* and *Romper Room*, I distinctly remember the opening title with an illustration of a banjo underneath from a show that left the air before my fifth birthday. Furthermore, my dad's recording of The Smothers Brothers performing "John Henry" at Rutgers is the first comedy I recall. "This baby's wet on me!" sent me into hysterics every time.

Therefore, my deepest thanks, appreciation and love go to my father, John J. Hayde, for recording that broadcast and many others. Without those tapes, I wouldn't have sought out the show's history or considered assessing its place in the legacies of folk music and television.

Having those tapes also enabled me to trade with a fellow *Hootenanny* collector: Paul Kattelman of Ohio. His collection included shows I didn't have and more complete versions of a few I did have. Thank you, Paul.

I'm sincerely grateful to those who appeared on the show and, over the years, shared their memories with me via regular mail, email, telephone and Zoom: Mike Kobluk of The Chad Mitchell Trio, Jeff Hyman of The Gaslight Singers, Dr. Molly Scott, John Madden of The Serendipity Singers, Naomi Brossart, Paul Prestopino and the late Jo Mapes. Others who were part of this story and graciously gave of their time: Don Connors and Brian Bolger of The Glencoves; Frederic Berney, producer of *Once Upon a Coffee House* (a.k.a. *Hootenanny-a-Go-Go*); Mark A. Bush of the College of William & Mary Class of 1965; and Robert S. Bader, producer of Shout Factory's *Best of Hootenanny* DVD set. For help in filling in some blanks and providing images and other assistance, I want to thank Emily Conner, Mike Devich, Hillary Mapes Levine and Ken Tiemann.

My thanks to the colleges and universities that hosted *Hootenanny* and have archived their student newspapers online. In chronological order, these are: Syracuse University (*The Daily Orange*), University of Michigan (*The Michigan Daily*), Brown University (*The Brown Daily Herald*), Pennsylvania State University (*The Daily Collegian*), Rutgers University (*The Rutgers Daily Targum*), University of Pittsburgh (*The Pitt News*), Southern Methodist University (*The SMU Campus*), UCLA (*The Daily Bruin*), Fordham University (*The Fordham Ram*), The University of Maryland (*The Diamondback*), University of Florida (*The Alligator*), College of William & Mary (*The Flat Hat*), Purdue University (*The Purdue Exponent*). All provided details that couldn't otherwise have been uncovered.

The following books were most helpful in providing insight and quotes:

Brown, G; *Colorado Rocks: A Half-Century of Music in Colorado*; 2004, Pruett Publishing

Colby, Paul with Martin Fitzpatrick; *The Bitter End: Hanging Out at America's Nightclub*; 2002, Cooper Square Press

Collins, Judy; *Trust Your Heart*; 1987, Ballantine Books

Collins, Judy; *Sweet Judy Blue Eyes: My Life in Music*; 2011, Three Rivers Press

DeTurk, David A. and A. Poulin, Jr. (Edited by); *The American Folk Scene: Dimensions of the Folksong Revival*; 1967, Dell Publishing

Gibson, Bob and Carole Bender; *I Come For To Sing: The Stops Along the Way of a Folk Music Legend*; 2001, Pelican Publishing Company

Shelton, Robert; *No Direction Home: The Life and Music of Bob Dylan*; 1986, Beech Tree Books (division of William Morrow)

Spizer, Bruce: *The Beatles Are Coming: The Birth of Beatlemania in America*; 2003, 498 Productions L.L.C.

Woliver, Robbie; *HOOT! A 25-Year History of the Greenwich Village Music Scene*; 1986, St. Martin's Press

Hundreds of newspaper articles about the show and its guest performers were found online at *newspapers.com*. To list each would take up enough pages to raise the cover price by a few dollars, so I've opted for economy. Original sources are usually cited after quote(s) within the text. A handful of articles were found among Richard Lewine's papers at the NY Public Library of the Performing Arts at Lincoln Center.

The following articles, from periodicals currently unavailable online, were essential:

Hentoff, Nat: "Requiem For Saturday Night Television," *Hootenanny*, May 1964. published by Hootenanny Enterprises, Inc.

Solomon, Linda: "I've Got a Right to Sing the Blues: Judy Henske," *Hootenanny*, December 1963.

Shelton, Bob: "Judy Collins: Why I Quit the A.B.C. Show," *Hootenanny*, March 1964.

Shelton, Bob: "The Kingston Trio vs. Beatlemania," *Hootenanny*, November 1964.

Uncredited: "A Republican Senator Defends Folk Music on Capitol Hill," *Hootenanny*, March 1964.

Uncredited: "Chad Mitchell Speaks His Mind," *ABC-TV Hootenanny*, January 1964, published by SMP Publishing Ltd.

Uncredited: "Helmsman of the Pilot Ship," *TV Guide*, July 25, 1964, published by Triangle Publications, Inc.

Along with *newspapers.com*, the following online sources were indispensable: *ancestry.com*; Google Books (*google.com/books*) primarily for back issues of *Billboard*; *worldradiohistory.com* for back issues of *Cash Box* magazine; *lantern.mediahist.org* for back issues of *Variety* through 1963; *singout.org* for back issues of *Broadside* and Ron Olesko's review of ***The Best of Hootenanny***; *ebay.com* and *outlet.historicimages.com* for vintage photos; *m.the-numbers.com* for *A*

Mighty Wind's box office figures; Texas Parks & Wildlife's *tpwmagazine.com*; *artpodell.com*; *bobgibsonfolk.com*; *brothersfour.com*; *budandtravis.com*; *chadmitchelltrio.com*; *cumberlandtrio.com*; *orrielsmith.com*; *paulwinter.com*; Stefan Grossman's Guitar Workshop (*guitarvideos.com*); *thenewchristyminstrels.fandom.com*; Colorado Music Experience (*colomusic.org*); *discogs.com*; *fultonhistory.com*; *people.com*; *theglobeandmail.com*; *terrascope.co.uk*; *tvparty.com*; The World Folk Music Association (*wfma.net*); *wikipedia.org*; and Historic Films (*historicfilms.com*), archive of most surviving *Hootenanny* kinescopes.

Also deserving of thanks are The Library of Congress for issues of *Sing Out!* and *Broadside*, as well as their Folklife Today blog (*blogs.loc.gov/folklife/*); Rob Stone of the Library of Congress Moving Image Research Center; Mark Quigley of UCLA Film & Television Archive; Jane Klain and Mark Ekman of The Paley Center for Media; Lyric Grimes of UNC Chapel Hill, Wilson Special Collections Library.

Others who were helpful in providing information, material, photos and/or encouragement over the years are Chuck Harter, Michael Henry, Steve Massa, John McElwee and Stuart Shostak. Thank you all. To my daughter Veronica Hayde, thank you for scanning all those album jackets. And, of course, thank you to Ben Ohmart and BearManor Media for believing in me and in this project.

My deepest love and devotion go to my very patient and supportive wife, Myra, and our four children. Most of all, thanks be to God the Father, the Son and the Holy Spirit for Your guidance and graces in this life.

All errors found in this book are my responsibility. Feel free to contact me with your corrections, complaints or compliments via email (MikeH0714@yahoo.com) or by writing in care of the publisher.

INDEX

NOTE: Colleges that hosted *Hootenanny* appear in **bold type** as do the page numbers that correspond to the entries for the show(s) taped there.

C

K

L

T